"No one who has read this book will ever read the *Iliad* in quite the same way."
—Gary Kamiya, *San Francisco Examiner*

"His book is a cogent, painful reminder that in the broken lives of Vietnam veterans we are still paying for what was distinctly unöriginal about that war as well as for its peculiarly original evils."
—*The New Yorker*

"Thank God for people like Jonathan Shay, trauma surgeons in their own right who can bear the truth about war."
—Gail Caldwell, *The Boston Sunday Globe*

"Jonathan Shay's book is one of the most fascinating accounts of the Vietnam War and one of the penetrating analyses of the warriors' experiences."
—Lt. Col. Arieh Y. Shalev, M.D., (Res.) IDF,
Chairman, Dept. of Psychiatry,
Hebrew University, Jerusalem

"For a combat veteran who has no formal training in the classics, *Achilles in Vietnam* is a bolt of lightning cracking through the ages. What was then is now, and I felt that in the author's analysis. For literary and historical scholars it is a challenge in its insight. For the psychologist and psychiatrist it gives me pause to wonder, what the hell have you been doing all these years? Pick up this work of art and use it."
—Rod Kane, author of *Veteran's Day*

"Poetry, psychiatry, and horror are joined in this remarkable book."
—Daniel Ford, author of *Incident at Muc Wa*

"Jonathan Shay has made an important and valuable contribution not only to the clinical body of work regarding PTSD and its treatment, but to the literature of the Vietnam War. This is not only a book for clinicians, but for veterans themselves, their loved ones, and all who wish to understand the Vietnam experience "
—Robert B. Rheault, Colonel, U.S. Army, Ret., Founder and
Director of Outward Bound for Veterans Suffering from PTSD

"*Achilles in Vietnam* poignantly illustrates both the parallels and the divergencies of two wars separated by twenty-seven centuries and their impact on the lives of the soldiers who fought in them. Must reading for mental health professionals who work with Vietnam veterans—or veterans of any war."
—John V. Sommer, Jr., Executive Director of the American
Legion and Vietnam veteran

"An audacious, erudite, and above all, profoundly humane book by an exceptional psychiatrist who illuminates the suffering of the Vietnam veterans he treats and the human experience of combat and grief in Homer's 3,000-year-old poem the *Iliad*. *Achilles in Vietnam* rattles the heart but bestows hope."
—Gloria Emerson, author of *Winners and Losers*

D0003 2250

"*Achilles in Vietnam* has a definite place in the classroom, offering students a bridge to the past. Shay makes Homer accessible to the modern psyche by demonstrating that many seemingly foreign aspects of the *Iliad*'s narrative are alive and well in any soldier's experience."
—*Bryn Mawr Classical Review*

"A heart-rending look at the permanent ruin war can wreak in any age."
—*Kirkus Reviews*

"*Achilles in Vietnam* is destined to become a modern classic, just like the ancient classic upon which the book is based. This is because the book gets to the essence of the veteran, and represents a delightfully brilliant integration of history, art, psychiatry, and science."
—Erwin Randolph Parson, Ph.D.,
The Journal of Contemporary Psychotherapy

"Shay has done a remarkable job of comparing and contrasting the Greek soldiers before Troy and U.S. grunts in Vietnam. This is a profoundly human book and a strong, realistic argument against modern warfare."
—ALA *Booklist*

"A summary gives no sense of the incredible power of this book. Shay's account of [the veterans'] pain overflows with understanding. We all lost our innocence in Vietnam. No one who reads this book will ever forget how radical the loss was."
—*Men's Journal*

"Carefully contrasting the legend of Achilles with his patients' debilitating traumas, Shay makes us understand that there are broad universal truths in the murky crossroads of morality and war."
—*Washington Post Book World*

"Shay's voice is informed and impassioned. *Achilles in Vietnam* should be required reading for all present and future government and military leaders. It is a valuable and inspirational text for all citizens."
—Philip K. Jason (U.S. Naval Academy,
Annapolis), *Magill's Literary Annual, 1995*

"If you want to read a book with great insight into the literature of war and a great understanding about the trauma and shattered lives of American combat soldiers, Jonathan Shay's book is a must."
—Tom Barden, Director of American Studies,
University of Toledo

"Once in a while a book comes along which is truly therapeutic. *Achilles in Vietnam* . . . has integrated for me many diverse elements, weaving and woven through the fabric of my own life and practice."
—E. Deborah Gilman, M.D., Women in Psychiatry column,
Psychiatric Times

"Order, meaning, and morality are fundamentally issues of religion, spirituality, and transcendence, and Shay's book brings a number of them to the fore."
—T. R. Hobbes, Professor of Old Testament,
McMaster Divinity College

ACHILLES IN VIETNAM

Combat Trauma
and the Undoing of Character

Jonathan Shay, M.D., Ph.D.

A TOUCHSTONE BOOK
Published by Simon & Schuster
New York   London   Toronto
Sydney   Tokyo   Singapore

TOUCHSTONE
Rockefeller Center
1230 Avenue of the Americas
New York, NY 10020

Copyright © 1994 by Jonathan Shay
All rights reserved,
including the right of reproduction
in whole or in part in any form.

First Touchstone Edition 1995

TOUCHSTONE and colophon are registered trademarks
of Simon & Schuster Inc.

Manufactured in the United States of America

5   7   9   10   8   6

Library of Congress Cataloging-in-Publication Data
Shay, Jonathan.
Achilles in Vietnam : combat trauma and the undoing of
character / by Jonathan Shay.
p.   cm.
Includes bibliographical references and index.
1. War neuroses. 2. Vietnamese Conflict, 1961–1975—
Psychological aspects. 3. Homer. Iliad. 4. Post-traumatic
stress disorder. 5. Veterans—Mental health—United States.
6. War—Psychological aspects. I. Title.
RC550.S53   1994
616.85'212—dc20   93-32034
                                                            CIP
ISBN 0-689-12182-2
0-684-81321-1 (Pbk)

Quotations from *The Iliad* by Homer. Copyright © 1974 by
Robert Fitzgerald. Used by permission of Doubleday, a division
of Bantam Doubleday Dell Publishing Group, Inc.

The Chosen and *Histories*, poems by William T. Edmonds, Jr.
Copyright 1993 by W. T Edmonds, Jr. Used by permission of the
author. All rights reserved.

Quotation from *Diagnostic and Statistical Manual of Mental
Disorders, Third Edition, Revised*. Used by permission of the
American Psychiatric Association.

I respectfully dedicate this book to the men of the Veterans Improvement Program (VIP) who have generously taught me and entrusted me with their experiences of war. In the larger sense they are the authors of this book.

These are their individual dedications:

IN MEMORY OF Brothers Earl A. Nickerson, Cecil Lee Dobson, Stephen M. Kenoffel, and Thomas John Protrack

IN MEMORY OF David Lee Hinz

IN MEMORY OF Capt. William "Blue" Casey, U.S. Cav.

IN MEMORY OF Fred J. O'Connor, Jr.

IN MEMORY OF 173rd Airborne (The Herd)

IN MEMORY OF Paul

IN MEMORY OF Jimmy English

IN MEMORY OF First Battalion, Ninth Marines

IN MEMORY OF Preacher

IN MEMORY OF A young guy named Dougy

IN MEMORY OF Timmy

IN MEMORY OF those in The Herd on Hill 875

IN MEMORY OF a black trooper named John Kennedy

IN MEMORY OF the nurses and Donut Dollies who served and died in Vietnam

IN MEMORY OF John Durham

CONTENTS

CONTENTS

CONTENTS

CONTENTS

ACKNOWLEDGMENTS

In addition to the men of the Veterans Improvement Program (VIP) and present and past members of the VIP treatment team— James Munroe, Lisa Fisher, Christine Makary, and Kathryn Rapperport—so many people have helped me with this that I tremble to think of who I have forgotten to thank by name.

Special debts of gratitude are due to the following: My companion, Vicki Citron, and my daughters, Tamar and Hannah Shay, have never compromised on the standards they have demanded for this book. To these wonderful critics I can only say, yet again, *thank you.* My editor, Lee Goerner, required painful cuts in the manuscript, but having made them, I am grateful to him for having brought about a better book. Without the encouragement of Harvard's Professor Gregory Nagy, this book would not have been.

Others whose help I gratefully acknowledge are: David Barber, Eliza Bergeson, Robert Berkowitz, Arthur Blank, William Boomhower, John Burkett, Michelle Citron, Tom Daley, Yaël Danieli, Kathleen Patrick Donohue, John Egan, Robert Fagles, Charles Figley, William Finch, Peace Foxx, Paul Fussell, Sallie R. Goetsch, Mary Harvey, Judith Lewis Herman, Katherine Hurbis-Cherrier, Mick Hurbis-Cherrier, David Read Johnson, Terence Keane, Wyn Kelley, David Kiley, Jon Lipsky, Aphrodite Matsakis, Jonathan Matson, John McDonough, Arthur Meara, Sarah Michaels, Shirley Moore, Laura Nemeyer, Martha Nussbaum, Dale Petersen, Ronald Pies, Roger Pitman, Kathryn Rapperport, Bob Rheault, Everett Rollins, Renato Rosaldo, Peter Saba, Ray Scurfield, Bennett Simon, Kalí Jo Tal, Richard Taylor, Steve Tice, Fred Turner, Mary Wertsch, and Graham Zanker. I have savored every word of their praise and encouragement, but it is their criticisms that I now thank them for.

AUTHOR'S CAUTION TO VETERANS, THEIR FAMILIES, AND THEIR FRIENDS

To any veteran of any war coming to this book, please pace yourself and take care of yourself while reading, even if this means stopping and putting the book down. Some of the experiences described here by your fellow veterans may trigger reactions in you that can disrupt your life. Take it slow; don't try to plow straight through. If stuff does get stirred up, find other veterans you trust and talk about it. Vet centers around the country are a good place to do this. You don't have to go through this alone—no veteran should have to!

To families and friends of combat veterans, if this book helps increase your understanding of what the person you love has lived with since his or her war, I am very pleased. But I do want to caution you that no book should give you the illusion that you "know what it was like." There is no substitute for listening to the particular experience of the person that you love—if he or she is able and ready to tell you about it, and if you are ready and able to hear and endure the emotions it will stir up in you. Two excellent books written primarily for wives of Vietnam veterans, but also valuable to others who share their lives with veterans, are *Recovering from the War* by Patience Mason (Viking, 1990) and *Vietnam Wives* by Aphrodite Matsakis (Woodbine House, 1988).

I don't know what the best general advice is about encouraging the veteran you love to tell his or her story. Some would say that the best advice is "Don't try this at home!" However, if you offer to listen to these experiences, you also need to pace yourself and take care of yourself. If the veteran you love thinks you are going to be injured by what he or she has to say, there will be silence. Most vet centers offer support groups for families of veterans of all wars, not only the Vietnam War. You shouldn't have to go through this alone either!

Jonathan Shay

INTRODUCTION

I am the psychiatrist for a group of American combat veterans of the Vietnam War who have severe, chronic post-traumatic stress disorder (PTSD). A number of years ago I was struck by the similarity of their war experiences to Homer's account of Achilles in the *Iliad*. This observation led to an article in the *Journal of Traumatic Stress*, "Learning about Combat Stress from Homer's *Iliad*," which led to this book. The thrust of this work is that the epic gives center stage to bitter experiences that actually do arise in war; further, it makes the claim that Homer has seen things that we in psychiatry and psychology have more or less missed. Homer's *Iliad* was composed about twenty-seven centuries ago; it is about soldiers in war. In particular, Homer emphasizes two common events of heavy, continuous combat: betrayal of "what's right" by a commander, and the onset of the berserk state.

To my astonishment, I was told that knowledge would also flow in the opposite direction—that scholars and critics of the *Iliad* would be better able to interpret the great epic if they listened to combat soldiers. This book came into being largely because of the encouragement of one of the world's leading *Iliad* scholars, Harvard's professor of classical Greek literature Gregory Nagy. The perspective of the combat soldier has never been applied in any systematic way to understanding the *Iliad*. It is a privilege to say *anything* new about a work of art so great that it survived the crash of the Greek civilization that created it and of later civilizations that passed it on.

However, my principal concern is to put before the public an understanding of the specific nature of catastrophic war experiences that not only cause lifelong disabling psychiatric symptoms but can *ruin* good character. I have a specific aim in doing this: to promote a public attitude of *caring* about the conditions that create such psychological injuries, an attitude that will support measures to prevent as much psychological injury as possible. It is my duty as a physician to do my best to heal, but I have an even greater duty to *prevent*.

What are the psychological injuries? Let us listen to the words of Vietnam combat veterans with severe PTSD as they tell what their life is like today:[1]

I haven't really slept for twenty years. I lie down, but I don't sleep. I'm always watching the door, the window, then back to the door. I get up at least five times to walk my perimeter, sometimes it's ten or fifteen times. There's always something within reach, maybe a baseball bat or a knife, at every door. I used to sleep with a gun under my pillow, another under my mattress, and another in the drawer next to the bed. You made me get rid of them when I came into the program here. They're over at my mother's, so I know I can get them any time, but I don't. Sometimes I think about them—I want to have a gun in my hands so bad at night it makes my arms ache.

So it's like that until the sun begins to come up, then I can sleep for an hour or two.

It wasn't any different when I was working for _____ before I lost it and they put me in the psych hospital. I remember the company doctor putting Valiums in my mouth, and they strapped me to a stretcher. I was screaming, and I thought the Gooks had overrun us and were pouring though the place. Everyone I looked at looked like a Gook.

I worked a lot of overtime and also went to school and had a second job. I didn't sleep any more then than now. Maybe two hours a night. But I sure made a lot of money. Workaholic. That's me—no, that *was* me. I was real lucky they kept me so long. They understood that sometimes I just had to leave work. And they never laughed at me when I hit the floor if there was a loud bang or something. I know guys here [in the treatment program] who work other places who had firecrackers lit off just to see them dive over a conveyer belt or something like that. Or their supervisors pushing them, mind-fucking them, pushing them till they lost it, so they could get rid of them. That never happened to me. Once a lamp in the ceiling exploded with a loud bang, and I dove into a tank of lubricant for the cutting machines. Oof! It was awful. But nobody laughed at me. They were real good to me, and they respected what I could do. They made me the head of the Emergency Response Team, like for explosions and injuries.

INTRODUCTION

Once a guy was burned real bad when some hydraulic fluid caught fire. I was the only one who didn't freeze. I got in there with the fire blanket—see, I still got the scars here on my leg where I got hit too with the burning hydraulics. I got through Vietnam without a scratch and get a Purple Heart for the _____ Company. [Laughs, then silence.] The smell of burning flesh fucked me up real bad afterward, though. I didn't notice it at the time the guy caught fire, but for the next few weeks I kept having flashbacks of the time the fast-mover [jet] laid a canister of napalm on my company. I couldn't get the smell out of my nose, out of my mouth.

I don't deserve my wife. What kind of life is it for her married to me? She says, "Let's take the kids out for dinner." And I say, "Sure, let's go." So we get to the restaurant and we walk in the door and I say, "Whoa!" when I look around and see all those people. So the hostess shows us to a table right in the middle, and I say, "How about there in the corner?" and she says, "There's people there," and I say, "We'll wait." Meantime my wife is looking at me and there's sweat running down my face. I can't sit with my back uncovered. If I know you're back there covering me, it's okay, but a bunch of strangers, and some of them Gooks—no way. I sit in the corner where I can see everyone who comes in and everyone who leaves. So after we wait thirty minutes for the table in the corner we start walking through the restaurant to it and my heart's pounding, pounding and the sweat's rolling off me and I say, "I gotta go." So they sit down and eat and I stand up in the parking garage, the second floor overlooking the entrance to the restaurant where I have a real good line on everything going on.

Or another thing, y'know my wife's real social, and of course I'm not. She understands now because of the couples therapy _____ did with her and me together. So we don't fight anymore about a lot of those things, and she even helps me now with the embarrassment. Like at my in-laws' she'll even make up something she forgot in the car when she sees that there's getting [to be] too many people in the room, so I can get out of there. But one thing she still don't understand is the mail. She gets so mad at me because I'll drive into town to buy cigarettes but I don't pick the mail up—it's right next to the 7-Eleven. What she doesn't understand is that every time I think it's _____'s kid sister writing me to find out how he died. She wrote to him every day—and I mean *every day*. Sometimes we wouldn't get our mail for six weeks, and when we'd get it there'd be more letters for him than for the rest of the platoon put together. It's better she don't know. If it was my big brother I wouldn't want to know the truth about the way *he* died.

Of course in another way I'm real good to her [laughs], compared to what I was like to other women before. [Pauses.] Whew! I was one mean motherfucker. She didn't want to know me. You didn't want to know me. You don't want to *know* the number of people I fucked up [pauses], or how I fucked them up.

I don't have very long to live. No, Doc, no, no, I'm not suicidal, it's just that sometimes I don't give a fuck. I don't care if I live or die. I've been waiting to die ever since I got back from Vietnam. When I get that way, my wife, my kids—and I really love them—it's "Get the fuck away from me!" Once when my daughter was younger and I was that way, she came up behind me and before I knew it I had her by the throat up against the wall. I can still see her eyes. I put her down and just walked out of the house without saying anything to anybody and didn't come back for a week. I felt lower than dogshit. I hate it that my kids behave so *careful* around me. I made them that way, and I hate it. Every time I see them being so careful I think of that look in her eyes and I get this feeling here [puts his palm on his belly] like a big stone sitting there.

I think I don't have long to live because I have these dreams of guys in my unit standing at the end of the sofa and blood coming down off them and up the sofa. I wake up screaming and the sofa soaked with sweat. It seems like if the blood reaches me I'm going to die when it does. Other nights I dream of the guys calling to me from the graveyard. They're calling to me, "Come on, come on. Time to rest. You paid your dues. Time to rest."

I never tried to kill myself, but a lot of the time I just don't care. For years I used to go down to the Combat Zone [the Boston red-light district] after midnight and just walk the alleys. If I saw someone down an alley in the dark, I wouldn't go the other way, I'd go down there thinking, "Maybe I'll get lucky." I'm amazed I wasn't killed. I guess I wanted to be killed. Once I came on a guy raping a hooker. She was screaming and screaming, and it was easy to tell he was hurting her bad. I yelled at him, and he turned around and started reaching behind his back. He was carrying. I ran on him so fast and had his elbow before he could pull out the piece [gun], and I pounded the shit out of him. That felt so-o go-o-od. I don't know what happened to the woman. I guess she screwed [ran away] while I was doing him. After that I started bringing a meat fork to the Combat Zone. You know like from a carving set with two—what do they call them—tines. I sharpened them real good. I didn't want to kill anybody, and I figured you could only stick that into somebody just so far before it stopped. When I went to the Combat Zone I never went with a gun. And there was a time I was really crazy and driving around town with a shotgun on the seat next to me.

I haven't spent a complete night in bed with my wife for at least ten years. I always end up on the sofa. It's safer for her, and I don't have to worry about waking her when I get up to walk the perimeter. When I was working sixteen hours a day I'd come home; she'd already be in bed. I'd do a couple hours of things around the house and meanwhile put away a case of beer and a fifth so I'd be able to sleep. Then I'd get in bed with her for two, three hours until it was time for work again. But after I couldn't work anymore, and really bad after I stopped drinking, I'd do this crazy shit at night. I once threw her out of bed so hard it broke her shoulder. I thought there was an NVA potato-masher [a grenade] come in on us. Another time I thought *she* was a Gook, and I had my hands around her throat before I woke up. So since I stopped drinking I never let myself fall asleep in bed with her. I lie there quiet until she's asleep and then get up, check the perimeter, and lie down on the sofa where I can see the door.

It's not much of a life for her, I guess. We haven't had sex in four years. She deserves better.

She says I always mess up a good thing—like I don't deserve it. At Christmas I try to make it perfect for the kids with a big, fresh tree trimmed just right and lots of presents, but it's like I'm watching them through a dirty window. I'm not really there and they're not really there, I don't know which is which. Maybe none of us is real. It's like I'm wrapped up in some kind of transparent cocoon and everything gets to me kind of muffled—oh fuck, I don't know how to explain it.

My son asks me if I'll come to his Little League game and I can't ever promise. He wants me to promise, but I can't. It's not that I don't want to go. I was in Little League myself, and I go sometime just at the last minute and watch from the tree line in the outfield. He has a great arm, and once he hit a home run into the trees where I was standing. I had to pull back real quick. You can't have somebody knowing where you'll be.

I'm so envious of all the normal people who can just go to the mall and hold hands with their wife and walk around. You see, I could never do that, because I'd be looking everywhere. Fuck! I even envy you. I see you walking up the street to the clinic and you're not checking the rooftops for snipers or looking between cars as you pass to make sure there's nobody going to jump you, and I'll bet you have *no idea* who's on the street with you. I can tell you every person two blocks ahead of me and two blocks behind me every second. I see you coming down the street, but you don't see me, because you're in your own world not looking for ambush. How come you're like that? I envy you.

You know, when I go into the men's room here at the clinic I have to pop open the door of each stall with my fist to make sure there's nobody waiting there for me. Sometimes there's guys in there taking a shit and they look at me like I'm a queer or something, but I got to do it or I'm too nervous to pee. Once I was in there and I was washing my hands and you walked in and just said, "Hi," and walked over to the urinal and peed without checking the stalls. How can you do that?

You know, people ask me if I work out. I look very healthy, athletic and stuff. I don't work out. I don't do anything. Maybe it's muscle tension that keeps me this way. But you know, I'm not really healthy. I went to the _____ Fair a bunch of years ago and they had a Take Your Blood Pressure for Free table, and they made me lie down and wanted to call an ambulance it was so high. They were afraid I was going to die on them right there. They worked me up at the hospital for a feo-something, a tumor that makes your blood pressure go through the roof, but they never found anything. Then when I told them that I had stomach pains a lot and vomit every morning, they told me I had ulcers and worked me up for something else, I can't remember the name, but again they thought it was another kind of tumor that makes your stomach pump out acid all the time by the bucketfull. They didn't find anything, but they gave me those pills to stop the acid, and now I don't vomit every day, only around my anniversaries. My skin is still all black in my groin from the jungle rot and Agent Orange, but my hands are better—see? It's only cracked a little here between the fingers and only kicks up during the summer. For years it was all around my waist cracked and oozing blood. My undershirt'd get caked to my skin and I'd have to change it three times a day or the smell would get to you. I was sprayed with Agent Orange during my second tour when we were working the Cambodian border. I thought they were spraying for mosquitoes, but it was Agent Orange, I found out afterward. This big plane came over putting out this big cloud behind it, and it came down on us like a mist, and I thought, "Ain't this amazing, they're spraying the mosquitoes all the way out here." But maybe it's all nerves, and not Agent Orange. That's what Dr. _____ told me. I don't know what to believe.

I know it all kicks up around the time of year we went into _____. I can't tell you what we were doing there, it's still secret and I've never been too comfortable with these dropped ceilings here in the clinic. It's just too easy to hide a microphone here. Maybe someday I'll be able to talk about it, but for now you never know who might be listening, and I'm not allowed to say anything about it. I shouldn't even have said we were in _____. I guess they need to keep tabs, because you know we still have our people over there who'd be dead in a minute if the wrong thing was said. There've been times I took every stick of furniture out of my house, took all the plates off the plugs in the walls and replaced every light fixture, and I had a guy sweep my house for bugs—cost me $600, but I still had the feeling I was being watched. I don't know if it was the NVA [North Vietnamese Army] or a CIT [U.S. Marine counterintelligence], or maybe both. You *know* the NVA has people over here disguised as refugees. Maybe that sounds paranoid, but I can't help thinking it. Here I did three fucking combat tours serving my country and I feel like a fucking fugitive.

It still makes me mad the way nobody understands what we did over there. When I first came back it was like I was living under a toilet and every five minutes somebody had diarrhea on me. There's nothing I can do. I feel like a complete freak, maybe like the Elephant Man—that's me. Nobody can understand, 'cept maybe another 'Nam vet. If only I could cry like I cried the day _____ had his face shot off. I haven't cried since then. Never.

Well, I guess it's something that I can even talk to you like this, and you not even a 'Nam vet and all. Remember how long it took me to say *anything*? I just had to watch until I could trust _____ and _____ and you. It was almost three years till I started to open up.

The people who read this book ain't going to believe any of this shit. And *you* better look out. Nobody's going to believe you when you tell them, and you'll end up an outcast like us.

These are voices of men as they are today, more than twenty years after their war service. About three-quarters of a million heavy combat veterans from Vietnam are still alive today, of whom a quarter million are still suffering in this manner.[2] I shall give a full explanation of combat post-traumatic stress disorder in chapter 10, but here is a summary of the key symptoms of PTSD and of the personality changes that mark its severe forms. All may be understood as the persistence of past traumatic experience in the present physiology, psychology, and social relatedness of the survivor. The symptoms can range in severity from mild to devastating, and not everyone will have all of the symptoms at the same time:

- Loss of authority over mental function—particularly memory and trustworthy perception
- Persistent mobilization of the body and the mind for lethal danger, with the potential for explosive violence
- Persistence and activation of combat survival skills in civilian life
- Chronic health problems stemming from chronic mobilization of the body for danger
- Persistent expectation of betrayal and exploitation; destruction of the capacity for social trust
- Persistent preoccupation with both the enemy and the veteran's own military/governmental authorities
- Alcohol and drug abuse
- Suicidality, despair, isolation, and meaninglessness

Such unhealed PTSD can devastate life and incapacitate its victims from participation in the domestic, economic, and political life of the nation. The painful paradox is that fighting for one's country can render one unfit to be its citizen.

I shall present the *Iliad* as the tragedy of Achilles. I will not glorify Vietnam combat veterans by linking them to a prestigious "classic" nor attempt to justify study of the *Iliad* by making it sexy, exciting, modern, or "relevant." I respect the work of classical scholars and could not have done my work without them. Homer's poem does not mean whatever I want it to mean. However, having honored the boundaries of meaning that scholars have pointed out, I can confidently tell you that my reading of the *Iliad* as an account of men in war is not a "meditation" that is only tenuously rooted in the text. The first five chapters track Homer's story of Achilles very closely: Agamémnon, Achilles' commander, betrays "what's right" by wrongfully seizing his prize of honor; indignant rage shrinks Achilles' social and moral horizon until he cares about no one but a small group of combat-proven comrades; his closest friend in that circle, his second-in-command and foster brother, Pátroklos, dies in battle; profound grief and suicidal longing take hold of Achilles; he feels that he is already dead; he is tortured by guilt and the conviction that he should have died rather than his friend; he renounces all desire to return home alive; he goes berserk and commits atrocities against the living and the dead. This *is* the story of Achilles in the *Iliad*, not some metaphoric translation of it.

This was also the story of many combat veterans, both from Vietnam and from other long wars. The reader will find some of the veterans' narratives disturbing. I have brought them together with the *Iliad* not to tame, appropriate, or co-opt them but to promote a deeper understanding of both, increasing the reader's capacity to be disturbed by the *Iliad* rather than softening the blow of the veterans' stories.

Names, specific units, and locations in Vietnam have been omitted or disguised to protect the privacy of my patients. I intend to go on working with these men—some of whom will read this book—so I have asked every veteran to review and approve his words and stories that I have used here, even though this is not legally required.

The clarity and eloquence with which the veterans tell their stories prove the truth of what Paul Fussell has written about the First World War:

> One of the cruxes of war . . . is the collision between events and the language available—or thought appropriate—to describe them . . . Logically, there is no reason why the English language could not perfectly well render the actuality of . . . warfare: it is rich in terms like *blood, terror, agony, madness, shit, cruelty, murder, sell-out* and *hoax*, as well as phrases like *legs blown off, intestines gushing out over his hands, screaming all night, bleeding to death from the rectum*, and the like. . . . The problem was less one of "language" than of gentility and optimism. . . . The real reason [that soldiers fall silent] is that soldiers have discovered that no one is very interested in the bad news they have to report. What listener wants to be torn and shaken when he doesn't have to be? We have made *unspeakable* mean indescribable: it really means *nasty*.[3]

One Vietnam combat veteran describes this social process of silencing the survivor:

INTRODUCTION

> I had just come back [from Vietnam], and my first wife's parents gave a dinner for me and my parents and her brothers and their wives. And after dinner we were all sitting in the living room and her father said, "So, tell us what it was like." And I started to tell them, and I told them. And do you know within five minutes the room was empty. They was all gone, except my wife. After that I didn't tell anybody I had been in Vietnam.

However, the fact that these veterans can speak at all of their experience is a major sign of healing. Unhealed war trauma can leave men as speechless as victims of prolonged political torture.

I have made no concessions to the stereotype of the veteran as uneducated Joe Six-pack. The men who have taught me have great intelligence, although some have had negligible formal schooling. I have learned that many veterans who dropped out of high school are now voracious readers who will be offended by talking down to them in any way. Some, who are among the most eloquent and terrifyingly intelligent, will not read this book, because they cannot read. Their wish has been that I write the best book I am able to write, not a Dick-and-Jane text that they might eventually be able to struggle through. The explanatory square brackets in quotations from the *Iliad* text (e.g., "windy Ilion [Troy]") are added for all readers who are not classicists, just as definitions of military terms (e.g., "RPG [rocket-propelled grenade]") are given for all those who are not Vietnam vets.

When I quote a veteran's words, I have done my best to preserve his voice—his sound and rhythms. Direct quotations are my own transcript of recorded interviews each generously given to help with this project, or are taken from my notes or from a veteran's written narrative. Transcripts have been lightly edited to remove "uh" and "you know" where these did not seem important to the tone. I have personally transcribed the tapes to preserve the exact words, not only as a mark of respect but also because of the poetry that flows through them.

By now there is a large body of Vietnam soldiers' memoirs, oral history, and testimony. The veterans' narratives in this book are an addition to this corpus. No disrespect for other veterans' published experiences is implied by the fact that I have used only unpublished material from men I know personally.

Nothing in this book is entirely new to mental health disciplines, in the sense that it has not been previously published in professional journals such as the *Journal of Traumatic Stress*. However, some of it is quite recent and by no means universally accepted in the field, such as the importance of the berserk state or of betrayal of "what's right" in the etiology of a chronic post-traumatic stress disorder after combat. I hope this book will educate and motivate mental health professionals who are just starting to work with combat veterans or are considering doing so. Those who are already in the field may be influenced by Homer's attention to the moral dimension of combat trauma, to the berserk state, to respect for the enemy, and to communalization of grief.

To *all* readers I say: Learn the psychological damage that war does, and work to prevent war. There is no contradiction between hating war and honoring the soldier. Learn *how* war damages the mind and spirit, and work to change those things in military institutions and culture that needlessly create or worsen these injuries. We don't have to go on repeating the same mistakes. Just as the flak jacket has prevented many physical injuries, we can prevent many psychological injuries.

I welcome feedback from readers
at the following E-mail address:

JSHAY@WORLD.STD.COM

PART I

Betrayal of "What's Right"

Every instance of severe traumatic psychological injury is a standing challenge to the rightness of the social order.
— Judith Lewis Herman,
1990 Harvard Trauma Conference

We begin in the moral world of the soldier—what his culture understands to be right—and betrayal of that moral order by a commander. This is how Homer opens the *Iliad*. Agamémnon, Achilles' commander, wrongfully seizes the prize of honor voted to Achilles by the troops. Achilles' experience of betrayal of "what's right," and his reactions to it, are identical to those of American soldiers in Vietnam. I shall describe some of the many violations of what American soldiers understood to be right by holders of responsibility and trust.

> Now, there was a LURP [Long Range Reconnaissance Patrol] team from the First Brigade off of Highway One, that looked over the South China Sea. There was a bay there. . . . Now, they saw boats come in. And they suspected, now, uh—the word came down [that] they were unloading weapons off them. Three boats.
>
> At that time we moved. It was about ten o'clock at night. We moved down, across Highway One along the beach line, and it took us [until] about three or four o'clock in the morning to get on line while these people are unloading their boats. And we opened up on them—aaah.
>
> And the fucking firepower was unreal, the firepower that we put into them boats. It was just a constant, constant firepower. It seemed like no one ever ran out of ammo.
>
> Daylight came [long pause], and we found out we killed a lot of fishermen and kids.
>
> What got us thoroughly fucking confused is, at that time you

turn to the team and you say to the team, "Don't worry about it. Everything's fucking fine." Because that's what you're getting from upstairs.

The fucking colonel says, "Don't worry about it. We'll take care of it." Y'know, uh, "We got body count!" "We have body count!" So it starts working on your head.

So you know in your heart it's wrong, but at the time, here's your superiors telling you that it was okay. So, I mean, that's *okay* then, right? This is part of war. Y'know? Gung-HO! Y'know? "AirBORNE! AirBORNE! Let's go!"

So we packed up and we moved out.

They wanted to give us a fucking Unit Citation—them fucking maggots. A lot of medals came down from it. The lieutenants got medals, and I know the colonel got his fucking medal. And they would have award ceremonies, y'know, I'd be standing like a fucking jerk and they'd be handing out fucking medals for killing civilians.

This veteran received his Combat Infantry Badge for participating in this action. The CIB was one of the most prized U.S. Army awards, supposed to be awarded for actual engagement in ground combat. He subsequently earned his CIB a thousand times over in four combat tours. Nonetheless, he still feels deeply dishonored by the circumstances of its official award for killing unarmed civilians on an intelligence error. He declares that the day it happened, Christmas Eve, should be stricken from the calendar.

We shall hear this man's voice and the voices of other combat veterans many times in these pages. I shall argue throughout this book that healing from trauma depends upon communalization of the trauma—being able safely to tell the story to someone who is listening and who can be trusted to retell it truthfully to others in the community. So before analyzing, before classifying, before thinking, before trying to *do* anything—we should *listen*. Categories and classifications play a large role in the institutions of mental health care for veterans, in the education of mental health professionals, and as tentative guides to perception. All too often, however, our mode of listening deteriorates into intellectual sorting, with the professional grabbing the veterans' words from the air and sticking them in mental bins. To some degree that is institutionally and educationally necessary, but listening this way *destroys* trust. At its worst our educational system produces counselors, psychiatrists, psychologists, and therapists who resemble museum-goers whose whole experience consists of mentally saying, "That's cubist! . . . That's El Greco!" and who never *see* anything they've looked at. "Just listen!" say the veterans when telling mental health professionals what they need to know to work with them, and I believe that is their wish for the general public as well. Passages of narrative here contain the particularity of individual men's experiences, bearing a different order of meaningfulness than any categories they might be put into. In the words of one veteran, these stories are "sacred stuff."

The mortal dependence of the modern soldier on the military organization for everything he needs to survive is as great as that of a small child on his or her parents. One Vietnam combat veteran said, "The U.S. Army [in Vietnam] was like a mother who sold out her kids to be raped by [their] father to protect her own interests."

No single English word takes in the whole sweep of a culture's definition of right and wrong; we use terms such as moral order, convention, normative expectations, ethics, and commonly understood social values. The ancient Greek word that Homer used, *thémis*, encompasses all these meanings.[1] A word of this scope is needed for the betrayals experienced by Vietnam combat veterans. In this book I shall use the phrase "what's right" as an equivalent of *thémis*. The specific content of the Homeric warriors' *thémis* was often quite different from that of American soldiers in Vietnam, but what has not changed in three millennia are violent rage and social withdrawal when deep assumptions of "what's right" are violated. The vulnerability of the soldier's moral world has increased in three thousand years because of the vast number and physical distance of people in a position to betray "what's right" in ways that threaten the survival of soldiers in battle. Homeric soldiers actually *saw* their commander in chief, perhaps daily.

AN ARMY IS A MORAL CONSTRUCTION

Book 1 of the *Iliad* sets the tragedy in motion with Agamémnon's seizure of Achilles' woman, "a prize I [Achilles] sweated for, and soldiers gave me!"(1:189)[2] We must understand the cultural context to see that this episode is more than a personal squabble between two soldiers over a woman. The outrageousness of Agamémnon's behavior is repeatedly made clear. Achilles' mother, the goddess Thetis, makes her case to Zeus: "Now Lord Marshal Agamémnon has been highhanded with him, has commandeered and holds his prize of war [*géras*, portion of honor]. . . ." The prize of honor was voted by the troops for Achilles' valor in combat. A modern equivalent might be a commander telling a soldier, "I'll take that Congressional Medal of Honor of yours, because I don't have one." Obviously, Achilles' grievance was magnified by his attachment to the particular person of Brisêis, the captive woman who was the prize, but violation of "what's right" was central to the clash between Achilles and Agamémnon.[3]

Any army, ancient or modern, is a social construction defined by shared expectations and values. Some of these are embodied in formal regulations, defined authority, written orders, ranks, incentives, punishments, and formal task and occupational definitions. Others circulate as traditions, archetypal stories of things to be emulated or shunned, and accepted truth about what is praiseworthy and what is culpable. All together, these form a moral world that most of the participants most of the time regard as legitimate, "natural," and personally binding. The moral power of an army is so great that it can motivate men to get up out of a trench and step into enemy machine-gun fire.

When a leader destroys the legitimacy of the army's moral order by betraying "what's right," he inflicts manifold injuries on his men. The *Iliad* is a story of these immediate and devastating consequences. Vietnam has forced us to see that these consequences go beyond the war's "loss upon bitter loss . . . leaving so many dead men" (1:3ff) to taint the lives of those who survive it.

VICTORY, DEFEAT, AND THE HOVERING DEAD

In victory, the meaning of the dead has rarely been a problem to the living—soldiers have died "for" victory. Ancient and modern war are alike in defining the relationship between victory and the army's dead, *after the fact*. At the time of the deaths, victory has not yet been achieved, so the corpses' meaning hovers in the void until the lethal contest has been decided. Victory—and the cut, crushed, burned, impaled, suffocated, frozen, diseased, drowned, poisoned, or blown-up corpses—mutually anchor each other's meaning.[4] Homeric participants in warfare understood a very simple relationship between civilians and the soldiers who fought to protect them: In defeat, all male civilians were massacred and all female civilians were raped and carried away into slavery. In the modern world, the meaning of the dead to the defeated is a bitter, unhealed wound, where defeat rarely means obliteration of the people and civilization. As we recently witnessed in the Persian Gulf War, defeat may not even bring the fall of the opposing government. At the level of grand strategy in Vietnam, the United States had been defeated, and yet American soldiers had won every battle.

For the veterans, the unanchored dead continue to hover. They visit their surviving comrades at night like the ghost of Pátroklos, Achilles' friend, visits Achilles:

> . . . let me pass the gates of Death.
> . . . I wander
> about the wide gates and the hall of Death.
> Give me your hand. I sorrow. (23:88)

The returning Vietnam soldiers were not honored. Much of the public treated them with indifference or derision, further denying the unanchored dead a resting place.

SOME VETERANS' VIEW—WHAT IS DEFEAT? WHAT IS VICTORY?

During a group therapy session, I once blundered into a casual mention of "our defeat" in Vietnam. Many veterans returned from Vietnam and found themselves outcast and humiliated in American Legion[5] and Veterans of Foreign Wars posts where they had assumed that they would be welcomed, supported, and understood. Time and again they were assailed as "losers" by World War II veterans. The pain and rage at being blamed for defeat in Vietnam was beyond bearing and resulted in many brawls.

These feelings reflect not only outrage at the heartless wrongheadedness of such remarks but also a concept of victory in war that left Vietnam veterans bewildered. "We knew that we never lost a battle," say the veterans. Winning, as far as I have been able to determine, meant to them being in possession of the ground at the end of the battle. So the hit-and-run or hit-and-hide small-unit tactics of the enemy always meant that we had "won" after a given engagement. However, many men experienced a deep malaise that their concepts of victory, of strength embodied in fire superiority and often in great local numerical superiority, somehow didn't fit, were futile. The enemy initiated 90 percent of all engagements but "lost" them all. Even battles like Dak To and Ap Bia Mountain (Hamburger Hill) were American victories in the sense that Americans held the ground when the last shot was fired.

Larger images of victory seem to have been formed out of newsreel footage of World War II surrender ceremonies and beautiful women weeping for joy at their liberation; defeat was a document signed in a railway carriage and German troops marching in Paris. As I listen to some veterans, there are times when it seems they believe that the Vietnamese *cannot* have won the war. Therefore, because we won all our battles, our victory was somehow stolen. Many veterans have a well-developed "stab in the back" theory akin to that developed by German veterans of World War I—that the war could have been handily won had the fighting forces not been betrayed by home-front politicians. My interest here is in the soldiers' experiences and not in the larger historical question of whether they were "sold out" by the politicians somehow brought under the spell of such still-hated figures as Jane Fonda.

Once or twice I have tried to explore with veterans these concepts of victory and defeat. I have abandoned these discussions, because the sense of betrayal is still too great and the equation of defeat with abandonment by God and personal devaluation still too vivid.

To return to my blunder in group therapy, a veteran whose voice is often heard in this book turned black with anger and, glaring at me, said, "I won *my* war. It's *you* who fucking lost!" He got up and left the room to remove himself from the opportunity to physically hurt me. Toward the end of the group session he returned and said, "What we lost in Vietnam was a lot of *good fucking kids*!"

More than a year after this experience I gingerly approached the subject with another veteran, prefacing what I was about to say (the paradox that we had "lost" the war while "winning" every battle) by saying that I knew that this was a very sensitive subject and that it made many vets very angry. When I had said it, he smiled in a not very friendly way and drew his finger across his throat. "It makes you want to cut my throat?" I asked. "Uh-huh," he replied.

DIMENSIONS OF BETRAYAL OF "WHAT'S RIGHT"

To grasp the significance of betrayal we must consider two independent dimensions: first, what is at stake, and second, what *thémis* has been violated.

ON DANGER IN WAR

"To someone who has never experienced danger, the idea is attractive," wrote the famous nineteenth-century military theorist Carl von Clausewitz.[6] So it appeared to many young men who volunteered—only about 10 percent of the men I see were drafted—for military service during the Vietnam War. For some it was a way to "prove" themselves to themselves, sometimes to their fathers and uncles who were World War II veterans. For some it was attractive as an expression of patriotic and religious idealism, often understood to be equivalent to anti-Communism:

> You get brought up with God an' country and—y'know, something good turned out bad. . . . They told me I was fighting Communism. And I really believed in my country and I believed everyone served their country.

Another veteran:

> It was better to fight Communism there in Vietnam than in your own back yard. Catholics had the worst of it. We had to be the Legions of God. We were doing it for your faith. We were told: Communists don't like Catholics.

For some the war was a cause that expressed an heroic ideal of human worth, in the words of one veteran, "the highest stage of mankind, willing to put your life on the line for an idea." For others it was the excitement, the spectacle of war. One veteran described his motive for joining the Marines: "I was bored. Vietnam was where it was happening, and in the Marines everybody went to Vietnam."

All knew that war was dangerous, but none were prepared for the "final shock, the sight of men being killed and mutilated [which] moves our pounding hearts to awe and pity."[7] They went to war with the innocence built from films in which war, in Paul Fussell's words, was

> systematically sanitized and Norman Rockwellized, not to mention Disneyfied. . . . In these, no matter how severely wounded, Allied troops are never shown suffering what was termed, in the Vietnam War, traumatic amputation: everyone has all his limbs, his hands and feet and digits, not to mention expressions of courage and cheer."[8]

Danger of death and mutilation is the pervading medium of combat. It is a viscous liquid in which everything looks strangely refracted and moves about in odd ways, a powerful corrosive that breaks down many fixed contours of perception and utterly dissolves others. Without an accurate conception of danger we cannot comprehend war and cannot properly value the moral structure of an army. We must grasp what is at stake: lethal danger and the fear of it.

THE FAIRNESS ASSUMPTION

Adults rightly think that a sense of proportion about petty injustice is intrinsic to maturity and hear their children shrilling "It's not fair!" as evidence of their childishness. The culture shock of civilians entering the stratified and ritualized military world is well known. It is also the world of "chickenshit." As Paul Fussell put it:

> If you are an enlisted man, you'll know you've been the victim of chickenshit if your sergeant assigns you to K.P. not because it's your turn but because you disagreed with him on a question of taste a few evenings ago. Or, you might find your pass to town canceled at the last moment because, you finally remember, a few days ago you asked a question during the sergeant's lecture on map-reading that he couldn't answer.[9]

Civilians and noncombat veterans often equate complaints about military life to adolescent whining because of the unexamined assumption that its injustices are always of this low-stakes variety. The experiences that Fussell invokes here undoubtedly cause anger and indignation, but the essential element of mortal danger is lacking. However, Fussell, himself a World War II combat veteran, continues the passage without a change in tone:

> Or, if you uttered your . . . [indiscretion] while in combat instead of in camp, you might find yourself repeatedly selected to take out the more hazardous night patrols to secure information, the kind, a former junior officer recalls, 'we already knew from daytime observations, and had reported.'[10]

Because we have entered the realm of mortal danger, the experience of betrayal merits full, respectful attention. Paradoxically, the reader must respond *emotionally* to the reality of combat danger in order to make *rational* sense of the injury inflicted when those in charge violate "what's right." If the emotion of terror is completely absent from the reader's experience of this book, crucial information about the experience of combat is not getting through.

A veteran recalls,

> Walking point[11] was an extremely dangerous job. The decision on who was going to do it was so carefree, so carefree, yeah. The decision was made politically [laughs]. Most of the time politically. Certain people got the shit. Certain people didn't. Certain people on the right side of certain people.

Another veteran:

> The CO had his favorites. Two companies, Delta [this veteran's company] and Charlie, always got sent out. The other two always stayed back on the hill at _____.

This may sound like a child complaining, "It's not fair!" about taking turns carrying out the trash, unless one grasps what was at stake. During the course of this man's year with Delta Company, it suffered more than 100 percent casualties, taking replacements into account. The companies that were the CO's favorites suffered few casualties. Contrary to what the young men anticipated in training and in watching war films, once they encountered the reality of battle, they fervently wanted to avoid it and wanted risk to be fairly distributed. Many aspects of the *thémis* of American soldiers cluster around fairness. When they perceived that distribution of risk was unjust, they became filled with indignant rage, just as Achilles was filled with *mênis*, indignant rage.

Soldiers grow most doubtful about the fair distribution of risk when they see that their commanders shelter themselves from it. Writing of the Vietnam War, a respected military historian commented:

> Officers in every armed force must find ways of inducing their men to fight and risk their lives—a most unnatural activity. . . . In modern warfare, where automatic weapons, artillery, and air power impose dispersal, men can rarely be pushed into combat; they must be pulled by the prestige of their immediate leader and the officers above him. Combat expertise that soldiers recognize and personal qualities of authority are important, but so is an evident willingness to share in the . . . deadly risks of war.
>
> . . . The deadly risks of combat must unfailingly be shared whether it is tactically necessary to do so or not, and junior officers cannot do all the sharing.
>
> If soldiers see that their immediate leader is exposed to risk while his superiors stay away from combat, they will be loyal to the man but disaffected from the army. . . . In Vietnam, the mere fact that officers above the most junior rank were so abundant and mostly found in well-protected bases suggested a very unequal sharing of the risk. And statistics support the troops' suspicion. During the Second World War, the Army ground forces had a full colonel for every 672 enlisted men; in Vietnam (1971) there was a colonel for every 163 enlisted men. In the Second World War, 77 colonels died in combat, one for every 2,206 men thus killed; throughout the Vietnam war, from 1961 till 1972, only 8 colonels were killed in action, one for every 3,407 men.[12]

The *Iliad* reminds us that military and political leaders have not always been thousands of miles away from the war zone. Agamémnon, the highest Greek political and military authority, personally shares every soldier's risk on the battlefield and is wounded in action (11:289ff); the King of Lykia, a Trojan ally, is killed in action (15:568ff). Only within the last few centuries has the era of "stone-age command" ended. Before the modern age the ruler and commander in chief were united in one person who was present and at risk in battle. Rear-echelon officers in Vietnam who attempted to micro-manage battles by radio from the rear were known as Base Camp Commandos; those who operated from a helicopter safely out of range of ground fire came to be called Great Leaders in the Sky. Martin van Creveld wrote:

> Under the conditions peculiar to the war in Vietnam, major units seldom had more than one of their subordinate outfits engage the enemy at any one time. . . . A hapless company commander engaged in a firefight on the ground was subjected to direct observation by the battalion commander circling above, who was in turn supervised by the brigade commander circling a thousand or so feet higher up, who in his turn was monitored by the division commander in the next highest chopper, who might even be so unlucky as to have his own performance watched by the Field Force (corps) commander.[13]

If American career officers in Vietnam did not share the risks of combat, cultural and institutional factors, rather than personal cowardice, were primarily responsible for this. The officers of World War II had a different culture, which focused on the substance of their *work* rather than on the institutional definition and status of their *jobs*, as in Vietnam. And compared to World War II, there were simply too many officers in Vietnam, leading them to become so absorbed in bureaucratic processes that the most elementary aspects of leadership dropped beyond their horizon.

Officers, the only soldiers we meet in the *Iliad*, went into danger in quest of "honor."

> What is the point of being honored so
> with precedence at table, choice of meat,
> and brimming cups, . . .
> And why have lands been granted you and me . . . ?
>   So that we two
> at times like this in the . . . front line
> may face the blaze of battle and fight well. (12:348ff)

Honor was conferred by others for going into danger and fighting competently. Honor was embodied in its valuable tokens, such as the best portions of meat at feasts, land grants, or, in Achilles' case, the prize of Brisêis. And so could honor be removed; a man could be dis-honored by seizure of the tokens of honor. Homer makes it plain that men were willing to risk their lives for honor and that the material goods that symbolized honor were not *per se* what made them face "a thousand shapes of death." (12:366) It is easy for us to caricature ancient warriors as simple brigands or booty hunters motivated by greed, but this is almost certainly a misunderstanding. The quest for social honor and avoidance of social shame are the prime motives of Homeric warriors. Achilles says,

> Only this bitterness eats at my heart
> when one man would deprive and shame his equal,
> taking back his prize by abuse of power.
> The girl whom the Akhaians chose for me
> I won by my own spear. A town with walls
> I stormed and sacked for her. Then Agamémnon
> stole her back, out of my hands, as though
> I were some vagabond held cheap. (16:61ff)

The rage is the same, whether it is fairness, so valued by Americans, or honor, the highest good of Homer's officers, that has been violated. In both cases life is at stake. In both cases the moral constitution of the army, its cultural contract, has been impaired under risk of death and mutilating wounds.

THE FIDUCIARY ASSUMPTION

Compared to the modern soldier, the Homeric soldier hardly depended on others at all, and when he did it was upon comrades he knew personally and called on by name without technology to assist his own voice. He depended upon himself for his weapons and armor; his eyes and ears provided most of the tactical intelligence he required. He did not need to rely on the competence, mental clarity, and sense of responsibility of a chain of people he would never meet to assure that artillery or air strikes meant to protect him did not kill him by mistake.

Consider the following "routine" event of combat in Vietnam: A man on night watch on the perimeter of a landing zone, using a starlight scope, observes enemy soldiers moving toward the helicopter landing zone (LZ) through the darkness. He calls this in to the command post (CP); his words awaken his comrades, lightly asleep beside him while not on watch. Meanwhile, the officer in the CP calls in a request for illumination shells and artillery fire to turn back or weaken the oncoming assault.

Note the dependency of every man on others: the sleeping men on the one on watch, the one on watch on night-vision equipment supplied by others, all of them upon the radio sets connecting the bunker with the CP. They depend upon the radio-telephone operator (RTO) on watch in the CP and the officer who calls in the request for fire support with the correct coordinates and correct munitions, upon the artillery watch officer issuing the correct orders for a fire mission to the nearby fire base, upon these being carried out with the correct munitions and the guns correctly laid— the wrong coordinates could bring the fire down *on* the Americans, ironically dubbed "friendly fire," the phrase invoked when the action of one's own arms results in any wounding or death.

The vast and distant military and civilian structure that provides a modern soldier with his orders, arms, ammunition, food, water, information, training, and fire support is ultimately a moral structure, a *fiduciary*,[14] a trustee holding the life and safety of that soldier. The need for an intact moral world increases with every added coil of a soldier's mortal dependency on others. The vulnerability of the soldier's moral world has vastly increased in three millennia.

The following narrative, which contrasts a respected company commander with his successor, illuminates both obvious and hidden dimensions of the fiduciary relationship:

I told you about that captain I liked, he kept moving us, you know, always move. We'd set up, we'd sleep, if you could sleep, and then get out of there. I think that we walked a lot of unbroken paths, off trails, never set up—see, my second captain, he'd come up and say, "Well, that's a nice NDP [night defensive position]. It's already dug, little foxholes. It's beautiful, we'll just set up right there." My captain wouldn't do that. He'd shake his head and say, "Uh-UH, we're going over there, and we're going to *cut*." . . . Cutting, cutting, cutting . . . My captain, I hated his goddamn guts, but I admired him, admired the living shit. I hated his goddamn guts because he was so hard. . . . He would always stay off trails, stay off used NDPs. Y'know, when he left and he was replaced, I thought I'd never get out of there. I'd never get out of there alive.

At first glance, this veteran appears simply to be contrasting a competent company commander with his incompetent replacement. The first captain understood that previously used NDPs were probably mined and booby-trapped, or that at the very least, enemy mortars and artillery had their coordinates. Existing trails, which would allow the company to move more quickly without the long labor of cutting through, were likewise mined and booby-trapped as well as invitations to ambush.

Why did the captain who replaced the admired commander not know these things? The answer to this question goes deep into the betrayals of trust of the higher officers who (1) designed a system of officer rotation that rotated officers (above second lieutenant) in and out of combat assignments every six months, (2) were responsible for training, evaluating, and assigning officers to combat command, and (3) placed institutional and career considerations above the lives of the soldiers under their responsibility.[15] By the time a company or battalion commander acquired knowledge of the enemy's habits, the terrain and weather, the strengths and weaknesses of his men and their arms, whose advice to heed among the junior officers and NCOs, and the arts of deception, he was replaced. Some canny commanders would set up in an existing NDP and then move out of it after dark to another position. Such skills are only slightly transferable from one officer to his replacement and mainly have to be acquired from experience.

However, these larger systemic failures such as too-rapid turnover, inadequate training, and incompetent selection of troop commanders misses another important point that was much more visible to soldiers. Was there no one to tell the new captain that he should not use existing trails? Of course there were NCOs and lieutenants to tell him. The old commander, whose way of moving was "cut, cut, cut," probably displeased his superiors who ordered him to move from point A to point B in two hours—a movement that could be done in that time only if he took his company along highly dangerous existing trails. Possibly he answered back, saying, "No, that can't be done."

Officers who *wanted* to stay in the field beyond six months were said to have "gone bush" or "gone native." They were suspected of not being "with the program" and of having nurtured a "personality cult" in which the troops were loyal to them as individuals rather than to the chain of command. The veteran quoted above continues,

I had a lieutenant who I loved. I would've walked into hell with him, walked right into hell. . . . Now, when he was supposed to leave the field, he wouldn't leave, they had to bring two armed guards, no lie. They brought a special bird [helicopter] out. They said, "Now get on the bird! You're under orders." He didn't want to go.

Neither the admired captain nor the beloved lieutenant were cowards, avoiding the enemy out of fear. As far as I can determine from this veteran's account, both were effective officers with real loyalty both to their military tasks and to the men under them. They did not place the self-interest of "looking good" to their superiors above the safety of their men. They were not swayed by bureaucratically structured measures of "productivity" derived from industrial processes. The most fundamental incompetence in the Vietnam War was the misapplication of the social and mental model of an industrial process to human warfare.

A full analysis of how war can destroy the social contract binding soldiers to each other, to their commanders, and to the society that raised them as an army deserves a whole book in itself. My purpose here is to draw the reader's attention to the importance in itself of betrayal of *thémis*, to the soldier's reactions, and to the catastrophic outcomes that often flow from these reactions. I shall do this primarily by focusing on those things that the *Iliad* brings into view but which long familiarity has made invisible to us.

Let us look further at the extreme state of dependence of the modern soldier on his army for *everything* he needs to stay alive in combat: his arms, his training, food and water, communications, knowledge of the enemy, and the skills of his superiors:

My personal weapon until just after this op. [Union I][16] was the M-14. It was heavy, but at least you could depend on it. Then we got the M-16. It was a piece of shit that never should have gone over there with all the malfunctions. . . . I started hating the fucking government. At least in Union I we had rifles we could depend on. The stocks [of the M-16] broke in hand-to-hand. I started feeling like the government really didn't want us to get back, that there needed to be fewer of us back home. This was a constant thing, they kept changing the spring, the buffer. It was like they was testing it. Our lives depended on them. We cleaned the damned things every day, but they were just no fucking good. There were times when we'd rather use their weapons than our own. I once took an AK [AK-47] from a dead NVA and used it instead of my Mattel toy [M-16].

> It was about a week or two into Union II. I was walking point. I seen this NVA soldier at a distance. We were approaching him and he spotted us. We spread out to look for him. I was coming around a stand of grass and heard noise. I couldn't tell who it was, us or him. I stuck my head in the bush and saw this NVA hiding there and told him to come out. He started to move back and I saw he had one of those commando weapons, y'know, with a pistol grip under his thigh, and he brought it up and I was looking straight down the bore. I pulled the trigger on my M-16 and nothing happened.

Obviously this soldier survived the failure of his arms to tell the story, but the experience of betrayal that he took from it has been far more destructive of his subsequent life than the grazing wound inflicted by the NVA. A vast number of military officers, civilian defense officials, and civilian contractors were involved in the specification, design, prototyping, testing, manufacture, field testing, and acceptance of the M-16. Yet as one retired military officer blandly put it, "Early models were plagued by stoppages that caused some units to request reissue of the older M-14."[17] The veteran quoted above experienced the deficiencies of design, manufacture, and especially field testing and acceptance of the M-16 as a gross betrayal of the duties of care and of loyalty by the officers who, by virtue of their office, held his life in trust.

Equipment failure is not new in modern warfare. I count nineteen instances of equipment failure in the *Iliad*, of which nine were fatal to the soldier in question. Each Homeric soldier, or his father, supplied his own equipment; its failure did not cast doubt on the moral structure of the army in which he served. The ancient soldier was far less dependent in every way on military institutions than his modern counterpart, whose dependency is as complete as that of a small child on his or her family.

> During one patrol in the dry season, _____'s squad ran out of water and was not resupplied. They walked for a day and a half in search of water in Vietcong–controlled territory. When men started to collapse from dehydration in the heat, an officer's plea for emergency resupply was heeded: A helicopter flew over and "bombed" the squad with cases of Tab, seriously injuring one of the men. The major whose helicopter dropped the Tab was recalled to evacuate the casualty. There was no enemy activity. _____ subsequently read

in the division newspaper that the major had put himself in for and had received the Bronze Star for resupplying the troops and evacuating the wounded "under fire."

Extreme dependency on others is fundamental to modern combat. We have become so accustomed to this that it easily escapes notice.

Shortages of all sorts—food, water, ammunition, clothing, shelter from the elements, medical care—are intrinsic to prolonged combat, if for no other reason than enemy attacks on the army's logistical support services. The fortitude of soldiers under such conditions, for example during the siege of Dien Bien Phu or Khe Sanh, is legendary. However, when deprivation is perceived as the outcome of indifference or disrespect by superiors, it arouses *mênis* as an unbearable offense.

> They had a fucking pet dog at the camp and they always got in fresh hamburger for the dog, but there were times we were out and starving, not even getting C-rations, because they wouldn't resupply us. The dog got sick and they had a chopper in there to fly it to Danang. I had a machete wound in my calf and had to walk for miles back to the base camp.

The shortage that the combat soldier finds most offensive, however, is shortage of competence.

> The first deaths in _____'s platoon were caused by "friendly fire" from adjoining sectors of the defense perimeter; the officer had neglected to inform them that he was sending men out on the berm. . . . In two successive helicopter-borne combat insertions the company left the landing zone in parallel columns and after a few "klicks" in the jungle lost track of each other until they met in a furious fire fight. Two men were injured in the first one, five in the second. _____ never heard of any investigation or disciplinary action.

Another veteran:

> There was just one stupid fucking thing after another. They decided to use tear gas on a ville [cluster of hamlets] after we had crossed a river neck deep, and of course everything was soaked, the canisters [of the gas masks] were soaked and they decided to use tear gas. Of course the masks didn't work. They gassed us almost to death.

No one has successfully defined where the inescapable SNAFUs—a World War II expression: Situation Normal, All Fucked Up—of war end and culpable incompetence begins.

Is betrayal of "what's right" essential to combat trauma, or is betrayal simply one of many terrible things that happen in war? Aren't terror, shock, horror, and grief at the death of friends trauma enough? No one can conclusively answer these questions today. However, I shall argue what I've come to strongly believe through my work with Vietnam veterans: that moral injury is an essential part of any combat trauma that leads to lifelong psychological injury. Veterans can usually recover from horror, fear, and grief once they return to civilian life, so long as "what's right" has not also been violated.

We now turn our attention to the soldiers' reactions to betrayal of "what's right." These are unchanged across three millennia. Indignant rage will occupy us for the remainder of this chapter. It opens the way for berserk rage, which I will describe in chapter 5.

SOLDIERS' RAGE—THE BEGINNING

Rage is properly the title of Homer's poem, and his audience may have known it by that name, not *Iliad*.[18] King Agamémnon causes a ravaging plague in the Greek army by his refusal to accept ransom for the daughter of a priest of Apollo, god of disease and healing. The plague ends only after Achilles mobilizes moral pressure on Agamémnon to return the captive woman. In doing this, Achilles forces him to do what a pious and prudent man would have done of his own accord. Agamémnon, however, takes it as a personal attack by Achilles and seizes Achilles' prize of honor, the captive woman Brisêis, to replace the one he gave up to save the plague-devastated army. Achilles' rage at this wrong is immediate:

> . . . in his shaggy chest this way and that
> the passion of his heart ran: should he draw
> longsword from hip, . . . kill
> [Agamémnon] in single combat . . . ,
> or hold his rage in check . . . ?
> . . . As he slid
> the big blade slowly from the sheath, Athêna

> . . . stepping
> up behind him, visible to no one
> except Akhilleus [Achilles], gripped his
> red-gold hair. . . .
> The grey-eyed goddess Athêna said to him:
>
> "It was to check this killing rage I came
> from heaven . . . " (1:221ff)

Achilles submits and withdraws. His *mênis*, restrained at the brink of cutting down Agamémnon, is diverted to hacking away emotional bonds and driving away those he used to love. In Vietnam men were not able, as Achilles was, to withdraw physically from combat. They did, however, have the freedom to withdraw emotionally and mentally from everything beyond their small circle of combat-proven comrades.

Homer's starting point, then, is *mênis*, indignant wrath. I believe it is also the first and possibly the primary trauma that converted subsequent terror, horror, grief, and guilt into lifelong disability for Vietnam veterans. Indignant rage is uncomfortably familiar to all who work with combat veterans.

Homer uses the word *mênis* for Achilles only in connection with the wrong done to him by Agamémnon, and never in connection with his berserk rage at Hektor for killing his friend Pátroklos. I prefer "indignant rage" as a translation for *mênis*, because I can hear the word *dignity* hidden in the word *indignant*. It is the kind of rage arising from social betrayal that impairs a person's dignity through violation of "what's right." Apart from its use as a word for divine rage, Homer uses *mênis* only as the word for the rage that ruptures social attachments. We now turn to this choking-off of the social and moral world.

CHAPTER 2

Shrinkage of the Social and Moral Horizon

Through [thémis] humans can make themselves stable. . . . Annihilation of convention [thémis] by another's acts can destroy . . . stable character. . . . It can, quite simply, produce bestiality, the utter loss of human relatedness.
—Martha C. Nussbaum,
The Fragility of Goodness: Luck and Ethics in Greek Tragedy and Philosophy

The social horizon of the unscarred soldier encompasses not only his family and other civilian ties but also all those military formations to which his unit belongs and with which it cooperates. Imagine the social world as a physical space, and then imagine a map of the space representing a soldier's sense of social connectedness. How does this map change after someone above the soldier violates "what's right"? Men fight mainly for their comrades; this has become conventional wisdom even among civilians. Prolonged exposure to danger and the profound strain of battle compel this contraction of loyalty to some degree in every war. However, soldiers sometimes lose responsiveness to the claims of *any* bonds, ideals, or loyalties outside a tiny circle of immediate comrades. An us-against-them mentality severs all other attachments or commitments.

ONE AMERICAN SOLDIER'S SOCIAL SPACE

This veteran speaks of his training in an elite unit:

> We were down in Kentucky, and you got to care about people there, everyone in that outfit, . . . you grew like a hand.

His social and moral horizon extended to his whole battalion. Then the battalion was sent to Vietnam. His experience there was a series of betrayals of "what's right," one of which is described here:

> You see, what you'd do is you'd set up an ambush. Now, Bravo Company's probably three miles away from you. And you make contact [with the enemy] and run towards Bravo Company. So what happened is we got into a fucking ambush and we couldn't get out of the ambush. And the motherfuckers wouldn't move. . . . <u>So from then on,</u> we didn't fucking [inaudible]. Y'know, <u>you wouldn't fucking tell them nothing.</u> "Fuck Bravo Company. <u>I hope all them motherfuckers die.</u>"

The social map of this soldier's world has shrunk and now excludes Company B, which it formerly included. In fact, it has shrunk to only the five men of his reconnaissance team:

> It was constant now. I was watching the other five guys like they was my children. . . . It wasn't seventy-two guys [in the company] I was worried about. It was five guys.

His social horizon, in the midst of lethal dangers to them all, has contracted to this small circle of comrades. As we shall see, Achilles' horizon shrinks even further, until it contains only one other person.

TRACKING ACHILLES THROUGH SOCIAL SPACE

We can map Achilles' social space, just as we surveyed that of the American sergeant in the previous section. The two maps are remarkably similar.

Achilles is a very high-ranking officer, so his social and moral horizon is in the beginning much wider than that of an enlisted man. As the *Iliad* opens, the god Apollo devastates the Greek army with plague. Agamémnon has brought this on by his arrogant refusal to accept ransom for the daughter of the priest of Apollo, captured during the sack of a city near Troy. Achilles calls an assembly of the army (1:64) to determine what is needed to propitiate Apollo and end the plague. Achilles cares about the *whole* army.[1] These broad sympathies and wide moral commitment are inseparable from Achilles' good character prior to the events recounted in the *Iliad*.

The seer Kalkhas makes the diagnosis and gives the prescription:
Return the priest's daughter. When Agamémnon balks at returning
the captive woman and demands an immediate replacement,
Achilles speaks of "we" for the whole army: "How can the army
make you a new gift? . . . we'll make it up to you." (1:156ff) However,
Agamémnon turns on him and orders the captive woman Brisêis,
Achilles' prize of honor, seized as the replacement. Homer makes
clear that this is undeserved, and not within Agamémnon's rights. In
the course of the *Iliad*, the other Greek officers say it was undeserved, and the gods and eventually Agamémnon himself agree.
Achilles' response is to withdraw his moral, emotional, and military
commitment from the army. He bitterly tells the assembled army, "I
swear a day will come when every Akhaian [Greek] soldier will
groan to have Akhilleus back . . . though a thousand men perish
before the killer, Hektor." (1:283ff) Homer reinforces this with the
rich symbol of the "great staff . . . Akhaian officers in council take . . .
in hand by turns, when they observe . . . due order in debate
(1:276ff). . . . [Achilles] hurled the staff . . . before him on the
ground." (1:292f) This is the same sentiment voiced in the previous
section by the American Airborne trooper when he said, "Fuck
Bravo Company. I hope them motherfuckers all die."

Significantly, as Gregory Nagy points out, the name Achilles
(*Akhí* + *lâuos*) means he "'whose **lâós** [host of fighting men] has
ákhos [grief]'. . . The Achilles figure entails **pêma** [pain, grief] for
. . . the Achaeans . . . when he withdraws from the war. . . ."[2] The
reason for withdrawal of commitment is the same for both the
American sergeant and Achilles: betrayal of "what's right."

After betrayal of *thémis* in warfare, an us-against-them mentality
takes hold in which everyone, no matter how close before, is either
an absolute ally or an absolute enemy. This simplification and
shrinkage of loyalties flows directly from the betrayal of "what's
right." Achilles' wrath has numbed him to any responsiveness to
the catastrophes of his fellow Greeks, for whom he has formerly
cared deeply. When a delegation of senior fellow officers begs him
to rejoin the fight, he castigates the one who is closest to him:

> "Old uncle Phoinix, . . . [do not speak]
> for Agamémnon, whom you must not honor;
> you would be hateful to me, dear as you are.
> Loyalty should array you at my side
> in giving pain to him who gives me pain." (9:739ff)

We have gotten only the briefest glimpse of Achilles' broad commitments prior to the moral injury inflicted on him by Agamémnon. However, as I shall show below, his moral horizon was broader even than the whole Greek army. Before the psychological injuries recorded in the *Iliad*, Achilles' habit was to respect enemy dead rather than defile them, and to ransom enemy prisoners rather than kill them. Achilles loses his humanity in two stages: He ceases to care about his fellow Greeks after betrayal by his commander, and then he loses all compassion for any human being after the death of Pátroklos. The *Iliad* is the story of the undoing of Achilles' character.

DESERTION

In response to Agamémnon's betrayal in the opening moments of the epic, Achilles prepares to desert:

> Now it is I who do not care to fight.
> Tomorrow at dawn when I have . . .
> . . . hauled my ships
> for loading in the shallows, if you like
> and if it interests you, look out and see
> my ships. . . .
> And if the great Earthshaker [Poseidon] gives a breeze,
> the third day out I'll make it home to Phthía. (9:436ff)

As the political and military head of an independent contingent,[3] Achilles could indeed leave if he wished. The modern soldier who does the same commits the gravest military crime. During a declared war, desertion can be a capital offense under American law. Rather than be diverted by generalities, let us listen again to the voice of the same reconnaissance sergeant we heard in the previous section:

> The only one who ever fucking did anything, anything right was fucking _____. He was sent home with _____'s body—and he didn't come back. He did the right fucking thing. When you had a guy get killed in our outfit, one of the team went home with him [a practice only in elite units, and only for part of the war]. And _____ went home with him. He took him back to New York. He quit. . . . Deserted, I guess—whatever you want to call it.

The dead man was the sergeant's closest friend. While the sergeant was hospitalized with pneumonia, his friend was killed when the team was sent out on a frivolous mission designed simply to get the men out of the camp. Betrayal and grief came to him and to the others on the team in one stroke. The sergeant stayed for three more combat tours to get revenge; another team member deserted. The sergeant's present judgment of the deserter: "The only one who ever fucking did anything, anything right."[4]

The moral strength of an army is impaired by every injustice, whether it personally touches an individual soldier or not. When Agamémnon wrongfully seizes Achilles' prize of honor, he inflicts an injury not on just this one man but on the whole army. I believe that commentators on the *Iliad* have overlooked this in their interpretation of the episode in Book 2, where the Greeks stampede for their ships after Agamémnon puts them to the bizarre "test" by telling them in Assembly:

> . . . let us act on what I say:
> Retreat! Embark for our own fatherland!
> We cannot hope any longer to take Troy! (2:157ff)

They are war-weary after nine years of fighting, to be sure, and their commander has just stood before them and ordered abandonment of the beachhead. Nonetheless, everyone—Agamémnon, the officers privy to his "test" of the army, and the gods themselves—is taken aback by the single-hearted response of the army:

> He made their hearts leap in their breasts, . . .
> and all that throng, aroused, began to surge
> as ground swells do. . . .
> . . . just so moved this assembly.
> Shouting confusedly, they all began
> to scramble for the ships. High in the air
> a dust cloud from their scuffling rose, commands
> rang back and forth—to man the cables, haul
> the black ships to the salt immortal sea.
> They cleared the launching ways, their hearts on home,
> and shouts went up as props were pulled away. (2:160ff)

I believe that this mass desertion by the Greek army is prompted more than anything else by the commander's betrayal of *thémis* that they witnessed at the prior Assembly.

27

Agamémnon's public betrayal of *thémis* with Achilles has pushed his soldiers to the brink of desertion and mutiny and will shortly cost them "loss on bitter loss." (1:3) Vietnam provides us with many parallels. Investigative reporter Neil Sheehan has written:

> [By 1969] it was an Army in which men escaped into marijuana and heroin and other men died because their comrades were "stoned" on these drugs. . . . It was an Army whose units in the field were on the edge of mutiny, whose soldiers rebelled against the senselessness of their sacrifice by assassinating officers and non-coms in "accidental" shootings and "fraggings" with grenades.[5]

SIMPLIFICATION OF THE SOCIAL WORLD TO A SINGLE COMRADE

Initially, Achilles' horizon shrinks from the whole Greek army (1:63) to his own troop, the Myrmidons. As wrath festers, his field of moral vision and emotional responsiveness shrinks further to just one man, his foster brother, Pátroklos (23:105):

> Ah, Father Zeus, Athêna, and Apollo!
> If not one Trojan of them all
> should get away from death, and not one Argive [Greek]
> save ourselves were spared, we two alone
> could pull down Troy's old coronet of towers! (16:115ff)

In this imagined apocalypse, everyone would die except Achilles and Pátroklos; not only the hated Agamémnon would be carried away, but friends such as Odysseus, Ajax, Phoinix, and all the Myrmidons. It bears remembering that at this point Achilles is unscarred by grief—betrayal of "what's right" alone has done this damage.

ACHILLES' CHARACTER
BEFORE HIS PSYCHOLOGICAL INJURIES

We see Achilles only briefly before his quarrel with Agamémnon, but cumulatively we learn much about his former character from the remarks of others throughout the *Iliad*.

RESPECT FOR THE DEAD

Achilles was not in the habit of defiling his fallen enemies, as he later does horribly to Hektor. Early in the *Iliad*, Hektor's wife, Andrómakhê, praises Achilles' past respect for the dead:

> "My father great Akhilleus killed when he
> . . . plundered Thêbê. . . .
> . . . He killed him, but, reverent at least in this, did not
> despoil him. Body, gear, and weapons forged
> so handsomely, he burned, and heaped up a barrow
> over the ashes." (6:484ff)

Enemy arms were legitimate spoils of war. In renouncing them, Achilles showed a generous, extra measure of respect to this fallen enemy beyond what was required by conventional piety. After Agamémnon's betrayal and Pátroklos's death, Achilles kills Hektor before the eyes of his wife and parents and then mutilates and atrociously debases his corpse.

Achilles' character has changed. Before, he was responsive to all *thémis* for the dead, the cultural definition of "what's right" toward enemy corpses. Achilles had earlier counted himself as part of the human community that encompassed both Greeks and Trojans. His brutal treatment of Hektor's body did *not* stem from mutual cultural ignorance or contempt, as was the case so often in Vietnam, where each side rejected the other's values and customs. Agamémnon acknowledges the shared *thémis* for the dead in Book 7 when the Trojans ask for a truce to permit them to burn their dead. He says, "As to the dead, I would withhold no decency of burning; a man should spare no pains to see cadavers given as soon as may be after death to purifying flame." (7:485ff)

TAKING PRISONERS ALIVE

We become aware of Achilles' prior attitude toward captives when Homer again puts Achilles' past conduct in the mouth of someone close to Hektor. This time it is Hektor's mother, Hékabê, addressing his corpse:

> Akhilleus captured other sons of mine
> in other years, and sold them overseas

> . . . That was not his way with you.
> After he took your life, cutting you down
> with his sharp-bladed spear, he trussed and dragged you
> many times round the barrow of his friend,
> Pátroklos, whom you killed—though not by this
> could that friend live again. . . . (24:895ff)

In all the *Iliad*'s fighting—and there are hundreds of pages of fighting—not a single prisoner is taken for ransom or for sale as a slave. Homer goes out of his way to emphasize Achilles' past practice of ransoming or selling prisoners rather than killing them. The former Achilles stands out as quite the humanitarian, especially when compared to his fellow warriors. Diomêdês and Odysseus kill Dolôn; Agamémnon talks Meneláos out of sparing Adréstos; the sons of Antímakhos beg to be taken for ransom, but Agamémnon kills them, having just dispatched Isos and Antiphos, whom Achilles had formerly ransomed; and Aías Oïliades takes Kleóboulos prisoner but kills him without discussion.[6] When Achilles kills Trôs (20:533ff) and later Lykáôn as he begs to be ransomed, *Achilles explicitly acknowledges his change of character*. He says to Lykáôn, who had just been ransomed home from Lemnos, where Achilles had shipped him after a previous capture:

> Young fool, don't talk to me of what you'll barter.
> <u>In days past, before Pátroklos died</u>
> <u>I had a mind to spare the Trojans, took them</u>
> <u>alive in shoals, and shipped them out abroad.</u> (21:116ff)

To summarize, we have direct evidence regarding Achilles' former moderation toward enemy dead and enemy prisoners. We have already seen that before Agamémnon's betrayal, Achilles had other marks of good character, such as concern for the well-being of his community as a whole, not merely his own private sphere.

MORAL LUCK

Greek tragic poets, starting with Homer, confront us with a harrowing dimension of human social existence. This is the possibility, as Brown University Professor Martha Nussbaum declares, that social betrayal can undermine our very humanity: "Annihilation of convention [Homer's *thémis*] by another's acts can destroy . . . stable character. . . . It can, quite simply, produce bestiality, the utter loss of human relatedness."[7] When this happens to a person, he or she has catastrophic *moral luck*. I offer a dialogue between two combat veterans in a therapy group:

> *First Veteran*: Well, at first, I mean when I just come there, I couldn't believe what I was seeing. I couldn't believe Americans could do things like that to another human being . . . but then I *became* that. We went through villages and killed everything, I mean *everything*, and that was all right with me.
>
> *Second Veteran*: <u>I was just lucky, that's all</u>. There were never, never any civilians up where I was. . . . We did some horrible, horrible things to NVA—but they were *soldiers*. . . . Killing babies, young girls, I would have *killed* an American I seen raping a nine-year-old girl without giving it a moment's thought. But where we were in the A Shau,[8] there just weren't any [civilians].

Here the veterans grapple with the question of moral luck: Can *any* workings of bad luck produce cruel or evil actions *in a good person*?

Our culture has raised us to believe that good character stands reliably between the good person and the possibility of horrible acts. In Book 10 of *The Republic*, Plato sarcastically calls Homer "the best of the poets and the first of the tragedians." Where is the tragedy in the *Iliad*? I have argued above that the *Iliad* is the tragedy of Achilles' noble character brought to ruin—*moral ruin in his own terms*. I displayed the evidence that prior to Agamémnon's betrayal of "what's right" and the death of Pátroklos, Achilles possessed a highly developed social morality. This was reflected in his care for the welfare of other Greek soldiers, respect for enemies living and dead, and a reluctance to kill prisoners. Achilles' moral unluckiness, his tragedy, was that events—simply what happened—created the desire to do things that he himself regarded as bad.[9]

The most ancient traditions of Western culture instruct us to base our self-respect on firmness of character. Many popular melodramas of moral courage provide satisfaction through the comforting fantasy that our own character would hold steady under the most extreme pressure of dreadful events. A permanent challenge of working with those injured by combat trauma is facing the painful awareness that in all likelihood one's own character would *not* have stood firm. Merely allowing ourselves to hear the combat veteran's story threatens our culturally defined sense of self-respect. We have powerful motives *not* to listen to the veteran's story, or to deny its truth.

The vulnerable relationship between child and parent is a metaphor for the relationship between a soldier and his army. It is also more than a metaphor when we consider the formation and maintenance of good character. The parent's betrayal of *thémis* through incest, abuse, or neglect puts the child in mortal danger. Despite intellectual limitations, the small child usually grasps the danger, although the child's mental representation of the danger differs from the adult's. The child's inner sense of safety in the world emerges from the trustworthiness, reliability, and simple competence of the family. Similarly, the child's acquisition of self-control, self-esteem, and consideration for others depends upon the family. Absent inherited mental disorders, good parenting will produce good character and all the other adult resources of dignity and maturity, including ideals, respect for others, self-respect, ambitions, self-care, prosocial rather than antisocial activity, reliable capacity to distinguish reality from fantasy, and so forth. Lurking behind these supposedly settled truths is the Platonic assertion that good character is a firm wall between a good person and evil acts, regardless of the betrayals of "what's right" and other blows, such as bereavement, that may simply happen to an adult. Often there is the invisible, unstated assumption that those who hold power in society exhibit loyalty and care in their fulfillment of *thémis*.

WAR DESTROYS THE TRUSTWORTHY SOCIAL ORDER OF THE MIND

Homer makes us witness to the weakening of Achilles' fine character by betrayal and its subsequent destruction by bereavement. Many veterans' narratives ask us to witness the same. This man did three Vietnam combat tours in tanks:

> I was eighteen years old. And I was like your typical young American boy. A virgin. I had strong religious beliefs. For the longest time I wanted to be a priest when I was growing up. You

know, I didn't just go to church Sundays, it was every day of the week. I'd come home from school and go right down to the church, and spend an hour in the church. And I was into athletics, sports. I was nothing unique. I was just a typical American boy—_____ High School, Class of 1965. . . . It was the way you were taught, like, "Whenever you're alone, make believe God's there with you. Would he approve of what you are doing?" That's basically—sure, I wasn't no angel, either. I mean, I had my little fistfights and stuff. It was, you're only human. But evil didn't enter it 'till Vietnam.

I mean real evil. I wasn't prepared for it at all.

Why I became like that? It was all evil. All evil. Where before, I wasn't. I look back, I look back today, and I'm horrified at what I turned into. What I was. What I did. I just look at it like it was somebody else. I really do. It was somebody else. Somebody had control of me.

War changes you, changes you. Strips you, strips you of all your beliefs, your religion, takes your dignity away, you become an animal. I know the animals don't—the animal in the sense of being evil. You know, it's unbelievable what humans can do to each other.

I never in a million years thought I would be capable of doing that. Never, never, never.

Revenge became this veteran's single value. No other value had any claim on him; all previous relationships ceased to have meaning. When he entered this berserk state, he stopped writing home, even ceased to care about the other men on his tank, except as instruments of his revenge.

I carried this home with me. I lost all my friends, beat up my sister, went after my father. I mean, I just went after anybody and everything. Every three days I would totally explode, lose it for no reason at all. I'd be sitting there calm as could be, and this monster would come out of me with a fury that most people didn't want to be around. So it wasn't just over there. I brought it back here with me.

This man's account makes clear that the changes combat brought about in him were not limited to the war zone.

Combat trauma destroys the *capacity* for social trust, accounting for the paranoid state of being that blights the lives of the most severely traumatized combat veterans. This is not a selective mistrust directed at a specific individual or institution that has betrayed its charge, but a comprehensive destruction of social trust. Lies and euphemisms by the soldier's own military superiors and civilian leaders of course undermine social trust by destroying confidence in language. Perversion of language and destruction of the trustworthy meaning of words by official lies were not new to the Vietnam War. This is well known and need not be elaborated here. What has been largely overlooked, however, is the way that enemy activities contribute to the destruction of a soldier's social trust. The enemy does severe damage to a part of mental function that is critical to the maintenance of social trust: the trustworthiness of perception.

In Vietnam the enemy struck not only at the body but also at the most basic functions of the soldier's mind, attacking his perceptions by concealment; his cognitions by camouflage and deception; his intentions by surprise, anticipation, and ambush. These mind games have been part of war since time immemorial, but never in American military experience have they been directed so skillfully and with such thoroughness at the enlisted man as in Vietnam. Our historical image of surprise and deception focuses on the strategies of leaders and commanders, such as Germany's surprise attack on the Soviet Union or the successful ruse that convinced German leadership that the invasion of France would land at Pas de Calais rather than Normandy. These deceptions were directed at the high command. Our images of the bitter fighting among the hedgerows of Normandy do not include booby-trapped wine bottles or French babies sitting in the road atop command-detonated mines. Only 3 to 4 percent of American casualties in World War II and Korea were from booby traps, while 11 percent of the deaths and 17 percent of the injuries in Vietnam were from these lowest-echelon attacks of surprise and deception.

American soldiers literally felt tortured by their Vietnamese enemy. Prolonged patrolling in Vietnam led to a decomposition of the normal, the familiar, the safe. Every familiar item of the physical world could be made to be or to conceal an explosive by the Vietnamese, whether a shiny aluminum rice carrier, a Parker-51 fountain pen, a bicycle, a coconut, Coke cans, C-ration cans, and discarded American artillery-shell casings. The trained, safest response to being fired upon was to take cover; the Vietcong prepared some ambush sites with small boards mounted with barbed spikes, which they would conceal in the vegetation, spike side up.

When American troops dove for cover, they would impale themselves on the spikes. In such warfare nothing is what it seems; all certainties liquefy; stable truths turn into their opposites.

I see a deep similarity between the experience of the Vietnam combat soldier and the victim of torture. Describing torture, Elaine Scarry writes,

> The contents of the [torture] room, its furnishings, are converted into weapons: the most common instance of this is the bathtub that figures prominently in the reports from numerous countries, but it is only one among many. Men and women being tortured . . . describe being handcuffed in a constricted position for hours, days, and in some cases months to a chair, to a cot, to a filing cabinet, to a bed; they describe being beaten with "family-sized soft drink bottles" or having a hand crushed with a chair, of having their heads "repeatedly banged on the edges of a refrigerator door.". . . The room . . . is converted into a weapon, . . . made to demonstrate that everything is a weapon, the objects themselves, and with them the fact of civilization, are annihilated: there is no wall, no window, no door, no bathtub, no refrigerator, no chair, no bed.[10]

Prolonged contact with the enemy in war destroys the soldier's confidence in his own mental functions as surely as would prolonged torture in a political prison. The opportunity to fight back, which the soldier enjoys but the prisoner does not, may not make much difference. Without confidence in one's own mental functions, ordinary economic, political, and domestic life becomes virtually impossible.

COMBAT IS A CONDITION OF CAPTIVITY AND ENSLAVEMENT

"War is only a branch of political activity . . . simply a continuation of political intercourse, with the addition of other means."[11] Before beginning this work, I would have understood this classic formulation by the famed nineteenth-century Prussian military theorist Carl von Clausewitz to refer to whole campaigns, the realm of generals' and national leaders in the conduct of contests between nations. But men who have actually fought in war have taught me another level of its meaning—for the people who were outside the perimeter in night listening posts, on the riverboats, behind the trees. They have taught me that even down to the individual soldier and his squad, war is profoundly political, because it is about power. For soldiers in prolonged combat, war is the mutual struggle to paralyze or control the will of enemy soldiers by inflicting wounds and death and creating the terror of these. Some combat units had printed "calling cards" or "death cards," the most common of which was the ace of spades. One veteran recalls, "We used to put it in the mouth of all the kills we got." The domination that a soldier seeks over his enemy is as total as the domination a master has over a slave, aiming for fear to so completely grip the enemy that he flees in panic, surrenders, or is too terrified even to move, let alone resist. When such domination is complete, a battle is a "walkover."

The struggle to dominate the will, however, is *reciprocal*. All the tools of physical warfare can be understood as attempts to create in the enemy the broken mental state of a slave. The enemy is a human enemy, not inanimate matter, and uses all possible social and psychological resources, such as training, unit cohesion, leadership, and coercion to resist this enslavement of the will and to inflict it in return. The enemy's attempts to dominate the soldier's will are inevitably met by counterdomination by his own side. The mind, the heart, the soul of the combat soldier become the focus of competing attempts to enslave.

The social institution of modern war makes the soldier a captive, but unlike other forms of captivity, the role of his captor is continuously shared by the enemy and the soldier's own army. Imagine for a moment a conventional war with a defined front line and rear areas on both sides of the front line. If a soldier flees the terror of the battle, it makes no difference in which direction he flees. He flees toward death or imprisonment no matter which direction he takes. If he flees toward the enemy he may be shot out of hand when his surrender is not accepted, or he may be imprisoned as a POW. If he flees toward his own rear, he may be summarily shot or imprisoned as a deserter. The front line is thus a narrow zone of fear and death lying between two prisons. In this narrow zone two massive social organizations compete to enslave the soldier. The social institution of war creates total captivity with opposing armies working in perfect harmony to keep the soldiers in place and at each other.

Terror, mortal dependency, barriers to escape—these are characteristics of modern combat that mark it as a condition of captivity and enslavement as harsh as any political prison or labor camp. The reader may think that this is overstated and reflects a prejudice against the American military. "It can't really be that bad . . . can it?" Necessity dictates strict discipline in time of war, does it not? I am not demonizing the American military but emphasizing that it is the world of war itself that creates conditions that add up to captivity and enslavement. The Vietnamese enemy and the American armed forces cooperated perfectly to create these conditions for the individual soldiers of both sides.

"DON'T MEAN NOTHIN'"—DESTRUCTION OF IDEALS, AMBITIONS, AFFILIATIONS

Homer and the Greek tragic poets held the terrifying view that apparently stable adult character *continues* to be dependent and vulnerable, even after it has been established by good nurturing in childhood. According to these tragic poets, good character is dependent on good-enough stability and reliability of *thémis* and remains vulnerable to high-stakes betrayal of *thémis* by power holders. The moral dimension of trauma destroys virtue, undoes good character.

Soldiers did not "set themselves up for it" when they received M-16 rifles that did not work. They did not "ask for it" any more than an eight-year-old girl or boy "asks for it" when he or she is raped by a relative. The insistence with which such reflexive equations as "set himself up for it" and "asked for it" push forward as an explanation for trauma is a reflection of how frightening and painful it is to believe accounts of high-stakes betrayal of "what's right." Normal adults wrap *thémis* around themselves as a mantle of safety in the world. Every trauma narrative pierces our adult cloak of safety; it challenges the rightness of *thémis* and leaves us terrified and disoriented. This is another powerful motive to deny the truth of trauma narratives, to avoid hearing them, or to forget them.

When ruptures are too violent between the social realization of "what's right" and the inner *thémis* of ideals, ambitions, and affiliations, the inner *thémis* can collapse. A veteran recalls a typical exchange between himself and other team members after deaths among them:

"Fuck it. They're dead. No big fucking deal. Move on."

"_____'s dead."

"Fucking _____ fucked up. He's dead."

"He shouldn't have *fucked up*. He wouldn't be *fucking dead*."

"Where, where's the compassion? Where's your sense of human—This is another fellow American."

Y'know? He didn't fuck up. He's dead. You know?

Why can't I feel? Y'know, why can't I grieve for him? That's where they put that hardening in you.

"Don't mean nothin'" and "Fuck it," the Vietnam combat soldier's mantras, spread out to engulf everything valued or wanted, every person, loyalty, and commitment.

CHAPTER 3

Grief at the Death
of a Special Comrade

The dignity of these humans is to weep.
—Martha Nussbaum,
Introduction to *The Bacchae*, p. xl

We can never fathom the soldier's grief if we do not know the human attachment which battle nourishes and then amputates. As civilians we have no native understanding of the soldier's grief. Combat calls forth a passion of care among men who fight beside each other that is comparable to the earliest and most deeply felt family relationships. The experiences of Vietnam combat veterans and the accounts of comradeship in Homer's *Iliad* illuminate each other, enhancing our understanding of the soldier's relationship to a special comrade, be it Achilles to Pátroklos or an American soldier to his buddy. We often hear that the death of a special friend-in-arms broke the survivor's life into unhealable halves, with everything before his death radically severed from everything after.

After probing the relationship to a special comrade, I shall examine grief *per se*. Vietnam and the *Iliad* again throw light on each other, clarifying the role of Thetis, Achilles' goddess mother, and the state of being "already dead" while still biologically alive.

Any blow in life will have longer-lasting and more serious consequences if there is no opportunity to communalize it. This means some mix of formal social ceremony and informal telling of the story with feeling *to socially connected others* who do not let the survivor go through it alone. The virtual suppression of social griefwork in Vietnam contrasts vividly with the powerful expressions of communal mourning recorded in Homeric epic. I believe that numerous military, cultural, institutional, and historical factors conspired to thwart the griefwork of Vietnam combat veterans, and I believe that this matters. The emergence of rage out of intense grief may be a human universal; long-term obstruction of grief and failure to communalize grief can imprison a person in endless swinging between rage and emotional deadness as a permanent way of being in the world.

SOLDIERS' LOVE FOR SPECIAL COMRADES— VIETNAM AND TROY

Pátroklos and Achilles were virtually brothers by adoption. The word *brother* appears as symbol in the everyday talk of Vietnam veterans, as in "How y'doin', bro?" or the much more deeply felt "I had to. He's my bro." The "brotherhood of soldiers" has become a dead metaphor in the mouths of political speechifiers and rear-echelon officers visiting the troops, but the reality of combat calls forth the language and emotion of the earliest and strongest family relationships in every place and era. A veteran, speaking of his closest friend-in-arms, says:

> It's a closeness you never had before. It's closer than your mother and father, closest [sic] than your brother or your sister, or whoever you're closest with in your family. It was . . . y'know, you'd take a shit, and he'd be right there covering you. And if I take a shit, he'd be covering me. . . . We needed each other to survive.

The kin relationship, brother, seems to be the most accessible and commonly spoken symbol of the bond between combat soldiers¹ who are closest comrades.

Modern American English makes soldiers' love for special comrades into a problem, because the word *love* evokes sexual and romantic associations. But *friendship* seems too bland for the passion of care that arises between soldiers in combat. Achilles laments to his mother that his *phílos*, his "greatest friend is gone." (18:89f) Much ink has been spilled over whether this word (and the abstract noun *phília*) and all its linguistic relatives should be translated under the rubric of "friend, friendship," etc. or of "love, beloved," etc. However, the difficulty of finding the right word reflects differences between ancient Greek and modern American culture that need to be made clear. "*Phília* includes many relationships that would not be classified as friendships. The love of mother and child is a paradigmatic case of *phília*; all close family relations, including the relation of husband and wife, are so characterized. Furthermore, our [word] 'friendship' can suggest a relationship that is weak in affect . . . , as in the expression 'just friends'. . . . [*Phília*] includes the very strongest affective relationships that human beings form, . . . [including, but not limited to] relationships that have a passionate sexual component. For both these reasons, English 'love' seems more appropriately wide-ranging. . . . [The] emphasis of *phília* is less on intensely passionate longing than on . . . benefit, sharing, and mutuality. . . ."[2] Many individuals who experience friendship as one of the central goods in their lives find that their employers will not recognize *phília* between people whose relationship is not familial. Veterans have lost their jobs because they left work to aid another veteran, in circumstances where the same absence would have been "understandable" and charged against sick or vacation time had the other been a spouse, parent, or child. Many people today view friendship purely as a leisure activity, or a sweetener that with luck arises among co-workers, neighbors, or members of a voluntary association such as a church or club but which will be put aside if it gives rise to any conflicting claims at work. Many veterans have also alienated their spouses because they would leave home to go to the aid of fellow veterans. The ancient Greeks, perhaps because their societies were so highly militarized (every male citizen was also a soldier), simply assumed the centrality of *phília*.

HOMER ON THE RELATIONSHIP BETWEEN ACHILLES AND PATROKLOS

Achilles, mourning the death of Pátroklos, recalls "how in his company he fought out many a rough day full of danger, cutting through ranks in war and the bitter sea." (24:7ff) Apart from military comradeship, Pátroklos may be Achilles' brother by adoption;[3] they grew up together in the same house. Pátroklos's ghost asks,

> "[Do not] inter my bones apart from thine
> but close together, as we grew together,
> in thy family's hall. . . .
> [Your father] adopted me
> and reared me kindly, naming me your squire [*therápon*].

41

So may the same urn hide our bones, the one
of gold your gracious mother gave." (23:98ff)

Homer makes clear that Achilles accepts this request (23:201ff);
burial in the same urn is an emblem of their family relationship.
While the kin relationship of brother seems to be the most frequent symbol of the relationship between combat soldiers who
are closest comrades, in our culture the powerful territory of feeling and symbolism of *mother* often seems to apply just as well.

Apart from being his figurative or legal brother, what else was
Pátroklos to Achilles? The word *squire* used by Fitzgerald in the
passage quoted above puts us on the wrong track. A better fit, militarily speaking, for the Greek word *therápon* is "second-in-command" or "executive officer." When Achilles commits his company
of Myrmidons to relieve the Greeks who are near collapse fighting
among their ships, he sends Pátroklos at their head, saying, "Now
go into action, prince and horseman!" (16:147f) Achilles and
Pátroklos customarily did military planning together, as
Pátroklos's ghost sadly recalls: "As living men we'll no more sit
apart from our companions, making plans." (23:91f)

Pátroklos also went with Achilles to Troy as his political adviser
and emotional stabilizer. Nestor recalls this to Pátroklos:

> ". . . these were [your father's] words to you:
> 'My child, Akhilleus [Achilles] is a higher being
> by his immortal blood; but you are older.
> He is more powerful but your part should be
> to let him hear close reasoning and counsel,
> even commands. He will be swayed by you
> for his good.'" (11:907ff)

Most adults who have not read the *Iliad* since high school or college cannot remember Pátroklos's name, only "what's-his-name,
you know, Achilles' friend." Virtually everyone who read the *Iliad*
in college and most who read it in high school have been told that
these two comrades were also lovers. This belief carries the ancient
authority of both Aeschylus and Plato, even though the plain sense
of Homer's text is devoid of evidence that these two comrades-in-
arms, Achilles and Pátroklos, were sexual partners.[4] Achilles' grief
for Pátroklos would not have been greater had they been a sexual
couple, nor less if they had not been. Many combat veterans are

denied compassionate understanding by civilians, because so many people cannot comprehend a love between men that is rich and passionate but not necessarily sexual. Veterans need to voice their grief and love for their dead comrades if they are to heal. However, many have learned to keep quiet because of their culture's discomfort with love between men that is so deeply felt.

Foster brother, closest friend, comrade-in-arms, second in command, emotional stabilizer—all together these constituted the relationship of Pátroklos to Achilles, and together they represent what Achilles lost when Pátroklos died. We must feel the value of this bond if we are to understand Achilles' grief when death broke it.

THE SPECIALNESS OF THE SPECIAL COMRADE

A veteran speaks of his dead friend this way:

> [He] was the kind of kid that grew on you. He couldn't *tell* a fucking joke. When he wanted to, he couldn't. Y'know, he would fuck up a two-word joke—and he'd take a half hour to tell it.
>
> If I'd get fucked up and I was drunk and being a nasty motherfucker, he would lead me back. If I was losing it—and there *was* times that I was losing it—I couldn't, I couldn't get my mind operational again. Y'know, he'd fucking shake me and it was like he was the fucking team leader, y'know? He'd pull me back into reality. "We got to move on. . . , c'mon." Y'know, "We gotta get going. We gotta get going". . . .
>
> Y'know, I remember at night, [he'd] be snoring and shit, making these weird fucking noises. . . . He go, "HHHsshh-WHEEeee". . . . And it seemed like he was always fucking far enough away so I'd have to fucking crawl across everyone to get to him. . . . You'd wake him up and [whispers], "Don't make no more fucking noises!"
>
> And he'd say, "You gotta stop this fucking drinking. You're getting paranoid and shit, y'know, hearing these fucking sounds." Or, uh. . . . He was fun to be with.
>
> Y'know, he would argue with me over the map. Like I'd be carrying a lot of shit with me, and he'd say, "Well, I'll carry some of the stuff."
>
> "You ain't carrying shit. You just carry that motherfucking radio, and shut the fuck up."
>
> I was close to the other guys, but I wasn't as close as I was to him.

The parallels here to Pátroklos's character—the buoyant heart, the generous, nurturing disposition—are very clear. In many combat veterans' descriptions of their lost friends-in-arms, we hear language strikingly similar to that used by Achilles to pay homage to Pátroklos.

One veteran of the 173d Airborne said,

> We called him "the Keeper of the Minds." He was the one who would not let you lose it. I can even remember guys calling out, "Get the Keeper over here!" when someone was losing it. His name was _____. When he was killed . . .

A person who is deeply loved and cared about can never be a replaceable part, a rank and MOS (Military Occupation Specialty) with just another service number on his dog tags. The *particularity* of the person, the specialness of the special comrade who has died, comes not from objectively unique traits but from the movement of the soul that we properly call love. The Marine in Larry Burrows's famous *Life* photo *Reaching Out, Battle for Hill 484, DMZ, 1966*, reproduced on the cover of this book, cares about the other wounded Marine in particular, not as a buddy-in-general, replaceable by any number of other Marines. Men learned in combat that to care passionately for the well-being of an individual person is to become vulnerable to pain and grief. Many soldiers drew the logical conclusion from this and say that after a special comrade was killed, they "just stayed the fuck away—didn't get close to nobody." Often they cannot remember the names or faces of anyone else with whom they served after that particular person was killed.

PORTRAIT OF PATROKLOS

A veteran in our program has written:

> Gentle people who somehow survive the brutality of war are highly prized in a combat unit. They have the aura of priests, even though many of them were highly efficient killers.

The *Iliad* makes clear that Pátroklos had precisely this kind of gentle character. It was in no way incompatible with being a formidable warrior: In Book 16 he kills twenty-four named warriors,

44

including Zeus's son Sarpêdôn, King of Lykia. We learn about Pátroklos's gentleness and compassion from our own observation and the reports of others.

In Book 11, for example, Achilles has sighted a wounded man in the distance being evacuated in Nestor's chariot, and he sends Pátroklos to learn his identity. When Pátroklos arrives at Nestor's hut, Nestor plants the idea that if Achilles cannot lead the Myrmidons himself to throw back the Trojans, he should at least allow Pátroklos to lead them in Achilles' armor as a tactical deception. "Taking you for him the Trojans may retire from the field and let the young Akhaians [Greeks] have a respite exhausted as they are." (11:926ff) What then follows reveals several aspects of Pátroklos's character, most significantly his compassion:

> At this, Pátroklos' <u>heart bounded within him</u>
> <u>and he went running back along the shipways</u>
> <u>toward Akhilleus.</u> Just as he passed the ship
> of great Odysseus . . .
> there came Eurypylos, the wounded man,
> . . . struck by the arrow,
> limping out of combat. Sultry sweat
> ran down his shoulders and his face, dark blood
> still trickled from his wound, but he limped on,
> unshaken spirit.
>   Seeing him, Pátroklos,
> <u>moved to compassion</u>, said . . . (11:933ff)

His enthusiasm, his loyalty to Achilles, and his desire to gloriously rescue the beleaguered Greeks send him running back with his heart pounding. But all of these are overridden by his compassion, which halts him by the wounded Eurypylos.

>   Supporting him
> with one arm round him, under his chest, [Pátroklos] led him
> into the hut. A squire put oxhides out
> on which [Pátroklos] laid the wounded man, then took
> his sheath knife and laid open the man's thigh
> to excise the biting arrow. With warm water
> he washed the black blood flowing from the wound
> then rubbed between his hands into a powder

over the wound a bitter yarrow root,
that dulled all pangs of pain. Now the gash dried
as the blood and powder clotted.[5] (11:957ff)

We see Pátroklos here in the intensely maternal role of an atten-
tive surgeon, one who is not only competent but who cares:

> Pátroklos stayed
> inside the shelter with Eurypylos
> to give him pleasure, talking, and to treat
> his aching wound with salve against the pain . . . (15:454ff)

At this moment Pátroklos hears the cries of Greek soldiers in pan-
icky retreat, and he continues his run back to Achilles from
Nestor. He arrives in tears at the mauling of the Greek fighters,
prompting Achilles to tease him:

> "Pátroklos,
> why all the weeping? Like a small girlchild
> who runs beside her mother and cries and cries
> to be taken up, and catches at her gown,
> and will not let her go, looking up in tears
> until she has her wish: that's how you seem,
> Pátroklos, winking out your glimmering tears. . . ." (16:7ff)

Because this teasing is so memorable, we tend to overlook the fact
that Pátroklos's tears are genuine and an important expression of
his character. He replies,

> "Akhilleus, prince and greatest of Akhaians,
> be forbearing. They are badly hurt. . . ." (16:25f)

We shall see below that Achilles' ridicule of his friend's tears is
contrary to the values of the Homeric warrior, even though it
seems natural to *us* that a soldier should sneer at tears.

Homer asks us to believe that gentleness and compassion really
were Pátroklos's leading character traits, equal to his fighting
prowess against the enemy. If we fail to perceive this, we will be
unable to comprehend the pain at his death. A convenient way to
sidestep Homer's emphasis on Achilles' anguish is to dismiss the
portrait of Pátroklos as idealized, to assume that it is exaggerated,

not real, too good to be true. How will the average mental health professional hear the following description of a veteran's dead friend?

> He wasn't a harmful person. He wasn't a dirty person. He had this head that was wide up at the top, and his chin come down to a point. He had this hair he used to comb to his right side, and he always had this big cowlick in back. Big old cowlick. And when he smiled—you ever hear "ear to ear"?—it was almost a gooney-looking smile. You know, it was just WA-a-ay—it was huge. He just had this big, huge smile. He never said nothing bad about nobody. He was just . . . he was a caring person.

Yet Homer's portrait of Pátroklos's character is unwavering: This young Greek is a formidable, efficient killer *and* a gentle, compassionate human being. While modern readers may find this implausibly idealized, there can be no doubt about what Homer intended us to believe about Pátroklos. After he is killed, diverse voices testify to the sort of person he was. Ironically, the first tribute to Pátroklos comes from Zeus, who has just engineered his death and now calls him "<u>gentle and strong</u>." (17:227) The next characterization of the dead friend also comes from a god: Athêna calls Pátroklos "glorious Akhilleus's <u>faithful</u> friend." (17:625)

Other soldiers, fighting to prevent Pátroklos's corpse from being captured by the Trojans, corroborate with homages of their own. Meneláos organizes the defense of the body while he looks for Nestor's son, Antílokhos, to take word to Achilles:

> "Remember poor Pátroklos, each of you,
> <u>his warmth of heart. He had a way of being</u>
> <u>kind to all</u> in life. Now destiny and death
> have overtaken him."

> Then Meneláos turned to search the field, . . .
> looking for Nestor's son, . . .
> and . . . red-haired Meneláos
> cried:
> "Antílokhos, come here, young prince,
> and hear sad news. . . .
> <u>Our best man,</u>
> Pátroklos, fell—<u>irreparable loss</u>
> <u>and grief</u> to the Danáäns [Greeks].

47

Here is your duty:
run to the ships, tell all this to Akhilleus [Achilles]. . ."

Hearing these words,

> <u>appalled and sick at heart, Antílokhos</u>
> <u>lost for a time his power of speech: his eyes</u>
> <u>brimmed over, and his manly voice was choked</u>. (17:757ff)

We not only hear that Pátroklos was warm of heart, kind to all, *and* the best fighter on the field that day, but we see here the effect that his death has on someone who has no kin or power relationship to him. Antílokhos, blind-sided by the news, is momentarily, perhaps dangerously incapacitated by grief, standing so near the edge of furious combat over the body.

Time and again Homer makes very sure that we understand that gentleness and kindness were Pátroklos's leading traits of character by bringing testimony to it from every conceivable quarter: gods, concubines, soldiers under his command, soldiers of higher rank unrelated to him, horses, and even the enemy themselves. Lykáôn, a prince of Troy whom Achilles has captured and is about to kill, knows of Pátroklos as Achilles' "friend, that <u>gentle and strong</u> soldier." (21:112) The grieving Myrmidons weep for their "<u>mildhearted friend</u>." Achilles' immortal horses mourn "their <u>splendid</u> charioteer, the <u>kind</u> man." (17:478ff, 23:324f)

We learn from the captive Brisêis, whom Agamémnon has returned to Achilles after Pátroklos's death, that his compassion extended also to the powerless:

> The girl
> Brisêis. . .
> saw Pátroklos lying dead
> of spear wounds, and she sank down to embrace him
> with a sharp sobbing cry, . . .
> "Pátroklos, very dear,
> most dear to me, cursed as I am. . . .
> Evil follows evil so, for me.
> . . . when Akhilleus killed my lord,
> . . . not a tear
> would you permit me: no, you undertook
> to see me married to the Prince Akhilleus

> . . . Now must I mourn
> your death forever, who were <u>ever gentle</u>." (19:309ff)

The Vietnam veterans who lost gentle comrades did not start out as the monsters of cruelty they became in their berserk states. *Philia* was reciprocal, as evoked in the veteran's words quoted above, "You'd take a shit, and he'd be right there covering you. And if I take a shit, he'd be covering me. . . . We needed each other to survive." Our culture insists upon the gender association of nurturance and compassion as maternal, whereas the ancient Greek culture understood *philia* to be equally available to both genders. Another veteran described his role in explicitly maternal terms:

> I became the <u>mother hen</u>. You know, "C'mon, c'mon, c'mon, c'mon, c'mon, get over here, get over here. Stay down. All right, now, now, everyone keep, y'know, y'know—the shit hits the fan, hit the fucking ground, don't worry about nothing, just stay down now."
>
> It was constant now. I was watching the other five guys <u>like they was my children</u>.

Veterans often speak of the gentle side of themselves as having died with the special comrade with whom they experienced mutual and reciprocal maternal love.

The terror and privation of combat bonds men in a passion of care that the word *brother* only partly captures. Men become mothers to one another in combat. The grief and rage that they experience when the special comrade is killed appear virtually identical to that of a child suddenly orphaned, and they feel that the mother within them has died with the friend.

THE GRIEF OF ACHILLES

Homer's dramatic method conveys Achilles' grief by showing his actions, such as blunt self-mutilation, weeping, and loss of appetite; by telling us his thoughts, such as his self-reproaches and his intrusive memories of the dead; and by poetic stratagems that make us understand that Achilles is "already dead."

Achilles has a premonition as he watches the battle from a distance, the moment Antílokhos reaches him with the news. (18:2ff)

After this moment of anticipatory "gloom and anger," Achilles' grief begins:

> A black stormcloud of <u>pain</u> shrouded Akhilleus.
> <u>On his bowed head he scattered dust and ash</u>
> in handfuls and befouled his beautiful face,
> letting black ash sift on his fragrant khiton.
> Then <u>in the dust he stretched</u> his giant length
> and <u>tore his hair</u> with both hands. (18:25ff)

Since Achilles' display of anguish bears similarities to biblical scenes of grieving,[6] it doesn't seem all that remote from what might come naturally to us. "Tearing one's hair" is idiomatic in English, usually representing anger, vexation, or frustration. In context here, however, it appears to be simple self-mutilation and self-inflicted pain. What comes next seems to confirm this by taking Achilles one step further toward impulsive suicide: Antílokhos grabs Achilles' hands to prevent him from slashing his own throat. (18:35ff) We do not learn Achilles' suicidal wish by overhearing his interior thoughts but rather by his friend's empathic understanding of what he is feeling. We hear nowhere else in the *Iliad* of a suicide after the death of a *phílos*. The impulse to suicide as a part of intense grief was apparently not a culturally assumed expectation. In some cultures suicide is a predicted complication of bereavement, such as among the West African LaDongaa, who tie the hands of mourners as a matter of "natural" precaution.[7] Neither was it so alien an idea to Homer's audience that they needed to have it explained to them.

What Homer shows us next, the condolences of Achilles' mother, the sea-goddess Thetis, makes us understand that Achilles is "already dead" before he begins his berserk frenzy. He weeps and wishes aloud to his mother that he had never been born, renounces this life, and hopes that his own death will come quickly. (18:79, 96f, 111) He proclaims his guilt (18:111ff) for not covering Pátroklos in battle. These aspects of grief—weeping, wishing one were dead, self-reproach—are all familiar to us, as are intrusive memories of the dead and loss of appetite:

> <u>Now pierced by memory</u>,
> he sighed and sighed again, and said:
>   Ah, once

you, too, poor fated friend, and best of friends,
would set a savory meal deftly before us
in our field shelter, when the Akhaians wished
no time lost between onsets against Trojans.
Now there you lie, broken in battle. Ah,
lacking you, <u>my heart will fast this day</u>
<u>from meat and drink as well</u>. (19:346ff)

The salty old soldier, Odysseus, rejects this impulse:

How can a fasting belly mourn our dead?
So many die, so often, every day,
when would soldiers come to an end of fasting? (19:447ff)

So far, Achilles' grief is familiar from our experiences in civilian life. However, unless one has had a terrifying misfortune of comparable extremity, there is little parallel in civilian experience for the role played in Achilles' life by his mother, the goddess Thetis. I submit that in addition to other dramatic and mythic roles that she plays, Thetis is an "imaginary companion" such as has sustained many in extreme danger and deprivation. One veteran in our program conversed regularly with a guardian angel while on long-range patrol in enemy territory. These dialogues became part of the shared life of his team, with his men asking him what the angel had said. Because we have become accustomed to condescending to Homer's gods as the products of "primitive" or "magical" thinking, or treating them as purely artistic or mythic symbols, we are prone to overlook their function as dramatized embodiments of combat soldiers' inner experience. Guardian angels, imaginary companions, and personal patron saints to whom one appeals *in extremis* are probably considerably more common and "normal" than mental health professionals care to admit.

BEING ALREADY DEAD

"I died in Vietnam" is a common utterance of our patients. Most viewed themselves as already dead at some point in their combat service, often after a close friend was killed. Homer shows Achilles as "already dead" before his death in a series of fine poetic stratagems. The transformation begins as soon as Achilles hears the news of Pátroklos's death from Antílokhos:

> "Here's desolation. . . .
> Lord Pátroklos
> fell [*keimai*]". . . .
> A black stormcloud of pain shrouded Akhilleus [Achilles]
> . . . . he scattered [grasped] dust and ash . . .
> and befouled his beautiful face. . . .
> Then in the dust he stretched [*keimai*] his giant length. . . .
> From the hut
> the women . . .
> flocked in haste around him,
> crying loud in grief. All beat their breasts. . . .
> His mother [the sea goddess, Thetis] heard him in the depths
> offshore . . . [and] cried in sorrow [*göoio*]. . . .
> Bending near
> her groaning son, the gentle goddess wailed
> and took his head between her hands in pity. . . . (18:20–79)

Homer affirms that Achilles is "already dead" through a decisive set of poetic parallels. "Darkness," a "dark cloud," or a "blinding cloud" covers a man's eyes when he is killed (e.g., 20:479). Dying men grasp, claw, grip, or clutch the earth with their hands (e.g., 11:485, 13:593, 17:353). Homer uses the same word, *keimai*, for Pátroklos falling dead in battle as for Achilles falling beside his body in grief. Words and conventional gestures associated with mourning the dead are used in reference to Achilles: Concubines and Nereids beat their breasts (18:33, 18:56); Thetis's cry for Achilles is called a death lament [*göoio*] (18:56). The same word is also used three times in this sense as death lament in Book 24 (lines 840, 894, 911). When Thetis comes to comfort her son, she "[takes] his head between her hands" (18:79), the gesture of the chief mourner in the funeral for a dead man.[8]

Speaking of the time after his closest friend-in-arms was killed, a veteran said:

> And it wasn't that I couldn't be killed. I didn't *care* if I was killed. . . . I just didn't care if I lived or died. I just wanted blood. I just wanted revenge, and I didn't care. <u>I didn't see myself going home</u>. No . . . nope . . . no, I didn't.

Achilles renounces his return home before Pátroklos's pyre:

> Apart
> from the pyre he stood and cut the red-gold hair
> that he had grown [as a vow for safe homecoming] for the river
> [god] Sperkheios.
> . . . In pain,
> he said:
> ". . . [The] vow
> to you meant nothing, that on my return
> I'd cut my hair as an offering to you. . . .
> Now, as I shall not see my fatherland,
> I would confer my hair on the soldier Pátroklos."
> And he closed his dear friend's hands
> upon it, moving all to weep again. (23:163)

Another veteran in our program wrote:

> In my wildest thoughts <u>I never expected or wanted to return
> home alive</u>, and emotionally never have.

The sense of being already dead may contribute to the berserker's complete loss of fear, which we shall see below. It may also be the prototype of the loss of *all* emotion that defines for combat post-traumatic stress disorder the prolonged states of numbness—the inability to feel love or happiness or to believe that anything matters.

GRIEF AND THE WARRIOR'S RAGE

The title of this section is borrowed from a paper by Stanford University anthropologist Renato Rosaldo, "Grief and a Headhunter's Rage,"[9] on the Ilongot headhunters of the Philippines. What I want to emphasize here is the rapid transformation of grief into rage. For many of the veterans in our treatment program for combat post-traumatic stress disorder, replacement of grief by rage has lasted for years and become an entrenched way of being. Much therapeutic effort aims at reawakening the experience of grief, which we regard as a process of healing, painful as it is. This reflects our *beliefs*, not conclusive scientific fact. We simply do not know which aspects of emotion are biological universals, like the heartbeat, and which aspects of emotion are culturally constructed.

In "Grief and a Headhunter's Rage," Rosaldo points out the Ilongot headhunters' unelaborated connection between grief and killing, to ease the pain of grief. Homer hints strongly at such a direct connection when one of Achilles' Myrmidons kills a Trojan and says:

> "By heaven now I've eased
> my heart somewhat of anguish for Pátroklos,
> tearing out a man's guts. . . ." (17:602ff)

The principal feature of Achilles' grief is, of course, his rage at Hektor and lust for revenge. Achilles tells his mother:

> "I must reject this life, my heart tells me, . . .
> if Hektor does not feel my battering spear
> tear the life out of him, making him pay
> in his own blood for the slaughter of Pátroklos!" (18:102ff)

Carrying out this revenge dominates the *Iliad* until Hektor's death near the end of Book 22.

The text of the *Iliad* shows many cultural roots of Achilles' rage. In Homer's culture a killing created a debt that could be discharged either by the blood of the killer or by substitute material compensation. Achilles phrases his own desire for revenge in the language of "blood-price," i.e., "making him [Hektor] pay in his own blood for the slaughter of Pátroklos!" (18:105f) This compensatory concept has already been voiced at 9:769f, "a normal man will take the penalty [blood-price] for a brother slain or a dead son," and reappears as a motif on the shield of Achilles at 18:572f, "two men at odds over satisfaction [blood-price] owed for a murder done."

The combat veterans that I treat are neither feral men nor lifelong misfits. Therefore, we need to ask whether the berserk rage that emerged out of their grief is a product of acculturated emotional responses (as, for example, the concept of vendetta), or whether it is a reaction that every human being in every age and society would experience in a similar circumstance. We simply don't know enough to settle this question now. I believe that the emergence of rage out of intense grief *is* a biological universal and that long-term obstruction of grief and failure to communalize grief can lock a person into chronic rage. This has not, to my knowledge, been established by controlled, prospective psychological research within our own culture, not to speak of cross-culturally.

I now turn to the communalization of grief in the *Iliad* and to the broad range of personal and social actions that I shall collectively refer to as griefwork. Griefwork of American soldiers in Vietnam provides a startling contrast to that of soldiers in the *Iliad*, a contrast that has enhanced my understanding of both the Homeric culture and our own.

COMMUNALIZATION OF GRIEF IN THE *ILIAD* AND IN VIETNAM

> My platoon was in a fucking fire fight at LZ _____. I was short[10] and wasn't supposed to be out in the boonies at all. I got the supply chopper back to _____ . . . and was in Southie [South Boston] forty-eight hours after getting shot at.

DEROS, the longed-for, lifesaving day when a man's twelve-month individual tour of Vietnam combat duty ended and a thirty-day home leave customarily began, came for most with a blessed fairness and reliability that marked few other experiences in Vietnam. Yet it carried a curse that was recognized by very few at the time: It prevented the communalization of combat traumas, which arises automatically from unit cohesion. There is a growing consensus among people who treat PTSD that any trauma, be it loss of family in a natural disaster, rape, exposure to the dead and mutilated in an industrial catastrophe, or combat itself, will have longer-lasting and more serious consequences if there has been no opportunity to talk about the traumatic event, to express to other people emotions about the event and those involved in it, or to experience the presence of socially connected others who will not let one go through it alone. This is what is meant by communalizing the trauma. The all-encompassing barrier that incest victims encounter in revealing their victimization is an essential part of what makes incest so injurious.[11] Bereavement is only one of the traumas of combat; how it was shared, or failed to be shared, is the main theme of this section. *Griefwork* encompasses the whole range of formal and informal social exchanges that soldiers at Troy and in Vietnam practiced after a death.

When and how did the Greek invaders of Troy mourn their dead? Who did what, and when? I ask these questions and take the trouble to answer them because they allow us to notice things about *American* soldiers' experiences in Vietnam that are so easily taken for granted that they are almost invisible. I shall concentrate on the Greeks because, like the Americans in Vietnam, they were foreign troops at a great distance from home overseas. Trojan dead, like locally based Vietcong, were in the hands of their own townsmen and families if the enemy didn't carry them off. The purpose here is not to reconstruct ancient Ionian or Mycenaean funeral practices but rather to illuminate our own recent conduct toward war dead and to speculate on its consequences.

As we work our way through the social and psychological processes of grief portrayed at Homer's Troy and compare them to those found among Americans in Vietnam, we shall have to untangle several separate sources of difference: contrasting cultures, changes in the nature of warfare, and institutional and historical factors peculiar to the Vietnam War.

During this comparison of Achilles' griefwork with that of Americans in Vietnam, we must also bear in mind *the enormous advantage that the powerful have over the powerless in the conduct of griefwork.* Communalization is virtually guaranteed and automatic when someone as powerful as Achilles grieves. My guess is that friends of the eight colonels killed in action between 1961 and 1972 had considerably more opportunity to communalize their grief than the enlisted men who lost friends. Homer also shows us the situation of the powerless:

> and the [slave] women wailed in . . . grief for Patroclus
> <u>calling forth each woman's private sorrows</u>. (Fagles trans.
>   19:357f)

Slaves are forbidden to weep except to mirror the mood of their masters; when their masters grieve, they have license to wail their personal sorrow.

WHEN WERE THE DEAD BROUGHT TO THE REAR?

Some things don't change much. In both Troy and Vietnam the dead were brought out of battle along with the wounded, either during the fighting or immediately after danger had passed. Greeks and Trojans took great personal risks to bring in the dead from the midst of the most ferocious combat, as was also true of Americans in Vietnam. I shall not dwell on this here. What has changed greatly is the utter disappearance of truces to collect or mourn the dead. A number of truces were held during the Vietnam War, but none for funerary purposes. Veterans have described private, infinitely fragile, unspoken truces that they observed to allow the enemy to collect their dead without being fired upon, particularly after engagements with the North Vietnamese. Reciprocal gestures of respect have also been reported: One veteran described a North Vietnamese practice of marking American bodies with lime to make them visible from the air and voiced the belief that they did this only for American soldiers who had fought well.[12] Unfortunately, such stories of mutual respect for the enemy's need to gather and mourn their dead are painfully rare, outnumbered a thousand to one by stories—on both sides—of the dead being used as booby traps or as bait for ambushes; of mutilation and degradation of the dead; and of cruelty and contempt for the bereaved.

We witness two funerary truces in the *Iliad*. In Book 7, many dead lie on the field following the tremendous battle that ensues when a Trojan breaks the truce that has been declared to end the war by single combat between Meneláos and Paris. Both sides want a pause to collect and cremate the dead. The Trojan herald comes to the Greek camp with an offer:

> "I am directed
> . . . to make this inquiry:
> Will you accept a truce in the hard fighting,
> allowing us to burn our dead? Next day
> again we'll fight, until inscrutable power
> decides between us, giving one side victory." (7:468ff)

Both for the stated reasons and for secret military reasons, the Greeks accept the offer:

Agamémnon responded to Idaíos [the herald]:
>   ". . . As to the dead,
> I would withhold no decency of burning;
> a man should spare no pains to see cadavers
> given as soon as may be after death
> to purifying flame. . . ." (7:482ff)

The scene at dawn the next day is remarkable both for its emotional power and for the fact that Greeks and Trojans weep freely within view of each other:

>   [the sun]
> had just begun to strike across the plowlands . . .
> when these two groups [Greeks and Trojans]
> met on the battlefield, with difficulty
> distinguishing the dead men, one by one.
> With pails they washed the bloody filth away,
> then hot tears fell, as into waiting carts
> they lifted up their dead. . . .
>   [The Greeks] piled
> dead bodies on their pyre, sick at heart,
> and burned it down. (7:502ff)

The closing lines of the *Iliad*, Book 24, lines 930 onward, describe the cremation and burial of Hektor during a truce granted for that purpose by Achilles to Priam, Hektor's father and king of Troy.

Time and safety to mourn were built into ancient warfare and were absent in Vietnam.

WHO BROUGHT THE DEAD TO THE REAR?

American dead in Vietnam were often handled in the field by medics, who were valued and socially integrated members of the dead man's combat unit. But very soon the dead passed into the hands of strangers, helicopter crews who had no personal connection to the surviving men of the combat unit and whose first priorities may have been other tasks, such as medical evacuation of the wounded, or resupply.[13] Medical evacuation crews legitimately focused their energies on getting the living wounded aboard and away to a field hospital; if there was room, the dead were sometimes quickly hauled or thrown aboard without ceremony. Medevac often came very soon after a call for it, so from the point of view of those left behind, a dead man sometimes virtually vanished. Sometimes he was gone before his closest friend-in-arms even knew he had been hit.

Once in the rear, American dead became the responsibility of personnel attached to Graves Registration, whose task was identification, preservation, preparation, and very prompt shipment of the bodies to the United States. One veteran in our program who dealt with every step of getting the dead out of Vietnam during his two tours in a transportation company states that a soldier's body often was actually aboard a plane, heading back to the United States, within twenty-four hours of being hit. These rear-echelon support troops usually had no social bond whatever to the combat unit the dead man came from. Sometimes a surviving friend would witness the way the body was handled by Graves Registration and experience this as indifference or disrespect. One veteran described going to Graves Registration in search of his dead friend and beating up the sergeant there because he was cooling beer in the chest holding the corpse.

The *Iliad* leaves the strong impression that a dead man's closest comrades, having fought to prevent his body from falling into enemy hands, carried it to the rear. For Greeks and Trojans this began a rich and densely varied series of activities by the bereaved for the dead and significant involvement of the bereaved with each other. In Vietnam, when the corpse disappeared from the battlefield the thread of griefwork snapped at its origin.

When Were the Dead Mourned?

Grief turns the attention of the survivor inward to feelings, memories, and imagined what-if scenarios; attention to the present sensory world is largely shut down. In Vietnam, American troops were exposed to attack twenty-four hours a day but were most often attacked at night. *There was no safe time to mourn.* Allowing one's attention to turn inward to grief could result in one's own death and the deaths of others. Night warfare reflects a change in the customs of war since Homer's time.

In the *Iliad*, combat is suspended every night. While there is no explicit mention that mourning took place at night, this is a reasonable inference. If it was safe enough to sleep, it was safe enough to grieve. In addition, there were funerary truces when grieving was not only safe and acceptable but socially compelled.

WHAT WAS THE LEVEL OF TRUST, SAFETY, AND SOCIAL COHESIVENESS IN THE REAR DURING MOURNING?

I have already indicated that a degree of security from enemy attack is essential for griefwork to proceed. During much of the Vietnam War, combat soldiers felt as unsafe in the rear as out in the field. Many veterans have told me, "There were two wars going on—one out in the boonies against the V.C., another in the rear between blacks and whites. I felt safer in the boonies." Virtually all combat units were racially integrated and mostly color-blind in combat, but when they came to the rear, social cohesion fell to pieces. Men segregated themselves rigidly along racial lines in the rear, preventing units from mourning together in relative safety. Racially motivated killings and riots were common in Vietnam. American soldiers in the rear were not safe *from each other*.

Men also felt unsafe in the rear because of the large number of Vietnamese civilians employed on American bases. In part this fear reflected racist identification of all Vietnamese as enemy "Gooks," and in part it reflected the reality that some of these civilians were gathering intelligence for the enemy, both on military operations in the field and for attacks on the rear-area bases themselves. For many years of the Vietnam War there was *no* safe rear area, because of the Vietcong's "unconventional" warfare. If you cannot let down your guard, you cannot grieve.

Among the many Greek contingents at Troy, we hear of nothing equivalent to racial antagonisms serious enough to make the men a danger to each other. Captive women must have sometimes sought revenge for their slaughtered families by fomenting hostility among their ultracompetitive slave masters, but we do not hear of this. The Greek units appear to have been internally very cohesive. Although we hear of some comings and goings from the beachhead, the overall assumption appears to be that everyone came over with his contingent, is there "for the duration," and will return with his contingent if he survives to do so, along with the bones of men who have died.

The individual (as contrasted to unit) rotation policy practiced in Vietnam, which moved individual men in and out of combat units on a preordained time schedule, systematically destroyed the unit cohesion of combat groups. Very, very few Vietnam veterans went over with the unit they had trained with, fought with that unit, *and* returned "to the world" with it.[14] I estimate that of the three-quarters of a million Vietnam combat veterans, only a few hundred or thousand did so. By contrast, my impression is that this was the majority experience in World War II, particularly in the Pacific. Even men who went over as individual replacements in World War II spent weeks or months with their units after fighting ended and universally returned by boat. "The long trip home" is generally credited as an opportunity for mutual support and communal reworking of combat trauma.

Survival and success in combat often require soldiers to virtually read one another's minds, reflexively covering each other with as much care as they cover themselves, and going to one another's aid with little thought for safety:

. . . if one of the Recon outfits, the shit hit the fucking fan, we'd be out the fucking door on the helicopters. And I don't care a shit if we were totally fucking exhausted. . . .

One of the teams got trapped, and . . . we got on a pickup. They picked us up, we flew in, and the pilot said, "Can't go in. They're receiving fire. Receiving fire." I'm on the radio [internal voice circuit of the aircraft] talking to this fucking pilot, and y'know, we're all sitting on the doors, three on each door.

And I said to the pilot, "Well, get down fucking close, and we'll kick ammo to them."

And the pilot said, "Okay, I'm going to make one fucking pass, so when we get down there . . ."

I said, "Well, you got to get like about ten, fifteen feet off the fucking ground. You gotta roll in, because I want to drop it right in on them."

"Oh, yeah, no fucking problem."

And then I whipped the fucking headset off, and I said to the guys, "Listen, when this motherfucker gets close, we gotta go."

An' we all went.

Now, you're talking about a fucking plane that's moving like a fucking tornado. And we crashed and burned, too. I remember my fucking head was all bruised and shit.

It didn't matter. It didn't matter getting out of that fucking helicopter.

And I was so fucking proud of the other five guys. Because they
went with it. . . .

Now we're all here. We kick some fucking ass. . . . Now the bond
begins. The bond begins of you can count on everyone. The other
team appreciated what we did. Y'know, they weren't alone. And I
knew if that same situation happened that I could count on six
more to come and get me. . . .

Half of us couldn't fucking walk after we got out of there, we
were so fucking bruised from the fucking brush and trees and
whatever else we landed on. But we weren't going to leave them,
even though the pilot said it was impossible to do this. . . . So you
gotta pull devious shit. Y'know what I'm saying?

This illustration of cohesion within an airborne reconnaissance
unit can be summed up in the words of this same veteran: "You
grew like a hand."[15]

USE OF MIND-ALTERING SUBSTANCES

The word *wine* apears fifteen times in Fitzgerald's translation of the
Iliad, sometimes as a figure of speech but most often to refer to
part of a meal or a libation. It was clearly available in quantity on
the Greek beachhead at Troy. To be sure, wine played a role in the
Homeric rituals of mourning—to quench the embers of the funeral
pyre (e.g., 23:274, 24:947). At no point do we see a soldier drowning his grief in wine, nor do we hear it mentioned. It is hard to
imagine that there was no wine at the funeral feast that Achilles
made for the Myrmidons (23:36ff), yet wine is not mentioned. Nor
is it mentioned in the brief notice of the funeral feast made by
Priam for Hektor. (24:959) This is a startling piece of cultural phar-
macology; we unthinkingly assume that "drowning one's sorrows"
is somehow natural and not culturally constructed.

Mind-altering substances of all sorts seem to have been the main
shrines to which American soldiers brought their grief. I shall give
two illustrations from the accounts of veterans of the days immediately after the deaths of their special comrades-in-arms:

And I cried and I cried and I cried. They started giving me I
don't know what kind of pills. They gave me some pills. And I had

to write down what happened, because there was no body to be identified. He would have been missing in action. So I wrote the letters.

This veteran believes that to the authorities in the rear, his tears were evidence of mental sickness that required a mind-altering medication. This soldier had never used alcohol or other drugs before this—and lest a jaded reader think this veteran used the episode to justify a subsequent addiction to the pills he was given, all subsequent substance abuse by this veteran involved alcohol.

The second account exemplifies widespread self-medication of grief with alcohol:

> I mean, I did it with the alcohol. And I did it when I was in the 'Nam. For that two days I stayed fucking shitfaced, just to numb it. Just so I wouldn't have to think about it.

This man had been a heavy user of alcohol before the death of his friend and remained so afterward. He came from a background where heavy drinking was customary at wakes for the dead.

WHO WEPT FOR THE DEAD, AND HOW WERE TEARS VALUED?

An American soldier who wept for a fallen friend was warned not to "lose it" and to "get your mind straight." One man, holding a dead friend, was told, "Stuff those tears!" and "Don't get sad, get even!" by his company commander. Open grief at the death of a comrade was fully accepted by the Homeric warriors. I count eight separate deaths to which soldiers in the *Iliad* responded with tears. Several of these are quoted in the course of this chapter and need not be repeated. The general answer to the question of who wept is: *everyone*. American military culture in Vietnam regarded tears as dangerous but above all as demeaning, the sign of a weakling, a loser. To weep was to lose one's dignity among American soldiers in Vietnam.

Homer's world valued tears as intrinsic to the dignity of war heroes. What evidence confirms that a social group places high value on a specific activity? I shall demonstrate the positive value placed upon weeping among Homer's warriors by showing (1) what other activities are displaced in order to engage in it, (2) the prestige within that social group of the people engaging in the activity, and (3) the language used to speak of it.

What could be more highly valued to a soldier than final victory? In the *Iliad*, however, the Greeks displace immediate exploitation of Hektor's fall, preferring the activities of weeping and burying:

> . . .[N]ow that the gods at last have let me
> bring to earth this man who wrought
> havoc among us . . .
> come, we'll offer battle around the city. . . .
> <u>Will they give up their strongpoint at this loss?</u>
> <u>Can they fight on, though Hektor's dead?</u>
>
> But wait:
> why do I ponder, why take up these questions?
> <u>Down by the ships Pátroklos' body lies</u>
> <u>unwept, unburied."</u> (22:450ff)

These priorities seem fantastic to our modern mind.

When we examine the social prestige of the Homeric characters engaged in weeping for the dead, we find consistently that this is a high-status activity. Achilles, the *de facto* king of the Myrmidons, repeatedly leads them in lamentations for Pátroklos: "Akhilleus led them in repeated cries of grief." (23:17ff, cf. 18:368) But even more telling is the scene after Pátroklos's cremation, when *all* the Greek commanders, including Agamémnon, are present and participate personally in collecting the bones:

> <u>"Son of Atreus [Agamémnon],</u>
> <u>noblemen of Akhaia's host</u>, begin
> by wetting down the pyre with tawny wine,
> . . . Then come,
> we'll comb the ashes for Pátroklos' bones! . . ."
>
> They did his will: . . .
> <u>Shedding tears</u>
> <u>for their mildhearted friend they gathered up</u>
> <u>his bones</u> into a golden urn (23:272ff)

This job, which our culture would declare to be a filthy one and assign to underlings, is done, weeping, by the highest Greek nobility with their own hands.

Let us for a moment recall Achilles' brutal teasing of Pátroklos: "Pátroklos, why all the weeping? Like a small girlchild who runs beside her mother . . ." (16:7ff) In one word, "girlchild," Achilles connects tears with two signifiers of low status in his culture, female and child, a very modern devaluation of tears customary in the American military in Vietnam. The series of scenes surrounding the death of Pátroklos proves how highly abnormal this disparagement was for the Homeric warrior.

The powerful are clearly at a great advantage for full communalization of their own grief. Achilles could write his own script for mourning Pátroklos; he had total control over what was done, when, and with whom. Contrast this to the utterly disempowered condition of the American grunt when he had lost an equally low-status and powerless friend. He could not even assert choice over his own time to weep or the social or physical location of his own body when he mourned. Even less could he arrange the weeping or feasting of anyone else.

Finally, the word *terpo*, which Homer uses about tears in the scene between Achilles and Priam, connects weeping to joy, satisfaction, and solace, indicating a positive value of mourning and tears. Fitzgerald's translation is particularly resonant when he speaks of the "luxury of tears":

But when Akhilleus' heart
had known the <u>luxury of tears</u> [*gööio tetárpeto*], and pain
within his breast and bones had passed away,
he stood then, raised the old king up . . . (24:617ff, cf. 4:758ff)

WHO WASHED AND PREPARED THE DEAD FOR CREMATION/BURIAL AND SHIPMENT HOME?

I have already noted that in Vietnam the service troops of Graves Registration had no organic social connection to the combat units from which the dead came—they were, in a word, strangers. Instead of launching a restorative period of grief by handling and washing loved, dead comrades, these men in Graves Registration were themselves traumatized by their gruesome duties to strangers. This is a paradox: The opportunity to see and care for

65

the dead body of a loved person reduces trauma to the bereaved, while seeing and handling the dead bodies of strangers is often traumatic in itself.

The following passage is important not for the details of what was done to prepare Pátroklos's body, but for who did it, and for the fact that it was done communally:

> With this <u>Akhilleus called the company</u>
> to place over the campfire a big tripod
> and bathe Pátroklos of his clotted blood.
> . . . <u>They bathed him then</u>, and took
> sweet oil for his anointing, laying nard
> in the open wounds; and <u>on his bed they placed him</u>,
> covering him with fine linen, head to foot,
> and a white shroud over it.
> <u>So all that night</u>
> <u>beside Akhilleus the great runner,</u>
> <u>the Myrmidons held mourning for Pátroklos</u>. (18:402ff)

Pátroklos's closest comrades prepared his body for cremation and burial. It is reasonable to infer that this was the case for all Greek soldiers who died at Troy.

One Vietnam veteran, answering how the death of a soldier in his unit was marked, said simply, "Zip." Another said that the battalion commander droned through the names and ranks of the men who had died since the last "debriefing" and then, without pausing for breath, concluded with, "The mess tent is open." In other units, a chaplain or the battalion commander said some words, but the prevailing impression I have been given is that communal recognitions of deaths were perfunctory, delayed, and conducted by rear-echelon officers who had no emotional connection to the dead or their comrades.

One veteran from an elite unit bitterly resents that nothing ceremonial marked the death of his closest comrade:

> They didn't even have a fucking stand-down for the fucking kid. They had a fucking stand-down for all the fucking pot-head motherfucking dope-stuffing motherfuckers. [Stand-down] is when guys in the outfit get killed, they'd bring the whole unit back, and they'd set his rifle up and put his helmet or his boonie cap on, and play taps and shit. Pay him fucking respect. They do this for all these mother-

fucking junkie motherfuckers around here. They can't do it for a fucking kid who did every fucking thing he was asked to do. Fucking kid never complained about nothing.

THE IMPORTANCE OF THWARTED GRIEF

If military practice tells soldiers that their emotions of love and grief—which are inseparable from their humanity—*do not matter*, then the civilian society that has sent them to fight on their behalf should not be shocked by their "inhumanity" when they try to return to civilian life.

The expectation in the *Iliad* appears to have been that the bones of the dead would be returned home at the end of the war:

> These corpses we must fire abaft the ships
> a short way from the sterns, that each may bear
> his charred bones to the children of the dead
> whenever we sail home again. (7:394ff)

Modern transportation makes possible swift repatriation of the intact dead body. Greek remains stayed with the combat unit for the duration; American remains flew away from the battle site sometimes in a matter of minutes and from Vietnam within days of death. I want to draw attention to this difference as a powerful symbol of the possibilities for griefwork by soldiers in these two wars. Needless to say, I am not advocating a return to the ancient practice, but I strongly urge that the needs of the dead soldiers' surviving comrades be considered in policies and practices regarding the handling, location, and transportation of the remains. Soldiers can mourn their fallen comrades without stealing grief from the families at home.

What Homer shows us of Greek and Trojan warriors in communal mourning indicates that it was intensely and positively valued. By contrast, accounts given by American veterans of the Vietnam War indicate that mourning was dreaded, perfunctory, delayed, devalued, mocked, fragmented, minimized, deflected, disregarded, and sedated. Obviously, the social and emotional processes of grief cannot proceed in the midst of active combat where it would endanger everyone, but elsewhere it can be encouraged. My guess is that the company, a unit of roughly a hundred, about the size of the troop of Myrmidons, is the largest group that can promptly meet the mourning needs of the bereaved soldier with a richness and authenticity that will make a difference in the rest of the soldier's life.

One of our veterans was spattered with blood and flesh when his closest friend was hit near him. "I was like *The Night of the Living Dead* after that," he recalls. Thwarted, uncommunalized grief is a major reason why there are so many severe, long-term psychological injuries from the Vietnam War.

CHAPTER 4

Guilt and Wrongful Substitution

> *I should've took the fucking round myself.*
> —Airborne veteran

The soldier's grief helps us comprehend the powerful bond that arises between men in combat. This bond may be so intense as to blot out the distinction between self and other, leading each to value the other's life above his own. But now the other is dead; the survivor still lives. "It should've been me!" is the cry of guilt that goes up in the midst of grief from a survivor condemned by his very survival.[1]

ABANDONMENT AND WRONGFUL SUBSTITUTION

Guilt torments one of our veterans, "Sarge," for the death of a younger man in his team while Sarge was hospitalized with a serious infection. He said:

> In my heart it's—if I was there, he wouldn't be dead. I didn't do my job. I didn't bring him home. . . . When it come the time, Doc, I didn't take care of him. <u>When he needed me, I wasn't there</u>. . . . <u>I should've took the fucking round myself</u>.

Another is similarly tortured by guilt for all the deaths in his platoon, which was wiped out in Cambodia while he was on home leave between combat tours. These accounts remind us that Achilles' guilt toward Pátroklos is also couched in terms of abandonment:

> I could not help my friend in his extremity.
> . . . He needed me
> to shield him or to parry the death stroke.

. . . Here I sat,
my weight a useless burden to the earth. (18:111ff)

These self-accusations, both by the veterans and by Achilles, appear at first glance to state the truth: Had each of them been there, rather than absent, the friend might be alive today. However, the guilt of the survivor does not spring from these "what if" possibilities, whether plausible or not. It seems to come from the twinlike closeness that the two soldiers shared, a closeness that allowed them to feel that each was the other's double.

Homer puts an interesting word in Achilles' mouth: He calls Pátroklos his *therápon*, his double, his substitute. (16:288ff) Achilles gives his armor to Pátroklos and sends him out as his *therápon*. This word originally meant "ritual substitute" or "stand-in," according to Gregory Nagy.[2] When Pátroklos dies, the substitution becomes a *wrongful* ritual substitute, rebounding like a religious taint on Achilles. Vietnam veterans have experienced this taint, even if they lack the theology to explain it. But in modern American life few veterans have found purification, although many have sought it in suicide. Homer takes the theme of guilty substitution even further when Achilles stands before Pátroklos's corpse and says:

> "My heart's desire had been
> that I alone should perish . . .
> here at Troy; that you should sail . . . [home]
> taking my son aboard your swift black ship
> . . . to introduce him to his heritage,
> my wide lands, my servants, my great hall." (19:362ff)

Achilles imagines Pátroklos as his *therápon* with his own son. Pátroklos's death was the wrong death, his substitution unintended.

"It should've been me!" can express many different levels of meaning at the same time. One man meant these words literally:

> And I says, "I guess I'll put the lean-to up." When you jump off a tank, we were always taught to jump off the right front fender. And that's exactly where I jumped. I jumped and I started clearing away some brush and shit, and going to put up the lean-to. And I started doing it.

70

And [he] yells down, he says, "I'll do it. Get that fucking pep—."
I had pepperoni, cans of raviolis, that's what I can remember. I had
other stuff, I don't know what the hell it was. But I remember the
pepperoni had all white furry stuff on it from the heat. I got back
up. I got back on, on the right side in the back sprocket, y'know,
crawled to the back, so the turret's in front. And the turret's here,
and here's my package. So I opened the package.

And [he]'s probably fifteen feet away. And when he jumped, he
jumped . . . ah-WHUH. . . . He jumped on a mine.

And there was nothing left of him.

We have met this veteran before, on page 47, and I repeat his portrait of his friend now in the context of his death:

He wasn't a harmful person. He wasn't a dirty person. He had this
head that was wide up at the top, and his chin come down to a point.
He had this hair he used to comb to his right side, and he always had
this big cowlick in back. Big old cowlick. And when he smiled—you
ever hear "ear to ear"?—it was almost a gooney-looking smile. You
know, it was just WA-a-ay—it was huge. He just had this big, huge
smile. He never said nothing bad about nobody. He was just . . . he
was a caring person.

And when you're on a tank, it's like a closeness you never had
before. It's closer than your mother and father, closest than your
brother or your sister, or whoever you're closest with in your
family. . . . Because you get three guys that are on that tank, and
you're just stuck together. You're there.

It should've been me.

I jumped first. It didn't blow me up. Sa-a-ame spot. Same spot.
Same exact spot.

Another veteran, a radio man of traditional Italian Catholic background, has recurrent dreams about a second radio man lying
dead across his lap, bleeding from a chest wound. Usually the two
men alternated nights, with one in the platoon command post and
the other outside the perimeter in position to ambush enemy soldiers approaching their night position. One night the other radio
man asked our patient to switch—he had a bout of malaria and
didn't want to go out on ambush (generally the more dangerous
and exhausting duty). During the night the command post was
mortared and the radio man was killed. Work on this recurring
dream revealed a visual connection to the image of the *Pietá*, the

dead Jesus lying across his mother's lap. The veteran further connected the substitute radio man with the doctrine that Christ died as our substitute, in punishment for our sins. This idea goes back at least to Anselm (d. 1109), although the words "Christ died for our sins" (1 Corinthians 15:3) apparently have other interpretations as well. Matthew 20:28, "Even as the Son of man came not to be ministered unto, but to minister, and to give his life a ransom for many," weaves together the ideas of nurturance, and dying as a substitute. Mark 10:45 is essentially identical. This veteran feels condemned *to* death, not redeemed *from* death, by the wrongful substitution.

DESERVING THE DEATH SENTENCE

As with Vietnam vets, Achilles makes the next step from guilt to passing sentence and the impulse to execute it in suicide:

> Antílokhos
> . . . [bent] to hold the hero's
> hands when groaning shook his heart: [Antílokhos] feared
> the man might use sharp iron to slash his throat. (18:35ff)

We learn of Achilles' suicidal wish through his friend's empathic understanding and protective action.

The boundary is not very clear between grief-stricken suicide to join the dead and guilty self-execution because "It should have been me!" The Larry Burrows photo on the cover of this book shows a Marine reaching out to another lying wounded on the ground. A third Marine is holding back the one who is reaching out. One veteran in our program interpreted the gesture of holding the man back as meaning, "You can't go with him [into death]."

Achilles makes his own sense of imminent, deserved death very vivid:

> . . . Thetis [Achilles' mother, a goddess] said:
> "You'll be
> swift to meet your end, child. . . ."

> Akhilleus the great runner ground his teeth
> and said:

> "May it come quickly. As things were,
> I could not help my friend in his extremity.
> Far from his home he died; he needed me
> to shield him or to parry the death stroke.
> For me there's no return to my own country.
> Not the slightest gleam of hope did I
> afford Pátroklos. . . ." (18:108ff)

Self-blame seems almost universal after the death of a special comrade, regardless of the presence or absence of a "real" basis for it. Yaël Danieli, speaking of European Jewish survivors of the Holocaust, teaches that such "baseless" guilt serves a resuscitative function in the inner reality of the bereaved—it makes the dead present, as if brought back to life.[3] The often "irrational" or "baseless" guilt of combat veterans, such as the tanker who failed to trigger a mine moments before it obliterated his friend, often represents the same inner process of bringing the dead into the present.

Some men undoubtedly felt such overwhelming guilt after the death of a comrade that they took their own lives in a direct and unconcealed manner. One veteran in our program witnessed another Marine, whom he knew only slightly, put a .45 to his head and blow his brains out.

Others recoiled from the stigma of suicide even as they pronounced a death sentence upon themselves. These sought the honorable compromise of death in battle and went berserk. They neither expected to survive nor wanted to. The few who inexplicably survived returned to civilian life with the double torment of death-deserving guilt and a ready capacity to go berserk.

HOMECOMING RENOUNCED

Grief and guilt often seem to merge in the wake of a closest friend's death in battle. Both slam the door on a happy homecoming for the survivor. Grief, as we saw in the previous chapter, can lead men to give up all desire to return home alive. The searing guilt of "it should have been me" has the same result. The reader will recall the wrenching scene of Achilles cutting his hair before Pátroklos's pyre and these veterans' own words, "I didn't see myself going home. No . . . Nope . . . No, I didn't," and "In my wildest thoughts I never expected to return home alive, and emotionally never have."

AN UNINTENDED OUTCOME
OF RELIGIOUS EDUCATION?

Christian scripture tells us, "There is no greater love than this: to lay down one's life for one's friends." (John 15:13) Soldiers in combat often hold the lives of their comrades dearer than their own and fear their comrades' deaths more deeply. In our culture this represents a convergence of Christian self-sacrifice, military training, and the spontaneous bonds of love and loyalty that develop among men who fight together. This willingness for self-sacrifice is endemic in combat and evidenced by thousands of unambiguously sacrificial deaths in war.

Religious instruction of children usually offers a strongly positive view of such self-sacrifice, often explicitly guaranteeing that the person who dies in this fashion will spend eternity in paradise as his reward. However, a second guarantee is usually implicitly made at the same time: God will see to it that the act of self-sacrifice, or even a sincere willingness to die, will *spare* the life of the comrade. Battle is full of bizarre ironies that seem to have been scripted for black comedy, such as the man in a bunker who throws himself on a grenade to save his comrades. The grenade is a dud, but because he is on the ground he alone survives when the enemy bursts into the bunker and guns down all the others. What happens when the sacrifice, or the sincere willingness to sacrifice, does not "work"? This is a situation experienced by many combat veterans with PTSD.

In an ethical universe run by a just, loving, and all-powerful God, the "person I was willing to die for" is not supposed to die. Incomprehensibly, he does die. Mortal soldiers discover that they differ from the immortals in this heartbreaking way: They cannot save, cannot protect, cannot resurrect the comrades they have come to value more than themselves. Homer shows us that the gods have *the power to save a mortal's life*: Paris is spirited away from an unequal duel by Aphrodítê (3:457ff), Aineías is saved by Aphrodítê and Apollo (5:361ff) and a second time by Poseidon (20:359ff), and Hektor is saved by Apollo (20:511ff). God as viewed by Christians, Jews, and Moslems also has the power to save, protect, and resurrect—*and when He does not*, He violates the covenant many thought had been passed down to them in religious instruction. The young man who took his religious instruction truly to heart found it unbearable when "I was willing to die

74

for him—but he's dead!" He was now guilty, and God was gone. This devastating sense of spiritual abandonment and meaninglessness, an unintended outcome of Judeo-Christian religious education, may not have afflicted Homer's polytheists.

SOLDIER'S RAGE—FATAL CONVERGENCE AND COMPLETION

The *Iliad* climaxes with Achilles' beastlike and godlike rampage. The berserk state is the most important and distinctive element of combat trauma. Everything that has gone before—detachment from moral and social restraints by prior betrayal of "what's right," grief and guilt at the death of the special comrade who has wrongfully substituted for the survivor, the sense of being already dead and deserving to be dead—all now converge on the berserk state.

CHAPTER 5

Berserk

*In his ecstasy of power he is mad for battle. . . . Pure
frenzy fills him.*

—*Iliad*, 9:288ff

A soldier who routs the enemy single-handedly is often in the grip of
a special state of mind, body, and social disconnection at the time of
his memorable deeds. Such men, often regarded by their commanders as "the best," have been honored as heroes. This chapter focuses on the triggers of this special state, its characteristics, and its
consequences for those who experience it—and survive.

I believe the word *berserk* is the most precise term available to
describe the behavior that I call to the reader's mind. I prefer this to
the more inclusive word used by Homer commentators since ancient
times, *aristeía*. *Berserk* comes from the Norse word for the frenzied
warriors who went into battle naked, or at least without armor, in a
godlike or god-possessed—but also beastlike—fury.[1] *Aristeía*, as it has
been used to describe episodes in the *Iliad*, applies to the whole
spectrum of epic, noteworthy valor, from clearly nonberserk to
berserk. The *aristeía* of Achilles (Books 19–22) is his epic moment.
Since ancient times Achilles has been the prototype of heroes.[2] Yet
his *aristeía* coincides exactly with his period as a berserker. The *Iliad*
charts the ambiguous borderline between heroism and a blood-
crazed, berserk state in which abuse after abuse is committed. The
narrator himself calls Achilles "shameless" (23:30ff) and his abuse of
the dead Hektor an "outrage." (22:467ff) Achilles, then, is also the
prototype of the berserker.

TRIGGERS OF THE BERSERK STATE

Here is a Marine veteran's narrative, a portion of which we have
heard earlier. I have used capitals for events that frequently trig-

ger the berserk state. Intermixed (underlined) are some character-istics of the berserk state:

We landed at a hot LZ. It was the beginning of Union II, just before I got shot. The chopper just didn't want to land and I got pushed out. THEY JUST PUSHED ME. It was about fifteen feet off the ground and I landed so deep in the mud that I couldn't move. I WAS GETTING FIRED ON FROM ALL OVER THE PLACE. I DIDN'T EVEN KNOW WHICH WAY TO HIDE, AND I COULDN'T MOVE. That was when I started hating the fucking government.

It was about a week or two into Union II. I was walking point. I had seen this NVA soldier at a distance. We were approaching him and he spotted us. We spread out to look for him. I was coming around a stand of grass and heard noise. I couldn't tell who it was, us or him. I stuck my head in the bush and saw this NVA hiding there and told him to come out. He started to move back and I saw he had one of those commando weapons, y'know, with a pistol grip under his thigh, and he brought it up and I was looking straight down the bore. I PULLED THE TRIGGER ON MY M-16 AND NOTHING HAPPENED. He fired and I felt this burning on my cheek. I don't know what I did with the bolt of the 16, but I got it to fire, and I emptied everything I had into him. THEN I SAW BLOOD DRIP-PING ON THE BACK OF MY HAND AND I just went crazy. I pulled him out into the paddy and carved him up with my knife. When I was done with him, he looked like a rag doll that a dog had been play-ing with. Even then I wasn't satisfied. I was fighting with the [medical] corpsmen trying to take care of me. I was trying to get at him for more. . . .

I FELT BETRAYED BY TRYING TO GIVE THE GUY A CHANCE AND I GOT BLASTED. I lost all my mercy. I felt a drastic change after that. I just couldn't get enough. I built up such hate, I couldn't do enough damage.

Everybody'd get hit, and the hate'd build up, ESPECIALLY SEEING WHAT THEY DID TO GUYS IN THE OUTFIT THEY GOT HOLD OF—CUT OFF THEIR DICKS, CUT OFF THEIR EARS. And I had to identify bodies at the morgue. It really fucked me up, them out in the sun all blown up like balloons. The stench—couldn't stand it.

Got worse as time went by. I really loved fucking killing, couldn't get enough. For every one that I killed I felt better. Made some of the hurt went away. EVERY TIME YOU LOST A FRIEND IT SEEMED LIKE A PART OF YOU WAS GONE. Get one of them to compensate what they had done to me. <u>I got very hard, cold, merciless. I lost all my mercy.</u>

"Couldn't get enough" is exactly what Homer shows us in Achilles' mistreatment of Hektor's corpse for twelve days after killing him:

> . . . at that hour he yoked his team, with Hektor
> tied behind, to drag him out, three times
> around Pátroklos' tomb. . . . Akhilleus
> in rage visited indignity on Hektor
> <u>day after day</u>. (24:16ff)

Returning to the veteran's narrative, betrayal of "what's right" figures prominently in it. He is trapped, he is wounded, his friends die, he sees enemy mutilation of American corpses.

Vietnam combat veterans who have been berserk (and survived) are usually very clear about the incidents that brought on the change, in contrast to generally clouded memory of the berserk state itself. One Marine veteran in my program received a high decoration for individual valor and has no memory of the event. Having lost the original citation, he has declined to request a copy of it.

When a soldier is trapped, surrounded, or overrun and facing certain death, the berserk state has apparent survival value, because he apparently has nothing to lose and everything to gain from reckless frenzy. Paradoxically, however, deliverance from certain death is also a common trigger of the berserk state:

<u>It was a mission we didn't have to be on</u>. We were lent to the Special Forces who were reinforcing a mountaintop that was under attack. We had been . . . [locating and destroying] the NVA mortar tubes around this mountain. They didn't have enough machines so they asked if we could lend some of ours, so we called ours in and two of us loaded ARVN [South Vietnamese] squads. There were three choppers going in. . . . The first landed and dropped its squad, but as it was taking off the command pilot got a bullet in his head. I know that because his right seat [copilot] came on the radio saying that his pilot had been killed and he was taking the machine back. I was third. The second guy didn't land his squad but went around [i.e., flew away without landing the troops and exposing his helicopter to enemy fire]. <u>I thought to myself, what the fuck is this?</u> We

were only four squads in Recon, so we always went in, we never went around, because if one of us was down there, we'd be dead if the other three didn't come in and back us up or get us out. I saw him go around and thought for a moment, maybe I should too, but then I thought, fuck it, we're Recon, and took it in.

Just as we're coming in I could see this NVA with his RPG [an infantry antitank weapon descended from the World War II bazooka] pointed straight at me. I said to my copilot, "You take it" [take control of the aircraft], and then at the last second the NVA shifted his aim to my [copilot] and fired. It hit the plastic and stuck halfway through but didn't go off. It just sat there vibrating. We landed and got the squad off. Then as we were taking off—I guess it was the vibration—it didn't explode, it burned. It sent a stream of flame right in my copilot's chest, and it literally melted him. The smell was beyond imagination.

After that I knew I couldn't be killed.

Unexpected deliverance from certain death often happens under circumstances in which others are killed, so distinction among triggering events of the berserk state is often unclear. The veteran who wrote the preceding narrative focused on unexpected deliverance, but betrayal and bereavement seem also likely to have contributed. This episode triggered the last of four distinct periods of berserking during this veteran's combat in Vietnam: the first, after betrayal by a commander that led to the death of his closest friend-in-arms; the second, after witnessing the results of enemy atrocities against civilian patients in a South Vietnamese hospital after the 1969 Tet offensive; the third, when he was overrun and trapped after crash-landing on a fire base; and the fourth, after his copilot was "melted" by the liquid-metal jet from the antitank shell fired at their helicopter.

Vietnam narratives reveal that the events that drive soldiers berserk are betrayal, insult, or humiliation by a leader; death of a friend-in-arms; being wounded; being overrun, surrounded, or trapped; seeing dead comrades who have been mutilated by the enemy; and unexpected deliverance from certain death. Except for the last, every one of these events plays a role in some of the *Iliad*'s five *aristeíai* that scholars conventionally recognize:[3] Diomêdês, Agamémnon, Hektor, and Achilles suffer betrayal, insult, or humiliation. Hektor, Pátroklos, and Achilles are bereaved of a friend-in-arms. Diomêdês, Hektor, and Achilles are wounded. In each instance Homer turns the heat up in the language he uses to describe their fury. Agamémnon sees himself as trapped just before he begins his *aristeía*. A messenger from the goddess Hêra treats Achilles to a vivid picture of likely atrocities against the corpse of Pátroklos.[4] Homer is an acute observer of the psychology of soldiers. Our appreciation is greatly enhanced when we come to the text with a knowledge of that psychology.

"DON'T GET SAD. GET EVEN!"

Preeminent among the triggers of the berserk state is of course bereavement, according to both Vietnam veterans and the *Iliad*. "Don't get sad. Get even!" was explicit advice given by officers and NCOs to weeping soldiers who had lost buddies. I have heard these words recalled from this situation by several veterans.[5] This apparently represented a conscious motivational technique by some in the American military during the Vietnam War that is conspicuously absent in the *Iliad*. Major and minor warriors at Troy often display the transformation of grief into killing rage, but there is not a single unambiguous instance of one man urging another to battle with anything equivalent to "Don't get sad. Get even!"

Consider how startling this contrast is. Ancient Greek culture explicitly approved of revenge killing—it was a kinsman's duty, not merely a thing permitted—and also approved of receiving monetary compensation [*poinê* = blood-price, indemnity] instead of taking revenge.[6] In this cultural context, where we have every right to expect it, we do not hear one soldier egging another on to revenge, as reflected in the Vietnam War refrain, "Don't get sad. Get even!" American culture explicitly rejects both revenge killing and the taking of *wergild*, blood-money as a substitute for revenge. Repeatedly, veterans have described their officers, comrades, and even chaplains urging them to exact a price in blood from the enemy for their fallen friends—to get a "payback."

CHARACTERISTICS OF THE BERSERK STATE

Several features of the berserk state have already emerged from the words of the veterans and of the *Iliad*, such as "I built up such hate, I couldn't do enough damage. . . . I got very hard, cold, merciless. I lost all my mercy," and "ecstasy of power . . . mad for battle . . . pure frenzy." I have listed these and other characteristics of the berserk state below. We find every item in this extensive list both in the accounts of Vietnam combat veterans and in Homer's *Iliad*.

CHARACTERISTICS OF THE BERSERK STATE

Beastlike
Godlike
Socially disconnected
Crazy, mad, insane
Enraged
Cruel, without restraint or discrimination
Insatiable
Devoid of fear
Inattentive to own safety
Distractible
Indiscriminate
Reckless, feeling invulnerable
Exalted, intoxicated, frenzied
Cold, indifferent
Insensible to pain
Suspicious of friends

After Pátroklos's death, Achilles—to use the words of our veterans—"lost it." When a veteran says he "lost it," what did he lose? What did Achilles lose? I believe that the veterans and Homer shared similar views on this subject. In the veterans' own words, they lost their humanity. Beast-god and god-beast replaced human identity.

A BEAST

Our most ancient cultural habits teach us to refer to the cruelty of one human to another as "animal" behavior.

> December 22, 1967, is <u>the day that the civilized me became an animal</u>. . . .

I was a fucking animal. When I look back at that stuff, I say, "That was somebody else that did that. Wasn't me. That wasn't me." Y'know, "Who the fuck was that?" Y'know, at the time it didn't mean nothing. It didn't mean nothing. . . .

War changes you, changes you. Strips you, strips you of all your beliefs, your religion, takes your dignity away, you become an animal. I know the animals don't. . . . Y'know, it's unbelievable what humans can do to each other.

This veteran recognizes that animals do not practice on their species-fellows the cruelty that humans do. Another veteran:

I became a fucking animal. I started fucking putting fucking heads on poles. Leaving fucking notes for the motherfuckers. Digging up fucking graves. I didn't give a fuck anymore. Y'know, I wanted—. They wanted a fucking hero, so I gave it to them. They wanted fucking body count, so I gave them body count. I hope they're fucking happy. But they don't have to live with it. I do.

These men speak of themselves as animals with pain and remorse after their berserking is over. The language they use parallels Achilles' description of himself at the climax of his berserking:

"Hektor, I'll have no talk of pacts with you, . . .
As between men and lions there are none,
no concord between wolves and sheep, but all
hold one another hateful through and through,
so there can be no courtesy [*philímenai*, lit. reciprocal *philía*]
    between us . . ." (22:308ff)

Achilles defines himself here as a lion or a wolf, not a human. This scene is laden with Homer's view of what it means to be human: to be willing to talk, to consider binding self-restraint embodied in agreements, to respect others as *possible* friends.

Homer compares attacking warriors to wild animals dozens of times. This was clearly a conventional metaphor used to praise warrior ferocity. For example, Diomêdês is compared to a lion, as are Agamémnon and Hektor. Pátroklos is compared to a diving hawk. However, when veterans and Achilles refer to themselves as animals they are not using conventional metaphors of strength and ferocity. Unlike Homer's narrator, who uses these as terms of praise, when soldiers speak of themselves this way they are speaking of a loss of human restraint, powerfully symbolized by Achilles' longing to eat Hektor's raw flesh.[7] The ancient Greeks saw the cooking of meat as a fundamental marker delimiting human from nonhuman. Animals are raw-meat eaters; humans restrain their hunger lusts and eat cooked, socially transformed meat. Animals are imagined to lack all mental, ethical, and social restraint; by their nature they are thought incapable of it. Presumed to be incapable, animals are beneath humanity.

A GOD

The berserker also feels like a god. The veteran who had four berserk episodes told me he experienced the third one when he was trapped after his helicopter was shot down on a fire base that was then overrun. The men were demoralized and not firing their weapons. In a berserk frenzy he grabbed a weapon and jumped up on the berm, firing at the North Vietnamese:

> Everyone was so shocked, all the firing stopped except me, and then I stopped. It was silent. <u>I felt like a god, this power flowing through me. Anybody could have picked me off there—but I was untouchable.</u>

Gods are immortal; man is mortal. Gods know no limit on their power (except other gods); man is often powerless and trapped. Gods are invulnerable; man is fragile, easily mutilated and killed. The berserker feels godlike in his power and acknowledges no limit to his power and invulnerability. He acknowledges no restraints of any kind. As beasts are beneath human restraints, gods are above them.

Achilles is compared three times to a "wild god." (20:572, 21:21, 21:266) Using poetic repetition, Homer evokes comparison—and contrast—with the god Poseidon:

> [Poseidon] stepped up into his car,
> and rolled out on the waves. Great fish beneath him
> gamboled from every quarter of the deep,
> aware their lord rode overhead; in laughter
> whitecaps parted, and the team full tilt

airily drew unwetted the axle-tree;
with leap on leap they bore him toward the beachhead. (13:29ff)

As for Achilles:

the sharp-hooved horses of Akhilleus just so
crushed dead men and shields. His axle-tree
was splashed with blood, so was his chariot rail,
with drops thrown up by wheels and horses' hooves.
And Pêleus' son [Achilles] kept riding for his glory,
staining his powerful arms with mire [feces let go by the terr-
    fied Trojans] and blood. (20:577ff)

Homer compares Achilles to the god Poseidon but reminds us that
his ride "for his glory" is not an airy swoop across sea-clean
whitecaps but across human bodies, shit, and blood.

It would be foolish and untruthful to deny the appeal of exalted,
godlike intoxication. Zeus even declares that the mere experience
of this power will compensate Hektor for his onrushing death:

"Ah, poor man,
    no least presage of death is in your mind,
    how near it is, at last. . . . Power for the time being
    I will concede to you, as recompense. . . ."
He bent his great head . . .
and made the arms [of Achilles] fit Hektor.
                    Then fierce Arês [the war god]
entered the man, his bone and sinew thrilled
with power and will to fight. (17:224ff)

Homer invites us to wonder if Hektor—or his widow—felt recom-
pensed.

We have seen the paradox that these godlike, exalted moments
often correspond to times when the men who have survived them
say they have acted like beasts.[8] Many Vietnam veterans I see in
the clinic swing painfully between a crushed, tainted mortality
and its nostalgically longed-for, but dreaded, godlike opposite.
Above all, a sense of merely human virtue, a sense of being valued
and of valuing anything, seems to have fled their lives. As products of a biblical culture, most veterans believed it is nobler to

85

strive to be like God than to want to be human. However, all of our virtues come from *not* being gods: Generosity is meaningless to a god, who never suffers shortage or want; courage is meaningless to a god, who is immortal and can never suffer permanent injury; and so on. Our virtues and our dignity arise from our mortality, our humanity—and not from any success in being God.[9] The godlike berserk state can destroy the capacity for virtue.

ABOVE AND BENEATH—DISCONNECTION FROM HUMAN COMMUNITY

Whether the berserker is beneath humanity as an animal, above it as a god, or both, he is cut off from all human community when he is in this state.[10] No living human has any claim on him, not even the claim of being noticed and remembered. Frequently, a veteran cannot remember the names or faces of any other soldiers he served with after he became a berserker:

> I wasn't close. I can't remember no one after that, and I was there over two years more. I can't remember that much. The people. I can't even remember the people.

To emphasize Achilles' social detachment, Homer heightens his standard practice for such scenes by using a dramatic device much like the cinematic trick of abruptly cutting off the sound track: The Greek army vanishes, leaving Achilles alone with the Trojan soldiers that he slaughters. All cooperation and coordination with his own men fall away. Contrary to the customs of ancient war Homer has shown us up to this point, Achilles hardly stops to strip the armor from the men he has killed, perhaps because this would have involved contact with his own people to carry the booty away. His countrymen suddenly reappear two books later to crowd around Hektor's corpse and stab it. (22:440ff)

LOSS OF ALL RESTRAINT

Restraint is always in part the cognitive attention to multiple possibilities in a situation; when all restraint is lost, the cognitive universe is simplified to a single focus. The berserker is figuratively—sometimes literally—blind to everything but his destructive aim. He cannot see the distinction between civilian

and combatant or even the distinction between comrade and
enemy. One of our veterans was tied up by his own men and taken
to the rear while berserk. He has no clear memory but suspects
that he had become a serious threat to them.

I see restraint as the fundamental thread that Homer draws
through the five major *aristeíai* of the *Iliad*.[11] The first *aristeía* in
the poem, that of Diomêdês, is the polar opposite of the last one,
Achilles'. Diomêdês exemplifies the self-controlled warrior,
Achilles the out-of-control warrior. Diomêdês' *aristeía* opens with
the goddess Athena's unexplained favor. (5:1ff) However, soon
after this divine inspiration, a second thing befalls the all-too-
human Diomêdês—he is wounded, a trigger for berserking. He
sees his blood spurting and prays to Athêna for revenge against
the archer who hit him. The goddess answers him promptly:

> "Courage, Diomêdês. Press the fight
> against the Trojans. Fury like your father's[12]
> I've put into your heart. . . .
> . . . <u>be sure you are not the man</u>
> <u>to dare immortal gods in combat</u>. . . ." (5:141ff)

Athêna's command, phrased as a warning not to battle the gods,
represents the all-important element of restraint. Much as a modern soldier should avoid firing on civilians or on the surrendering
enemy, Diomêdês checks to make sure he is not taking a god
under fire, even during the slaughter phase of his *aristeía*.

The most striking example of Diomêdês' restraint ends his *aristeía*. Glaukos, a Trojan ally, comes out to challenge him.
Diomêdês, who has just devastated the Trojan ranks, demands to
know whether this "young gallant stranger" is a god, and if not,
who is he. Diomêdês and Glaukos discover that they are each
other's *phílos* through their grandfathers (6:140ff), and they make
a private truce. This outcome is astonishing to our modern mentality, but for my purpose here the point is Diomêdês' restraint.
His scheme of values remains complex, irreducible to a single
point such as revenge for his wounding.

Important restraints in other *aristeíai*: Agamémnon is
restrained by pain; Hektor is restrained by prudent and pious
avoidance of Ajax; and initially, at least, Pátroklos abides by
Achilles' order to limit himself to throwing the Trojans out of the
beachhead. After the death of a friend, a fellow Myrmidon,

Pátroklos goes berserk and loses all restraint. (16:657ff) The restraints he sheds are prudent self-preservation, Achilles' instructions, and even rational appreciation of what is humanly possible:

> Now three times Pátroklos
> assaulted the high wall at the tower joint. . . .
> . . . then
> a fourth time he flung himself against the wall,
> more than human in fury. (16:805ff)

No restraint of any kind limits Achilles during his berserk state— no prudence, ethics, piety, personal gain, compassion, fatigue, or physical pain, not the rational requirements of victory nor even fidelity to his dead friend. The ghost of Pátroklos reproaches Achilles for the whole urgent enterprise of revenge against Hektor, just as the living Pátroklos spoke against Achilles' obsession with revenge against Agamémnon because it shut out other things that Achilles valued:

> "Thou hast forgotten me,
> Akhilleus. Never was I uncared for
> in life but am in death. Accord me burial
> in all haste: let me pass the gates of Death.
> . . . I wander
> about the wide gates and the hall of Death.
> Give me your hand. I sorrow." (23:80ff)

The ancient Greeks believed that the unburied dead continue to suffer dreadful misery until covered by the earth. Achilles has violated "what's right" for the dead, not only in his abuse of Hektor's corpse but also in delaying Pátroklos's burial until revenge is carried out.

Achilles even flirts with cannibalism. He taunts the dying Hektor:

> ". . . Would god my passion drove me
> to slaughter you and eat you raw. . . ." (22:412f)

His pain and cannibal rage are mirrored by Hektor's mother, Hékabê:

*"I could devour the vitals of that man [Achilles],
leeching into his living flesh!"* (24:255f, emphasis in source)

Hearing Achilles' cannibal longing may have struck Homer's listeners with reverberating reminders of Diomêdês' restraint, and
beyond that of his father's lack of it. According to ancient commentators, Athêna was about to confer immortality upon
Diomêdês' father, Tydeus, as he lay dying from wounds taken in
his fight with the Theban Melanippos, who was also dying. What
stopped the goddess was her disgust at what she saw: Tydeus was
eating the brains of Melanippos.[13]

REVENGE AS REVIVING THE DEAD

The berserker's manic obsession with revenge is not only destruction to gratify rage. At some deep cultural and psychological level,
spilling enemy blood is an effort to bring the dead back to life.
One veteran recalls the following interior chant to his dead friend
at every kill:

> Every fucking one that died, I say, "_____, here's one for you,
> baby. I'll take this motherfucker out and I'm going to cut his fuck-
> ing heart out for you."

He spoke to his dead friend as if he were alive and present, psychologically bringing him back to life. In the *Odyssey* Homer
makes explicit the idea that revenge killings attempt to revive the
dead, when he says that the dead regain their faculties whenever
they get to drink a libation of blood.[14] Achilles may have acted
upon this notion when he took twelve Trojan soldiers alive
(21:31ff) "to pay the price for dead Pátroklos":

> "I have brought twelve radiant sons of Troy
> whose throats I'll cut, to bloody your great pyre. . ." (23:29f)

Achilles addresses these words to the still-unburied Pátroklos,
promising their execution in the blood-pouring manner of animal sacrifice. Hektor's mother alludes to Achilles' atrocities
against the dead body of Hektor as an attempt at resuscitative
magic:

89

"After he took your life, cutting you down
with his sharp-bladed spear, he trussed and dragged you
many times round the barrow of his friend,
Pátroklos, whom you killed—though not by this
could that friend live again. . . ." (24:895ff)

Parallels between the veteran's words and Achilles' are inescapable. During berserk rage, the friend is constantly alive; letting go of the rage lets him die.

In addition to reviving the dead, revenge denies helplessness, keeps faith with the dead, and affirms that there is still justice in the world, even if this is manifested only in the survivor's random vengeance.

THE BERSERKER IN THE EYES OF OTHER SOLDIERS

An enduring paradox of prolonged combat is the attraction that the berserk warrior sometimes has for the soldiers around him. He has lost all concern for the safety of others, as much as for his own. After the death of this veteran's special comrade, even the rest of the team ceased to matter:

> Before, I'd let two Dinks pass, one Dink pass. After that I don't let no passes. You know, I was endangering five other people. But I wasn't worried about that. . . . Y'know, they were seasoned. If they want to come along for the fucking ride, come along. Hardened. I didn't want them motherfuckers [i.e., the other team members]. . . . That's when I didn't give a fuck anymore. That's when I started standing up on ambushes and doing stuff I normally wouldn't do. Instead of fucking letting 'em have it from the fucking brush, I'd stand up and let the motherfuckers see me and then let 'em have it. I'd use my knife. I didn't give a fuck anymore. I didn't give a fuck about anything. They couldn't kill me. No matter what they'd fucking do.

In an ambush, the greatest safety for the ambushers lay in hitting the middle of an enemy patrol, hence, "I'd let two Dinks pass." Now that he is obsessed with revenge, however, his own safety and that of his team no longer matter. All the diversity and multiplicity of social morality have been replaced by the single value of revenge. However, the berserker's sense of godlike invulnerability seems to make others feel safe. They often volunteer to go on patrols with the berserker, despite his visible indifference to their safety.

We look in vain for the *Iliad*'s Greeks to criticize Achilles' conduct. This is hardly surprising, considering that he has just won the war for them and is still visibly crazed even after the first funeral feast for Pátroklos. (23:43ff) No one is tactless or foolhardy enough to tell Achilles that his treatment of Hektor's corpse is, in the words of our veterans, "really out there," although a number who are beyond the reach of his spear and sword do speak up: the ghost of the dead Pátroklos, the gods, and the narrator.[15]

FLAMING ICE—BERSERK PHYSIOLOGY

No one has ever drawn a syringe of blood or cerebrospinal fluid from a berserk warrior nor mapped the electrical activities of his nervous system. No one knows how much of the large literature on the physiology of extreme stress can be applied to berserking, on which there is no established physiological literature. It is plain that the berserker's brain and body function are as distant from everyday function as his mental state is from everyday thought and feeling.

How ironic it is that this book about a war now a generation past and a poem almost three thousand years old may remain fresh for years; and yet if I make many references to scientific work published just this year, the book is likely to be "dated" very quickly. So I am reluctant to speculate here on any of the specifics of the physiology of the berserker, because anything I might say is likely to be out of date as soon as this book appears. Understanding brain and hormonal changes in severe combat PTSD is a rapidly advancing field, as are the profound influences of stress hormones on memory, on health, and on aging.

Veterans are well aware of the sensations that accompany the autonomic and endocrine hyperarousal that is the most obvious bodily concomitant of combat. The heart pounds, the muscles tense, the senses are on extreme alert. This is widely known as the "fight-or-flight reaction." Says one veteran: "Well, I mean, you're scared at the same time, but your adrenaline and the training makes you fucking mad, now." There may be a "burning in the gut" or a feeling "like electricity coming out of me." Adrenal hormones reduce sensibility to pain and fatigue and sharpen the senses. Bodily strength at such times seems superhuman:

> Now Hektor picked a boulder. . . .
> The strongest pair of men . . .
> . . . could not . . . heave up
> this boulder from the ground. . . .
> Lightly Hektor handled it alone . . .
> so Hektor, lifting up the stone, went forward
> to the high double doors. . . . (12:496ff)

Some people experience the "adrenaline rush" as intensely pleasurable and willingly refer to the berserk state as exaltation or intoxication. Some combat veterans speak of it as "better than sex." Achilles speaks of anger as pleasurable:

> "Ai! let strife and rancor
> perish from the lives of gods and men,
> with anger that envenoms even the wise
> <u>and is sweeter than slow-dripping honey</u>. . . ." (18:122ff)

Apart from adrenaline, the adrenal glands release other hormones in response to emergencies. Hektor's fatal encounter with Achilles occurs under the eyes of Hektor's parents, who watch from the walls of Troy. As Achilles approaches, Hektor loses his nerve and bolts, with Achilles in pursuit. Three times they circle the city in this famous chase. However, in the absence of divine intervention, as mere mortals neither Hektor nor Achilles could have remained alive for more than thirty seconds in the absence of cortisol—both would have collapsed and died. The human body is not adapted to *constant* emergency mobilization.

Prolonged combat also brings bodily changes that deaden pain, hunger, and desire, resulting in an emotional coldness and indifference. The neurochemical basis of this change may be the release of opiatelike substances by the brain itself in response to terror and pain, as well as corelease of such substances with adrenaline by the adrenal gland. One veteran recalls with amazement his tiny food intake:

I ate the equivalent of maybe a third, a third of a bologna sandwich a day. And that's all I ate. I don' know. I just didn't want to eat. Once a week they'd fly us out liver and onions. And I hate liver and onions. On a Sunday afternoon and I never ate it. Never, never ate it.

Why I became like that? It was all evil. All evil. Where before, I wasn't. I look back, I look back today, and I'm horrified at what I turned into. What I was. What I did.

Homer gives a high profile to Achilles' refusing food:

> "I will not swallow
> food or drink—my dear friend being dead,
> lying before my eyes. . . .
> Slaughter and blood are what I crave, and groans
> of anguished men!" (19:230ff)

Finally, the berserker is hyperalert and ready to see even the smallest novelty in the environment or in people as a sign of imminent attack. This has demonstrable survival value in combat:

> We used to laager out [the armored equivalent of circling the wagons] at night, the five tanks. And I'd go out, go out by myself. They all thought I was fucking gone. I was. But I couldn't see it.
> I was so finely tuned, I could smell the Gooks coming. Nobody else, I could smell those fucking Gooks, whenever they come near.[16]
> I was just finely, finely tuned. I was in a state of hyperalertness.

Persisting hyperalertness years after its survival value has gone may originate in other changes in the parts of the brain that process incoming sensations for signs of danger and connect sensations with emotion.

The true physiological relationship between the burning rage of the berserker and his icy deadness remains uncharted territory. We see the paradox that the same human being may burn with fury while cold as ice, incapable of hunger, pleasure, or even pain from his wounds.

Homer shows cold deadness fueling a conflagration of revenge in the famous scene when Priam's son Lykáôn surrenders to Achilles and begs to be taken alive for ransom, as Achilles has already done once before:

> . . . Priam's son pled for his life,
> but heard <u>a voice of iron</u> say:

"Young fool, don't talk to me of what you'll barter.
In days past, before Pátroklos died
I had a mind to spare the Trojans, took them
alive in shoals. . . .
<u>Come, friend, face your death, you too.</u>
<u>And why are you so piteous about it?</u>
Pátroklos died, and he was a finer man
by far than you. You see, don't you, how large
I am, and how well-made? . . .
. . . Yet death waits for me. . . . "

                         . . . Akhilleus
drew his sword and thrust between his neck
and collarbone, so the two-edged blade went in
up to the hilt. . . .
                    . . . Akhilleus picked him up
by one foot, wheeled, and slung him in the river. . . . (21:113ff)

Achilles is so cut off from human compassion that he even addresses Lykáôn as "friend" (*phílos*) as he tells him that the only possible community between them is that of death—and executes him. This so-called "consolation" to Lykáôn is nothing but the chilling cruelty of the berserker; a warmer reading of this scene is ruled out by Achilles' gratuitous mistreatment and mocking of Lykáôn's corpse.

ARISTEIAI OF AMERICAN SOLDIERS IN VIETNAM— THE DIFFERENCES

We have already seen one important difference between Homeric warrior berserking and the killing rages of American soldiers in Vietnam: Bereaved American soldiers were often urged, "Don't get sad. Get even!" by their military superiors, but Homeric warriors never were. Other differences are also noteworthy.

The *aristeíai* recorded in the *Iliad* are generally of very brief duration, compared with berserk episodes of Vietnam veterans. One veteran went berserk after the death of his closest friend-in-arms and remained in that state for two years, until his behavior became so extreme that his own men tied him up and took him to the rear:

It was like two years, I was like that. I remember re-upping. I definitely remember. I wanted revenge. I didn't get it out of me. I wanted it, I wanted it, I wanted it. . . . It was unbelievable, the revenge never left me for a minute. It was there. It was there and it was powerful. And it consumed me. It consumed my mind. It consumed my body. It consumed every part of me.

They took . . . my life. Somebody had to pay them back for that. And it was me, because it was my life. That's how I looked at it. I couldn't get enough. I could have had my hands around ten Gooks' throats a day and it wouldn't be enough.

I carried this home with me. I lost all my friends, beat up my sister, went after my father. I mean, I just went after anybody and everything. Every three days I would totally explode, lose it for no reason at all. I'd be sitting there calm as could be, and this monster would come out of me with a fury that most people didn't want to be around. So it wasn't just over there. I brought it back here with me.

This man's berserk state persisted in his physiology long after he left the battlefield. He credits an adrenaline-blocking drug with finally bringing it under control.

The *Iliad* usually shows the onset of an *aristeía* coming shortly after the triggering events. The interval between Agamémnon's betrayal of *thémis* in seizing Achilles' prize of honor and the onset of Achilles' berserk state was about two weeks; between Pátroklos's death and Achilles going berserk, overnight. In all other instances the interval between trigger event and berserking was only a matter of minutes or hours. Undoubtedly, this is partly due to the dramatic compression that Homer favored. His enormous epic covers only fifty-three days, with Books 2 through 22 encompassing only five days. Vietnam veterans often report that berserking began shortly after the death of a special comrade, but often the time interval after a betrayal of "what's right" was longer than in the *Iliad*, and often there was one major betrayal in the midst of a series of lesser ones. The betrayal most bitterly recalled by one veteran, the awarding of individual medals, Combat Infantry Badges, and a unit citation for an attack on unarmed civilians, occurred six months before the death of his closest comrade, the death that began his berserking.

The *Iliad* mentions such terms as "blood-lust" but offers little of soldiers talking about revenge. Mostly, we *see* Achilles' revenge.

Thankfully, I hear veterans talk about revenge much more than I see it. These are the words of one veteran:

> After [he] died, I was hurting, hurting bad. Then I went on a fucking vendetta. All I wanted was to fucking hurt people. All I wanted to do was rain fucking destruction on that fucking country. If it fucking burned, I burnt it. I used more fucking ammo in the next three months than the whole fucking time I was there. . . . A lot of fucking air power, too. [He was in a position to request and usually get air strikes.] Before, I used Puff the Magic Dragon [a fixed-wing aircraft gunship fitted with several 7.62mm multibarreled machine guns, each capable of firing six thousand rounds per minute]. Puff was more efficient and human. . . . How could you say bullets are fucking humanized? But they were. To see what napalm does—napalm was for *revenge*. Napalm would suck the air right out of your breath. Take it right out of your lungs.

Here are the words of another veteran, speaking of the obliteration of his closest friend-in-arms by a mine and the hunger for revenge that followed:

> And we looked and looked and looked. And the only thing that was left was, it almost looked like a wig. It was just his hair. Just his hair. And we put that in the body bag. And I was crying like a baby. And a convoy was going by and there was soldiers and they were looking at me, and I just didn't give a fuck.
>
> And I cried and I cried and I cried. . . . And I stopped crying. And I probably didn't cry again for twenty years.
>
> I turned. I had no feelings. I wanted to hurt. I wanted to hurt. And I wanted to hurt.

Homer's narrative and veterans' narratives agree that betrayal of "what's right" is a conditioning event that prepares a soldier to go berserk at the death of a closest friend-in-arms. I cannot say for certain that betrayal is a necessary precondition. However, I have yet to encounter a veteran who went berserk from grief alone, as in the second phase of Pátroklos's *aristeía*, or from betrayal alone, if the betrayal did not cause a death or wound. I also cannot say which came first in American military culture, suppression of grief or the motivational ploy of nudging grief into berserking rage.

ACHILLES IN VIETNAM

NAKED BERSERKERS AND ACHILLES' INVULNERABILITY

Berserking American soldiers invariably shed their helmets and flak jackets. They had no other armor. As one veteran said, "Got rid of my helmet, got rid of my flak jacket. I just wanted to kill." All the berserker feels he needs is a *weapon*; everything else is in the way. Achilles wants to go after Hektor just moments after he hears the grievous news of Pátroklos's death, despite the loss of his own armor, which Pátroklos was wearing. Once we grasp the psychological attractiveness of going into battle naked, the following passage makes complete sense, when Achilles roars at his mother:

> ". . . Do not attempt to keep me from the fight,
> though you love me; you cannot make me listen." (18:146f)

He remembers well that he has no armor; only a moment before he told his mother this, but he still has his great Pelian spear. Thetis (a goddess, after all) holds him back from rushing into battle *baresark*, that is, "bare shirt," without armor.[17] In the destruction and slaughter that follow, we see the loss of all other restraint.

My claim throughout this book is that the *Iliad* can be legitimately read as a text concerning the human experience of combat. The main purpose of this chapter has been to show the broad range of phenomena associated with the berserk state, the most salient of mental states of the combat soldier. The crucial trait that emerged from this analysis is the absence of restraints—apparently *any* restraint—when berserk. This appears to be the feature that differentiates the unequivocally praiseworthy *aristeía* of Diomêdês from the demonic and questionable berserk state of Achilles.

The god Apollo—although a prejudiced witness who is partisan to Troy—gives a striking picture of the wreckage of Achilles' good character:

> Murderous Akhilleus . . .
> a man who shows no decency, implacable,
> barbarous in his ways. . . .
> The man has lost all mercy;
> he has no shame. . . .
>   . . . A sane one may endure

97

an even dearer loss: a blood brother,
a son; and yet, by heaven, having grieved
and passed through mourning, he will let it go. . . .
Not this one: first he took Prince Hektor's life
and now he drags the body, lashed to his car,
around the barrow of his friend [Pátroklos]. . . . (24:46ff)

CLINICAL IMPORTANCE OF THE BERSERK STATE

On the basis of my work with Vietnam veterans, I conclude that
the berserk state is ruinous, leading to the soldier's maiming or
death in battle—which is the most frequent outcome—and to lifelong psychological and physiological injury if he survives. I
believe that once a person has entered the berserk state, he or she
is changed *forever*.

This is not an historical curiosity. More than 40 percent of
Vietnam combat veterans sampled in the late 1980s by the con-
gressionally mandated National Vietnam Veterans Readjustment
Study reported engaging in violent acts three times or more in the
previous year. We're talking about 300,000 men here. The percentage of combat veterans who reported averaging more than
one violent act a *month* was almost five times higher than among
the sample of civilian counterparts.[18] A growing body of recent
physiological evidence suggests a relationship between disorders
of specific brain neurotransmitter function and impulsive violence.

Episodic recurrence of the berserk state in civilian life after
war is not new. As Kipling wrote toward the end of World War I,
"You went Berserk . . . you'll probably be liable to fits of it all your
life."[19]

If a soldier survives the berserk state, it imparts emotional
deadness and vulnerability to explosive rage to his psychology and
a permanent hyperarousal to his physiology—hallmarks of post-
traumatic stress disorder in combat veterans. My clinical experience with Vietnam combat veterans prompts me to place the
berserk state at the heart of their most severe psychological and
psychophysiological injuries. Clinical investigation of the berserk
state is an embryonic field of study, so we cannot say exactly what
components and intensity must be present to result in lifelong
physiological and emotional damage. Homer helps us to hear

what many veterans have been trying desperately to tell us about going berserk.

This completes the evolution of combat traumas, told in the order that Homer unfolded them in his story of Achilles. The next section takes up themes that do not fall into a specific sequence in the *Iliad* or in the stories of Vietnam combat veterans, but which pervade both. They are no less important than the sequential themes and are often deeply connected to them.

PART II

CHAPTER 6

Dishonoring the Enemy

*Thy servant slew both the lion and the bear: and this
uncircumcised Philistine shall be as one of them.*
—1 Samuel 17:36

To our modern mind the enemy is detestable—by definition.
"Well, he's the enemy, ain't he?" said one veteran. "You couldn't
kill them if you thought he was just like you." This apparently self-
evident truth—that men cannot kill an enemy understood to be
honorable and like oneself—is something this veteran learned as
part of his culture. Even those who condemn this attitude on ethical and religious grounds, such as Rev. William Mahedy, think it is
a given fact of the human species:

> The enemy must in some way be dehumanized, degraded to less
> than full human status. Collectively, the population [and soldiers]
> of the other country must become "gooks," "Nips," "Japs,"
> "Krauts," or "Huns." One must first hide from the full humanity of
> the opponent before [one] is able to kill him.[1]

Vietnam-era military training reflexively imparted the image of a
demonized adversary: The enemy soldier was pictured as evil and
loathsome, deserving to be killed as the enemy of God and as
God-hated vermin, so inhuman as not really to care if he lives or
dies. Debased images of the enemy are very old in our culture,
dating from the Bible.

By contrast, the *Iliad* emphatically portrays the enemy as
worthy of respect, even honor. For example, Agamémnon, the
Greek commander in chief, speaks of "holy Ilion [Troy]" *in the
presence of his troops* (4:199ff). It's hard to imagine General
Westmoreland, commander of U.S. forces in Vietnam, speaking
of "holy Hanoi" under any circumstances at all. This chapter
compares images of the enemy voiced by Vietnam combat veter-

ans with those used in the speech and actions of soldiers on both sides at Troy. These in turn will be compared with what was said about and to the enemy in 1 Samuel 17, the biblical anti-epic of David and Goliath. I make this comparison because I believe that the modern cultural habit of dehumanizing the enemy originates in biblical religion. Hektor, Aías [Ajax], Diomêdês, and Glaukos all treat the enemy with great respect while displaying exceptional military prowess. They are not unusual or deviant in Homer's world; indeed, they represent the ideal from which Achilles falls away.

THE ENEMY *AS* ENEMY:
IMAGES IN COMMON TO VIETNAM AND TROY

The official position of the U.S. government was that North Vietnam intended to enslave the people of South Vietnam and that mass executions and torture of political opponents would follow the defeat of South Vietnam. Some veterans in our program believe that North Vietnam did pursue a policy of genocide in the South after the war. As individuals, they personally witnessed the results of North Vietnamese and Viet Cong atrocities against the living and mutilation of the dead. One veteran was the first to enter a civilian hospital in Kontum, the North Vietnamese having just retreated after overrunning it.[2] The North Vietnamese had systematically hacked from the patients' bodies any limbs they had found bandaged with American bandages or hooked up to American I.V.s.

In Homer's *Iliad*, too, the enemy *is* the enemy and plans the most brutal mayhem possible. The reader should not sentimentalize Homeric combat. The Greeks know that if their beachhead is overrun, the Trojans intend to burn their ships and slaughter them to the last man. The Greeks, for their part, have vowed, in the words of Odysseus, "never to turn back till they plundered Troy" (2:331) and set it in flames. Their war aims go beyond mere seizure and destruction of property, as is spelled out by the Greek elder statesman, Nestor:

Therefore let no man press for our return [to Greece]
<u>before he beds down with some Trojan wife</u>. (2:415f)

In their own words, the Greeks plan no mercy for the Trojans. From the Trojan perspective, there is no doubt about the malignity of Greek intentions. Here, the fearsome Greek purposes are starkly visualized by Priam:

> My sons brought down, my daughters dragged away,
> bedchambers ravaged, and small children hurled
> to earth in the atrocity of war,
> as my sons' wives are taken by Akhaians'
> ruinous hands. (22:66ff)

In both Vietnam and Troy, the enemy *was* the enemy. Americans and Homer's warriors held in common just a few other ideas, such as that the war was fought for a just cause and that the enemy was deceitful and treacherous. Otherwise, images of the enemy contrast very sharply.

IMAGE OF THE VIETNAMESE ENEMY

The American soldier's image of his Vietnamese enemy appears little changed from the stereotype of the Japanese enemy in World War II, who were thought of as monkeys, insects, vermin, child-like, unfeeling automata, puny, incapable of any competencies worthy of notice, bent on world conquest, comical, inscrutable, uniquely treacherous, deranged, physiologically inferior, primitive, barbaric, and devoted to fanatical suicide charges. I shall illustrate some of these images from the words of several veterans in our program:

> Charlie [the Vietnamese enemy]—he had no feelings. Charlie never cared whether he lived or died. He didn't care. And that's what I seen. They come charging the tanks all wired up. We'd shoot them, and y'know, they just didn't care. They had no concept of life. And I guess I got into the same thing.

> Then-n-n you run into somebody that you start firing at, and you say, "Well I'm going to kick his fucking little fucking Gook ass." And all of a sudden this motherfucker got you pinned down. Y'know, I mean, he's tearing up the fucking trees you're hiding behind. And you start saying to yourself, "These motherfuckers are

serious. Well, what they're doing." Y'know, "I'm going to break his fucking balls when I get ahold of him." Well, I mean, you're scared at the same time, but your adrenaline and the training makes you fucking mad, now. "I'm going to kick his <u>little motherfucking ass</u> when I get my hands on him."

   <u>You know, they told me I was fighting Communism</u>. And I really believed in my country and I believed everyone served their country. <u>You know, they said we were fighting Communism, that they were peasants [who used] pitchforks and homemade weapons</u>.

The hit-and-hide tactics of the Viet Cong were seen as cowardly rather than competent and resourceful, and the Viet Cong were viewed as "not real soldiers." Stateside instructors portrayed them as ill equipped and not to be feared, as inert matter to be ground down by the superior American war machine. All Vietnamese were lumped as Asian peasants and described as primitive, ignorant, superstitious, and not rational. Americans went to war ignorant of the martial culture dating back centuries, shared by all Vietnamese classes, including rural peasants. In Vietnam, when Americans witnessed the determination and self-sacrifice of enemy soldiers, they were taught that enemy soldiers placed no value on their own lives. They were called madmen and animals and were said to lack any emotions. In addition to being dirty and smelling bad, the enemy were puny and ugly, perhaps an outward sign that they were enemies of God.

HOMER: VALOR DOES NOT DEPEND ON CONTEMPT FOR THE ENEMY

Homer's warriors kept a respectful image of the enemy, which directly contradicts what we think of as natural in soldiers. At Troy, fighters on both sides viewed their opponents as men much like themselves, as competently armed, formidable fighters. They were worthy of honor and capable of imparting honor even if one suffered defeat at their hands. The Greeks viewed the Trojans as the legitimate inhabitants of a holy place, made holy by worship of the same gods who might, at the end of the day, favor the Trojan defenders and not the Greek expeditionary force. Greeks and Trojans each acknowledged that the highest gods might favor the enemy.

When Achilles lost his respect for the enemy, he was behaving abnormally and unnaturally for his culture. The following analyses will establish that respect for the enemy was normal and natural for the most honored warriors on both sides of the Trojan War.

ENEMY SOLDIERS TALK TO EACH OTHER AT TROY

The effective range of spears and swords is well within the reach of the human voice. Combat with these weapons is face to face, hand to hand, personal. When face-to-face combatants share a common tongue, complex speech occurs between them. The American Civil War was the last time in our own history when both sides spoke the same language. The *Iliad* shows cultural and linguistic unity between Greeks and Trojans as great as that between Union and Confederacy in the Civil War.

Homer has us listen to a large number of verbal exchanges between combatants. However, since direct speech on the battlefield between enemies almost always reflects "mind games," i.e., attempts to manipulate the enemy according to one's own agenda, direct speech may be skewed either toward respect, when the enemy's cooperation is sought, or toward contempt, when the goal is to intimidate, distract, enrage, or otherwise "throw off" the enemy. Keeping these reservations in mind, direct speech still has much to tell us.

The private battlefield truce between Diomêdês, a Greek, and Glaukos, a Trojan ally (6:140–280), shows the cultural chasm that separates us from the world of the *Iliad*. In all modern armies, both soldiers would be guilty of serious, possibly capital offenses in reaching a private truce. Modern folk culture would question the battle-willingness of one or both of them for even thinking of such a truce. Glaukos, the Lykian second-in-command, approaches to take on Diomêdês. Diomêdês asks him:

> Young gallant stranger, who are you?
> I have not noticed you before in battle—
> never before, in the test that brings men honor—
> but here you come now, far in front of everyone,
> with heart enough to risk my beam of spear.
> A sorrowing old age they have whose children

face me in war! If you are a god from heaven,
I would not fight with any out of heaven. (6:140ff)

The first thing we note is the respectful way he addresses the
enemy. The possibility that this respect comes from a worry that
Glaukos might be a god in disguise does not weaken the force of
the example: An American soldier who admitted the possibility that
God appeared to him as an enemy soldier would have been considered a traitor or insane. When we look at Diomêdês' other fights
(e.g., in Book 5), never once does he speak disrespectfully to his
enemy. As the scene with Glaukos unfolds, they exchange genealo-
gies and discover that their grandfathers had been each other's
xénoi, or guest-friends. This discovery has many reverberations,
considering that the whole war was being fought over the betrayal
of Meneláos by a former *xénos*, Paris. Diomêdês and Glaukos
declare a private truce with each other, and Diomêdês says:

> "I am your friend,
> sworn friend, in central Argos. You are mine
> in Lykia, whenever I may come.
> So <u>let us keep away from one another's</u>
> <u>weapons in the spear-fights of this war</u>.
> Trojans a-plenty will be left for me,
> and allies, as god puts them in my path;
> many Akhaians will be left for you
> to bring down if you can. ·
>   <u>Each take the other's</u>
> <u>battle-gear; let those around us know</u>
> <u>we have this bond of friendship from our fathers</u>." (6:265ff)

They advertise their truce; no one even looks askance, not to
speak of placing them under arrest. Subsequent events in the
Iliad prove them both to be fierce fighters, not the least weakened
by this private truce.[3]

An even more telling example of respect for the enemy is the
single combat between the Greek champion, Aías [Ajax], and
Hektor, the Trojan commander (7:243ff). The duel ends with their
exchange of gifts, which would constitute a punishable offense in
any modern army, or at least call for a psychiatric examination.
The terms Hektor proposes for the duel are no more than *thémis*,
the social morality, "what's right" in treating the dead that Greeks

and Trojans already share. That is, the body of whichever fighter loses the duel will be returned to his own people for religiously correct cremation and burial. Hektor's challenge is also notable for what it does *not* say. He makes no boasts of a god's favor, even though he knows he has it and cannot be killed that day. With Achilles withdrawn from the army, the Greeks are as fearful of Hektor's challenge (7:106) as the Israelites are of Goliath in 1 Samuel 17:11.

The long and furious duel ends in a draw at nightfall. Hektor tells Aías, "We'll meet again another time—and fight until the unseen power decides between those hosts of ours, awarding one or the other victory." (7:343ff) Homeric warriors clearly do not think of the enemy as god-hated vermin, and they admit that they do not know whose side the gods are on. Hektor continues, "Afterwards they'll say, among Akhaians [Greeks] and Trojans: 'These two fought and gave no quarter in close combat, yet they parted friends.'" (7:357ff) The contrast to fighting "Gooks" in Vietnam cannot be sharper.

I have classified in the *Iliad* all instances of direct speech between enemies according to who is speaking and whether the tone and content are respectful or contemptuous.[4] The result shows that the Greeks insult their enemies much more often than they speak respectfully to them. The Trojans are more civil, addressing their enemies with respect a bit more often than not. The Greeks—the eventual winners, after all—are quite insulting to the Trojans' faces; perhaps their cultural attitudes are more like ours, because they, our forebears, wiped out their respect-weakened adversaries. The text does not support this, however, when we observe that some of the most formidable Greek fighters treat their enemies with respect; this refutes any idea that prowess somehow requires contempt for the enemy.

SOLDIERS TALK ABOUT THE ENEMY AT TROY

We probably learn the truth of soldiers' attitudes when we have a chance to listen in on what comrades say to each other about the enemy. Both Greeks and Trojans show great readiness to speak well of the enemy in the *Iliad*. Among themselves, Greeks speak respectfully of the enemy twice as often as they speak critically, and the Trojans *never* insult the enemy in private.[5] When Homer's

Greek and Trojan fighters talk to their fellows about their own local defeats, these losses are often attributed to the respect-worthy excellence of the enemy. American soldiers' culture in Vietnam virtually outlawed this way of viewing enemy successes. Here are the words of one veteran in our program:

> We were down for a while [on] a base camp there, because they wanted us to work the Cambodian border.... They had all these fucking towers and shit. And they're all in their bunkers. With showers—you know, these motherfuckers trying to start their own city or something? And <u>they had more fucking Gooks on that fucking base than they had Americans</u>, y'know? And we kept saying [to the people in the base camp], "Are you guys serious? Y'know, these motherfuckers are going to maul the fuck out of you." And we were there for about two months, and they got overrun one night we were there.... They shot up the fucking place and ran out the other side. It was crazy. That's when you wanted to get back out in the fucking field. <u>Because everyone in the rear didn't know what the fuck they were doing</u>. They were shooting at each other.... "Fuck that. I'm out of here!" Y'know, "C'mon, c'mon, I'm getting back out in the fucking jungle where it's safe."

Blaming one's own tactical defeat on the evil spying of the enemy or on the culpable incompetence of the leadership were culturally available ways of thinking and speaking; respect for the enemy's military excellence (including the gathering and use of intelligence) was not.

The *Iliad* contains no derogatory nicknames for the enemy used by soldiers when talking among themselves; we hear no hint of ancient equivalents of "Gook," "Dink," "Zip," or "Slope," used so freely at all levels of the American military in Vietnam. If it sounds like Homer's warriors suffered from an excess of politeness or had no flair for insulting language, the reader should consider the rich lexicon of abuse that Greek heaped on Greek and Trojan on Trojan. Yet I have not identified a single instance of Trojans scorning the enemy in an insulting, contemptuous, or even critical manner. On the Greek side I find only two mild instances: Aías calls the Trojans "lesser men than we," (15:592) and Agamémnon criticizes them for breaking the ritually sworn truce made for single combat between Paris and Meneláos. This passage is noteworthy in a number of respects.

> <u>They've ground the truce under their heels.</u>
>   <u>. . .all the more they'll pay</u>
> <u>for their misdeed in lives, in wives and children</u>!
> For this I know well in my heart and soul:
> the day must come when <u>holy Ilion</u>
> is given to fire and sword, and Priam perishes,
> <u>good lance though he was</u>, with all his people. (4:184ff)

Agamémnon is grief- and guilt-stricken at Meneláos's wound by the truce-breaking arrow shot. Even in this emotionally charged moment when he fears his brother is a dead man, with his troops listening, when Agamémnon relishes hope of divine retribution for breaking the sworn truce, he refers to Troy as "holy Ilion" and calls Priam "good lance though he was."[6]

Why is this mentality so alien to us? Undoubtedly racism has played a large role in the psychology of American soldiers in Asia, and this must not be underestimated. However, the religious roots of the enemy as vermin have largely been ignored.

Religious Roots of the Enemy as Vermin: Biblical Anti-epic in 1 Samuel 17

When modern American soldiers and their leaders dehumanize the enemy, they affirm their loyalty to God, expressing a cultural tradition powerfully engraved by biblical scripture. The story of David and Goliath from 1 Samuel 17 offers an illuminating contrast to Homeric warriors in the speech of enemies about and to one another.

The Bible's anti-epic opens with Goliath's arming scene:

> And there went out a champion out of the camp of the Philistines, named Goliath, of Gath, whose height was six cubits and a span [around nine feet].
>
> And he had an helmet of brass upon his head, and he was armed with a coat of mail; and the weight of the coat was five thousand shekels of brass [more than two hundred pounds].
>
> And he had greaves of brass upon his legs, and a target of brass between his shoulders.
>
> And the staff of his spear was like a weaver's beam; and his spear's head weighed six hundred shekels of iron: and one bearing a shield went before him.

Compare this with Agamémnon's arming scene given in chapter 8, on pages 141–142.

> And he stood and cried unto the armies of Israel, and said unto them, . . . choose you a man for you, and let him come down to me.
>
> If he be able to fight with me, and to kill me, then will we be your servants: but if I prevail against him, and kill him, then shall ye be our servants, and serve us.

Note the contrast between these terms and those of the single combats between Paris and Meneláos and between Hektor and Aías. The "pagan" enemy is presented as a moral monstrosity as well as a physical monster, not conceivable as a counterpart in political settlement, like the one agreed for the duel between Paris and Meneláos in the *Iliad*'s Book 3.

> When Saul and all Israel heard those words of the Philistine, they were dismayed, and greatly afraid. . . .

The Greeks are similarly afraid at 7:107 when Hektor calls for a duel with a Greek champion. But David takes up the challenge, defying Goliath by equating him with a beast:

> And David said to Saul, Let no man's heart fail because of him [Goliath]; thy servant will go and fight with this Philistine.
>
> And Saul said to David, Thou art not able to go against this Philistine to fight with him: for thou art but a youth,. . . .
>
> [David answered,] <u>Thy servant slew both the lion and the bear: and this uncircumcised Philistine shall be as one of them</u>, seeing he hath defied the armies of the living God.
>
> David said moreover, <u>The LORD that delivered me out of the paw of the lion, and out of the paw of the bear, he will deliver me out of the hand of this Philistine</u>. And Saul said unto David, Go, and the LORD be with thee. . . .

David's arming scene, made to appear comical, disparages the cultural prestige of armor:

> And Saul armed David with his armour, and he put an helmet of brass upon his head; also he armed him with a coat of mail.
>
> And David girded his sword upon his armour, and he assayed to go; for he had not proved it. And David said unto Saul, I cannot go with these; for I have not proved them. And David put them off him.

Goliath's subhuman status is reaffirmed in action:

> And he took his staff in his hand, and chose him five
> smooth stones out of the brook, and put them in a shepherd's bag
> which he had . . . ; and his sling was in his hand: and he drew near
> to the Philistine. . . .
>
> And when the Philistine looked about, and saw David, he
> disdained him: . . .
>
> And the Philistine said unto David, <u>Am I a dog, that thou
> comest to me with staves</u>?

Goliath, no brainless lout any more than Aías [Ajax], grasps immediately that David defines him as subhuman—indeed, David has just said that to Saul a few lines earlier. His warrior pride is also offended because this Israelite champion, David, is not an honorable foe according to the warrior ethos. He has no "name"; in fighting him Goliath lowers himself, and in killing him he can win no honor, which is so central to the single combat between Ajax and Hektor.

> And the Philistine said to David, Come to me, and I will
> give thy flesh unto the fowls of the air, and to the beasts of the field.
>
> Then said David to the Philistine, Thou comest to me with a
> sword, and with a spear, and with a shield [all cultural prestige
> items in the epic world]: but I come to thee in the name of the
> LORD of hosts, the God of the armies of Israel, whom thou hast
> defied.
>
> This day will the LORD deliver thee into mine hand; and I
> will smite thee, and take thine head from thee; and I will give the
> carcasses of the host of the Philistines this day unto the fowls of the
> air, and to the wild beasts of the earth; that all the earth may know
> that there is a God in Israel.
>
> And all this assembly shall know that the LORD saveth not
> with sword and spear: <u>for the battle is the Lord's, and he will give
> you into our hands.</u>[7]

The story proclaims the power of the God of Israel, divine favor for Israel, and the religious merit of David's faith in his God. Rejected here is all merely human *thémis*, along with respect for the enemy and any possibility of honorable defeat, so prominent in the duel between Ajax and Hektor, described above on pages 108–109 Hektor does not boast of divine favor, even though he knows he has it.

Modern habits of nationalism and racism have blended with the biblical idea (e.g., Exodus 17:14ff, Deuteronomy 13:14ff) that God's enemies should be exterminated like vermin. One Marine veteran summarized the element of religious war conveyed by his drill instructor:

> It was better to fight Communism there in Vietnam than in your own backyard. Catholics had the worst of it. We had to be the Legions of God. We were doing it for your faith. We were told: Communists don't like Catholics.

From 1954 onward, Francis Cardinal Spellman "declared that Vietnam was vital to the preservation of the American way of life and Catholicism," according to Spellman biographer John Cooney. Spellman promoted a public belief that Vietnam was largely a Catholic nation, though it was and still is predominantly Buddhist. The "winsome young Catholic doctor working in Vietnam named Tom Dooley" was a favorite of Spellman's. A "Roman Catholic sainthood investigation in 1979 uncovered his C.I.A. ties."[8]

Another Marine veteran was cast into deep confusion by the contradiction between how he was raised and what he saw:

> [When I was a child] I spent hours and hours and hours on my knees, concentrating so as not to have the pain. . . . We had the children's services in the main church. It was so big. It gave me the feeling, "This thing goes back thousands of years, this has a history, this is a monument to God.". . . We had good priests there, they wore cassocks and taught us to respect everyone and be tolerant of other religions. That was real important to them.
>
> Well, we were put on trucks and taken to a place in the jungle near _____ in the middle of nowhere, this huge Buddhist temple, the biggest building I ever saw in Vietnam. . . . It was like something out of *National Geographic*, y'know, exotic, beautiful, and *old*. This place went back centuries, it had the same feeling of going back, back, back in history, a monument to God, like St. _____ [his church]. . . . We're standing around gaping at this when suddenly all these fucking Zips come up in trucks, pile off, and start destroying this thing, going at it with sledgehammers and pry bars, knocking over these old statues and smashing them. . . . I asked _____ [a three-tour NCO], "What the fuck?" He was laughing, "They're Catholics!". . . It dawned on me we had been trucked there to pro-

tect the Catholics while they wrecked the temple. Y'know, maybe we was in Vietnam to protect the Catholics.

This veteran had been raised by Catholic educators to respect other religions and to believe that the U.S. Constitution provided for separation of church and state. In Vietnam he developed the suspicion that his life was placed at risk by his government in pursuit of an unconstitutional policy on behalf of a church that he now suspected had lied to him all along.

Twentieth-century nationalism has taken over the biblical tendency to measure loyalty by how vehemently one dehumanizes the enemy. When American soldiers and their commanders in Vietnam debased the enemy, they echoed very ancient proofs of their faith in God and of their own religious merit.

The Judeo-Christian (and Islamic) world view has triumphed so completely over the Homeric world view that dishonoring the enemy now seems natural, virtuous, patriotic, pious. Yet in the *Iliad* only Achilles disrespects the enemy. In Homer's world, this is not a natural but an inhuman state into which Achilles has tragically fallen. Homer's warriors are never weakened by respecting the enemy.

CLINICAL IMPORTANCE OF HONORING OR DISHONORING THE ENEMY

Restoring honor to the enemy is an essential step in recovery from combat PTSD. While other things are obviously needed as well, the veteran's self-respect never fully recovers so long as he is unable to see the enemy as worthy. In the words of one of our patients, a war against subhuman vermin "has no honor." This is true even in victory; in defeat, the dishonoring absence of human *thémis* linking enemy to enemy makes life unendurable. J. Glenn Gray, writing of World War II in the Pacific against Japan, describes the effects of such a war:

> The ugliness of a war against an enemy conceived to be subhuman can hardly be exaggerated. There is an unredeemed quality to battle experience under these conditions which blunts all senses and perceptions. Traditional appeals of war are corroded by the demands of a war of extermination, where conventional rules no longer apply. For all its inhumanity, war is a profoundly human

institution. . . . This image of the enemy as beast lessens even the satisfaction in destruction, for there is not proper regard for the worth of the objects destroyed. . . . The joys of comradeship, keenness of perception, and sensual delights were lessened. . . . It is probable that the war . . . was particularly revolting not because the terrain on which it was fought was treacherous and unsuited for conventional warfare. It was ugly because [of] the image of the enemy. . . . No aesthetic reconciliation with one's fate as a warrior was likely because no moral purgation was possible. Thousands of veterans can testify to days that were grim and relentless and terrible, utterly without beauty and almost without human quality of any sort.[9]

This description of the alienation of the soldier from his task and his world could have been written about many of our patients as they are today: numb, incapable of pleasure, tortured by a pervasive sense of taint.

Homer tells us it is not necessary to see the enemy as vermin to be motivated to fight. Our patients tell us that turning the enemy into vermin exacted a terrible price from them *after* the fight was over. Here is an example from my clinical practice with Vietnam combat veterans:

I was visiting C. in his hospital room a few weeks after he attempted suicide by hanging. He had been successfully resuscitated after being found not breathing and pulseless. At the time of the attempt he was in the company of a hallucinated Vietnamese soldier, a frequent flashback visitor in his life.

I asked C. to tell me about the Vietnamese man. During his first tour C.'s work was to go from landing zone to landing zone making deliveries. On one such circuit he was accompanied by a "cherry" (a newly arrived replacement) who "didn't know anything, but I liked him." They were unloading the helicopter at one of their stops when "this Gook jumped out of the grass and cut off [the cherry's] head" with a burst from his AK-47. C. emptied the clip of his M-16 into the enemy soldier, opening his belly, spilling his intestines, and knocking him backward. "The fucking Gook was dead!" A movement caught his eye and he turned as he slammed in another clip. When he turned back, the "dead" man had gotten to his feet with his intestines hanging out and was bringing his weapon to bear on C., who emptied the second clip, partially severing his head. "I was so mad about [the new soldier] that I tore this Gook's head off and threw it into the grass. That was the first Gook I killed." Then he put the other American's body and head in a body bag from the helicopter, searched frantically for the head he had flung away, found it, and put the Vietnamese in another body bag with his head. C. subsequently requested transfer to a rifle company and became an expert and determined combat soldier.

During the twenty years after discharge C. attempted suicide several times, usually in the presence of the hallucinated Vietnamese soldier or his head. Also, he was almost always visited by the Vietnamese soldier during his family's Thanksgiving or Christmas dinner.

I said, "Honored guest!"

This barely considered remark struck the patient like an illumination. "Yeah, he was dead but he got up anyway to get at me." I commented that he himself had become such a determined soldier and would have probably done the same thing even when mortally wounded; and that this Vietnamese soldier was a worthy adversary, deserving of the honor that the veteran showed him. Over the months that followed the patient reported that the hallucinated visits were less frequent and were no longer terrifying as they had been in the past.

ABUSE OF THE DEAD ENEMY

Unlike the Greeks, we believe that the dead are beyond harm, so we often overlook the toxic residue left behind by disrespectful treatment of enemy dead. One of our men has intrusive memories every Christmas that center on "this dead Gook we hung on a tree with a big banner that said 'Merry Fucking Christmas.'" Another has intrusive memories of Viet Cong dead he was digging out of a collapsed tunnel. Apparently as much from curiosity as malice, he cut open the chest of one corpse with his knife to "see what his lungs looked like." Another veteran has flashbacks of the episode I have given previously, which began his berserking:

> I pulled him out into the paddy and carved him up with my knife. When I was done with him, he looked like a rag doll that a dog had been playing with. Even then I wasn't satisfied. I was fighting with the corpsmen trying to take care of me. I was trying to get at him for more.

He is haunted not by killing the enemy soldier, whose bullet could easily have blown out his brains, but by his abuse of the dead soldier's corpse.

Homer's critique of Achilles' loss of respect for the enemy pervades the *Iliad*. Much of what Homer depicts of Diomêdês, Aineías, Glaukos, Hektor, and Aías serves mainly to draw attention to Achilles' loss of humanity and moral disintegration. Homer contrasts Achilles' conduct toward the dead Hektor with the *thémis* for the dead, accepted by both Greeks and Trojans. Achilles' prewrath character was marked by generous sympathy for the plight of others outside his immediate circle, unwillingness to kill prisoners, and respect for the dead enemy. He was value-rich rather than value-simple.

One of the most astounding features of this massive war story is its reluctance to make anyone a villain. Even the wrongdoer Paris is sympathetically shown as willing to sacrifice himself to end the war. Perhaps this seems strange to us only because we have grown up on Judeo-Christian-Islamic, i.e., biblical, culture, which insists on turning every story into a war of good and evil and a drama of blame and punishment. Homer is not a propagandist for either Greeks or Trojans, and he does not dehumanize the warriors of either side, inflaming our emotions against them as evil monsters or subhuman vermin.

In this chapter I have emphasized the religious roots of dishonoring the enemy and its toxic psychological results. However, *any* ideology that debases the enemy endangers the lives of soldiers while they fight. As historian John Dower has convincingly demonstrated, the Pacific war in World War II provides devastating examples of how racist stereotypes *on both sides* of the conflict led to disastrous underestimation of the enemy.[10]

Among the Japanese, Americans were considered too soft to endure the mental and physical strain of extended submarine duty; the Japanese dismissed antisubmarine capability as unneeded and neglected to create any, with catastrophic results.[11] Westerners were also thought too selfish and egotistical to engage in a long fight in distant places. On the eve of the battle of Midway, Admiral Chuichi's intelligence concluded that Americans "lack the will to fight." Japanese left important papers behind in the field, on the assumption that Westerners would never figure out how to read them or how to crack their codes. Because Westerners were so soft, the logic ran, the Allies would agree to a compromise peace when confronted with the pure spirit of Japanese self-sacrifice.[12]

On the British and American side, prior to Pearl Harbor, the Japanese were regarded as physical and mental defectives: too nearsighted and prone to vertigo to fly a combat aircraft; too fearful to fight in jungles, which they supposedly believed were inhabited by ghosts and demons. Here again the consequences of these stereotypes were disastrous. Japanese aircraft swooped in on the Philippines nine hours *after* Pearl Harbor and wiped out MacArthur's air force on the ground. They sank the *Prince of Wales* and the *Repulse*. Neglect of the Zero fighter plane by top military planners did not come from Japanese secrecy or lack of available information, which Claire Chennault in China and examination of a downed Zero had provided in abundance; rather, it was the certainty that "our little brown brothers" could not independently design and manufacture high-performance combat aircraft nor fly them in complex combined operations.

This dangerous incapacity to see virtues in the enemy is similarly built into the way our children are taught the story of the Trojan Horse. The prevalent educational tradition (1) assumes that the Greeks are the good guys, taking sides in a way that Homer never does;[13] (2) teaches that the enemy are credulous boobs, preparing the ground for subsequent racist dehumanization and underestimation of the enemy; (3) unthinkingly perpetuates hostile biblical propaganda against pagan cultures by equating them with superstitious dependence on talismans.

The impulse to dehumanize and disrespect the enemy must be resisted, whether its basis is religious, nationalistic, or racist. The soldier's physical and psychological survival is at stake.

CHAPTER 7

What Homer Left Out

Contrasting Homeric combat with American practices in Vietnam has brought many of our own previously invisible assumptions into view. In this chapter I shall reverse focus, to reveal some things that Homer left out or drastically understated in his account of war. Homer minimized to the point of falsification these four universal realities of war: casualties from "friendly fire," "fragging," the suffering of the wounded, and the suffering of civilians, particularly women. And he entirely omitted the soldier's experience of shortage and privation. We have no way of knowing whether he played down or ignored the things he did because of his own invisible cultural assumptions, because of conscious artistic decisions, or out of pressure to censor things that put his audience in a bad light or that they didn't want to hear. The *Iliad* is a work of poetry, not sociological or historical scholarship, but hearing what it does *not* say will also add to our understanding.

DEPRIVATION

Shortage, privation, and daily physical torment play no role in the *Iliad*. Battlefield shortage of everything at one time or another was treated by Homer as if it never happened. His complete silence on the deprivations suffered by men in combat screams out for correction. Where are thirst, hunger, lack of sleep, maddening heat, and agonizing cold? Where are filth, squalor, an inability to wash the body, pants sticky and reeking from dysentery, the utter lack of privacy? Where are lice, rats, fire ants, scorpions, snakes, mosquitoes?

I shall not attempt a comprehensive review of deprivation in Vietnam combat.[1] Every Vietnam combat veteran has his own stories. I shall use one 101st Airborne veteran's narrative to speak for all, not because it includes examples of every known privation but because of his poet's eye for the inwardness of the experience:

First off, you were overloaded. . . . You carried eighty, ninety pounds. The average guy over there weighed 125 pounds. I weighed 125, so you take a guy like that. I don't exaggerate. [This veteran's normal weight is around 160.]

You were always exhausted, always. Even when something happened, you're usually relieved you can fall down and get comfortable for a minute.

It was the water, the cleanliness. We didn't have any soap and water. We doused down with insect repellent every night. We didn't bathe like for four, five weeks at a time. We didn't change clothes. The heat, the dehydration. The living situation was just as bad on us as facing the enemy, because you weren't always facing the enemy and you were always facing these conditions of jungle rot, dysentery, dehydration, hunger, fatigue, despair, all the time. Almost wishing you'd get hit. . . .

One of the most outstanding things . . . was that the conditions we had to live under were animal, purely animal. And your thoughts went the same way. You live like an animal, you started thinking and eating like an animal and behaving like an animal. Filthy rotten pig, pig, stink! And then how're you supposed to feel good about anything? Y'know, you can't feel good. You always hoping something would happen so you could fall down and get a rest. Those thoughts went through my head.

We just got two, two meals. One in the morning and one at night. That was it. All we ate. Food would be in the way of ammunition that we could carry. I think the ammunition was more important, so we would carry I think six days, five or six days of meals, when we were really full, . . . plus everything else you carry. But you only ate—in the morning when you got up, you ate, and then you humped [went cross-country on foot with full combat equipment] for twelve hours, and then at six at night you ate. And that was it. They were C-rations. They're not very filling; they're not very filling at all.

So we were starving—we were always stealing each other's food. Always—stealing. And we all knew it. I'd steal from you, and you knew I was stealing from you. But you were stealing from me. So you know, if you went out on a RIF or Recon,[2] I'd run over to your rucksack and I wouldn't hide it. I'd just do it. I mean, if you have half a canteen of water I'm going to take it [laughs]. Sorry. That's the way it was. We had guys stealing little cans of pimento cheese and shit, and eating it.

We had a profound time with the terrain and the weather. The terrain was—I think the terrain equaled the NVA, it was so bad. It was so goddamn bad. By the time you got into a fire fight or something, you were so fucking tired I don't think you cared that much. Don't care. That's the way I see it.

I cannot say how much deprivation, *per se*, psychologically injures combat soldiers, apart from combat itself. Creating shortage for the enemy by capturing, destroying, or halting supplies has been a basic operational goal since ancient times. The gigantic American effort against the Ho Chi Minh Trail had this aim. Every American helicopter shot down, truck destroyed by a mine, or ammunition dump blown up reflected the enemy's effort to do the same.

The National Vietnam Veterans Readjustment Study has attempted statistically to distinguish four clusters of traumatic war experience and to assess their separate contributions to post-traumatic stress disorder. These four clusters are exposure to combat, exposure to abusive violence, deprivation, and loss of meaning and control.[3] The four clusters are all aspects of war trauma, and PTSD symptoms are the lasting results for the veterans after the war. No one who has read Part I of this book will find it surprising that the cluster most powerfully correlated to PTSD symptoms is the one directly connected to the berserk state, exposure to abusive violence. However, the second-strongest correlation was deprivation, with exposure to combat third and loss of meaning and control the weakest. The differences are not enormous, but it is significant that deprivation alone was so strongly correlated with PTSD symptoms. Homer was not a witness to the Trojan War, living two or three centuries later, but if deprivation is a permanent feature of war, why would he have left it out? Homer belonged to a class of traveling artists who made their living performing in the houses of the great. The noble families that constituted Homer's audience probably traced their ancestry to several Greek and/or Trojan warriors named in the *Iliad*. The *Iliad*'s large cast of characters, particularly the minor ones, may have originated in the ancestral names and birthplaces of the bards' patrons, as Homer and his predecessors tailored each series of performances to the identities of their hosts. As the bards went from noble house to noble house, they would have found it safest to reflect honor on *all* of the warriors who fought at Troy, regardless of the current political alignments or animosities among the powerful. If this speculation is correct, it explains a number of features of the *Iliad*. First of all, an ancestor must have died honorably at Troy to be of use as a source of present family prestige and political legitimacy. Deprivation cannot be shown in the *Iliad*, because this would stigmatize the ancestor as poor, reflecting dishonor. This also rules out death by fragging, disease, or friendly fire. There is not a single named warrior who dies in any of these ways. Finally, the bards' need to stay in the good graces of hundreds of Ionian nobles who, through intermarriage, traced ancestry to *both* sides of the Trojan War may account for the astounding absence of villains.

FRIENDLY FIRE

I have described the total and terrifying dependence of the modern combat soldier on the competence and trustworthiness of others in the army. This all-inclusive dependence not only means relying on the army to provide ammunition, intelligence, food, water, and medical evacuation, but also relying on your own *not* to kill you with weapons intended for the enemy. The soldier's vulnerability is never more dramatically apparent than when artillery, bombs, or napalm intended to support troops in a fight with the enemy kill the very men they are meant to protect. The most famous such incident in the Vietnam War was the accidental bombing of a company of paratroopers near Dak To in November 1967. Less dramatic were the deaths by ones, twos, and fours that would occur when platoons from the same company fired on each other; when a grenade jauntily (and irresponsibly) worn by its pin dislodged in the mess tent; when a helicopter gunship mistook Americans for the enemy.

This tank gunner's experience was but one example of something every veteran of prolonged combat has witnessed:

Let's see, I worked places like _____, _____, and _____. It was during that time, the seventeen tanks worked together once. The seventeen tanks got on line. There was infantry in front of us. The captain ordered everyone back because the fight was getting too heavy for them, and we pushed up. And we got the order. Seventeen tanks opened up at once, and the fucking jungle just fell in front of us. Needless to say, there was four infantry still in front. And they died. They just didn't have control of all their men. I think these guys were from the Big Red One [First Infantry Division].

And that's the only thing we found out there, was four dead of our guys. Didn't find any [enemy dead].

According to Colonel David Hackworth, 15 to 20 percent of American deaths in Vietnam were due to "friendly fire."[4] My purpose is not to sit in judgment but to emphasize the painfulness and universality of death and wounds from one's own arms.

About half of Homer's massive poem is devoted to direct description of battle. There are more than a dozen examples of a weapon (arrow, spear, stone) missing the enemy soldier it was aimed at but killing another nearby. Suspiciously, there is not a single example of hitting a "friendly" warrior. No one cuts a comrade with the backstroke of his sword, knocks him down with his chariot, or hinders a movement of his comrade's shield to deflect a fatal spear throw. In this highly specific and detailed account of armies fighting, there is only one episode of deaths from friendly fire:

> Not far from [Achilles] . . .
> Athêna shrieked . . .
> Three great cries
> [Achilles] gave above the moat. Three times they shuddered,
> whirling backward, Trojans and allies,
> and <u>twelve good men took mortal hurt</u>
> <u>from cars and weapons in the rank behind</u>. (18:259ff)

The goddess Athêna is heavily involved here, as if to say that such things do not happen in ordinary battle. The men who died, despite their presence in the front ranks, are not named, just as no Greek who dies of the plague is named.

FRAGGING

Fragging is Vietnam slang for assassination of one's military superior. British military historian Richard Holmes, deputy head of

125

the Department of War Studies at England's Royal Military Academy at Sandhurst, explains:

> The term was derived from the use of a fragmentation grenade, conveniently rolled into the victim's hooch at night, although assassination with small-arms fire in the confusion of a firefight was not unknown. . . . Fragging is not new. . . . [The] major commanding the 15th Foot at [the eighteenth-century Battle of] Blenheim turned to address his regiment before the battle, apologizing for his bad behavior in the past, and asking that, if he had to fall, it should be by the enemy's bullets. A grenadier shouted "March on, sir; the enemy is before you, and we have something else to do than to think of you now." The action over, the major turned to the troops and raised his hat to call for a cheer: he was promptly shot through the head by an unknown marksman.[5]

The *Iliad* opens with an interrupted fragging. When Agamémnon orders that Achilles' prize of honor be seized in compensation for the captive woman he has given up to stop the plague, Achilles has his sword halfway out of its sheath before the goddess Athêna intervenes:

> "It was to check this killing rage I came
> from heaven. . . .
> Enough: break off this combat, stay your hand
> upon the sword hilt. Let him have a lashing
> with words, instead. . . ." (1:243ff)

Agamémnon's betrayal of Achilles, his lack of balanced judgment and self-control, cost the Greeks "loss on bitter loss," yet not a single Greek except Achilles contemplates killing him. Agamémnon receives blunt criticism from Diomêdês (9:36ff) and Nestor (9:123ff), but no one thinks of avenging the needless deaths of their friends.

Among Vietnam combat veterans, however, fragging has been a widely acknowledged impulse. How many Vietnam combat veterans daydreamed of executing General Westmoreland, or the whole U.S. Congress, or Secretary of Defense McNamara, or Presidents Johnson and Nixon for the deaths and suffering of their friends? More to the point is the actual murders or attempted murders of officers and NCOs in Vietnam. Richard Holmes cites an estimate that 20 percent of American officers who died in

Vietnam were assassinated by their own men.[6] Richard Gabriel, who served twenty-two years in the U.S. Army, writes:

> When forced to serve under officers whom they believe to be incompetent and therefore dangerous, soldiers throughout history have resorted to the simple yet effective device of killing them. . . .
>
> At least 1,013 documented killings of superiors or attempted killings . . . were reported [for the Vietnam War].[7]

SUFFERING OF THE WOUNDED

Homer does not hide the frightful wounds that soldiers inflict on each other. Nonetheless he denies the *suffering* of the wounded by declaring them dead within moments of being cut, stabbed, or crushed. In reality, to die of war wounds is usually to die in lingering agony and madness.

Homer's casualty figures are implausible. Statistical analysis[8] reveals a startling ratio of killed to wounded in Homer's account (about eight killed for each wounded), compared to Vietnam (about one killed in action for every six wounded). This makes sense if Homer counted as killed in action every recipient of a wound that would *eventually* prove fatal from blood loss or infection. All those wounded who required hospital care in Vietnam would certainly have been dead men at Troy. It is hard to say what proportion of walking wounded—all of the wounded in the *Iliad* fall in this category—would have died from tetanus or other infections. War's changing technology also has an impact on the kinds and lethality of wounds. Exploding munitions produce a spectrum of sizes, shapes, and velocities of projectiles, presumably increasing the variety of injuries done to the human body. Searing heat is produced not only by fire weapons *per se*, such as napalm, but by other explosives as well as by hydraulic, fuel, and ammunition fires started in tanks and armored personnel carriers. No one is burned in the *Iliad*. Only spears, swords, arrows, and rocks appear as weapons at Troy. I have not found a single instance in which one weapon throw or thrust afflicted more than one enemy. Modern soldiers are trained not to bunch together for a great many reasons, one of which is the ease with which a single high-velocity bullet or shell fragment can injure more than one soldier. This can happen by a bullet passing "clean" through one soldier and striking another, but often the second man is struck by a body part of the first. I have heard of a man whose eyes were put out by his friend's teeth.

Much of the civilian public has some grasp of wound pain through experience with surgery or injury. Still, the overwhelming majority of surgical wounds are not infected. Modern care of contaminated wounds from accident or assault aims at eliminating infection through use of antibiotics, and by surgical removal of foreign bodies and devitalized tissue where infections will prosper despite aggressive antibiotic therapy. While infection after injury is more common than infection after surgery, prevention and cure are the rule, not the exception. As a result, relatively few civilians have experienced or witnessed the toxic delirium of serious bacterial infection or the delirium of hemorrhagic shock. Modern military surgery has the same immediate objectives as civilian surgery after an auto accident or criminal assault: halting and replacing blood loss, preventing and combating infection, restoring burned or ripped-off skin, and restoring function. War wounds tend to be more massive, and more massively contaminated by soil, clothing, and wood, which may be driven in by explosion. High-velocity bullets transfer so much kinetic energy to human tissue that it "cavitates," making an instantaneous internal steam explosion that kills a large volume of living matter. When a high-velocity bullet hits bone or teeth it creates violently destructive "secondary projectiles." Because of the massiveness of contamination, tissue destruction, and injury to blood vessels, modern military medicine, even at its best, cannot always succeed against infection. In ancient times there was limited understanding of how to stop or replenish blood loss. The ancients also grossly misunderstood infection and had no means to combat it. For example, ancient physicians believed that pus was *required* for a wound to heal.[9]

Wounded soldiers died in physical and mental agony. The screams and groans of the wounded must have lacerated the spirit of their comrades. The great battle that rages after a Trojan violates the truce in Book 4 ends only at nightfall with the indecisive single combat between Hektor and Aías. (7:31ff) Sometime that evening the Greeks and Trojans agree to a funerary truce to start the next day. There has been no opportunity to bring in the wounded. Why do we not hear their cries in the darkness? The dead of both sides are jumbled together (7:506ff); it is simply not believable that there were no wounded among them.

Homer censors the suffering of the wounded while vividly displaying the gruesomeness of the wounds.[10]

CIVILIAN SUFFERING

As with the wounded, Homer shows us only part of the suffering of civilians. One narrowly selected aspect of civilian suffering is fully presented: bereavement after the combat death of a son, husband, or father. Other agonies falling on civilians during war, and exclusively upon women after defeat, are either passed over in complete silence or minimized.

SUFFERED BY ALL CIVILIANS DURING WAR

Homer displays the full agony of bereaved civilian men and women when their sons, husbands, and fathers die in war. Homer involves us in the lives of Hektor's wife, son, father, and mother, then forces us to share their grief when, standing on the battlement of Troy, they see Achilles chase Hektor around the walls to kill and defile him. His placement of Hektor's family in the foreground augments the pervasive theme of the loving—and now bereaved—families that war has savaged. As Oxford classicist Jasper Griffin observes, Homer's famous thumbnail "obituary notices" sound this theme throughout the epic like a musical pedal point:

> In the *Iliad* the lesser heroes are shown in all the pathos of their death, the change from the brightness of life to a dark and meaningless existence, the grief of their friends and families; but the style preserves the poem from sentimentality on the one hand and sadism on the other. Stripped of . . . [these] passages it would lose not merely an ornament, but a vital part of its nature.[11]

When a "lesser hero" falls in battle, Homer lingers for a moment and brings out the significance of his death:

> Then Aías . . . knocked down
> . . . Simoeísios,
> in the full bloom of youth. On slopes of Ida
> descending, by the banks of clear Simóeis

129

> his mother had conceived him, while she kept
> a vigil with her parents over flocks;
> he got his name for this. To his dear parents
> he never made return for all their care,
> but had his life cut short when Aías' shaft
> unmanned him. In the lead, as he came on,
> he took the spear-thrust squarely in the chest
> beside the nipple on the right side; piercing him,
> the bronze point issued by the shoulder blade,
> and in the dust he reeled and fell. (4:570ff)

This is the first such obituary in the *Iliad*, and it sets the pattern for most of those that follow: They show the particularity of the human being who has died through the loss suffered by those who loved him. Homer's soldiers do not die in general, as impersonal aggregate casualty statistics or as another man's metaphorical body part—such as "Today at Troy, Agamémnon mauled Hektor's right flank. . . ." Even Homer's "minor" soldiers die as particularly themselves, through reference to the specific parents, wives, children, and friends who will grieve each soldier's death.

Hektor's family and their grief are given full realization in the final books of the *Iliad*. In the moments before the duel between Achilles and Hektor, both his parents stand on the wall at the city gate and implore their son to come to safety inside:

> [Hektor's father] wrenched at his grey hair and pulled out
> hanks of it in both his hands, but moved
> Lord Hektor not at all. The young man's mother
> wailed from the tower across, above the portal,
> streaming tears, and loosening her robe
> with one hand, held her breast out in the other,
> saying:
>   "Hektor, my child, be moved by this,
> and pity me, if ever I unbound
> a quieting breast for you. Think of these things,
> dear child; defend yourself against the killer
> this side of the wall, not hand to hand.
> He has no pity. If he brings you down,
> I shall no longer be allowed to mourn you
> laid out on your bed, dear branch in flower,

born of me! And neither will your lady,
so endowed with gifts. Far from us both,
dogs will devour you by the Argive ships." (22:92ff)

Civilian suffering as bereavement, which earlier in the epic was a buried but pervasive theme, comes fully to the forefront of the audience's experience at the end of the poem. Thus, civilian bereavement—grief at the death of sons and husbands who are soldiers—appears subtly and continuously as accompaniment to soldiers' grief for each other, a major motif in Homer's song.

However, the same cannot be said for other dimensions of civilian suffering. Troy was besieged for ten years. Even though the blockade was quite permeable, there must have been periods of famine. Homer is silent on this hardship. Besieged cities are as notorious for pandemics of infectious diseases as military camps are. The only plague Homer mentions is in the Greek camp, never in Troy.

Terror is notably absent from Homer's picture of civilians, except to strengthen the impact of the death of a soldier. For example, Andrómakhê, Hektor's wife, overwhelmed with fear and anticipation of his death, meets Hektor as he hurries back to the battlefield:

> No more comfort,
> no other warmth, after you meet your doom,
> but heartbreak only. Father is dead, and Mother.
> My father great Akhilleus killed when he
> besieged and plundered Thêbê, our high town, . . .
> Then seven brothers that I had at home
> in one day entered Death's dark place. Akhilleus,
> prince and powerful runner, killed all seven
> amid their shambling cattle and silvery sheep. . . .
> Father and mother—I have none but you,
> nor brother, Hektor; lover none but you!
> Be merciful! Stay here upon the tower!
> Do not bereave your child and widow me! (6:481ff)

Civilians have everything to fear from defeat: death by fire, genocidal massacre, rape, enslavement, separation forever from everyone loved or merely known, destruction of a society. Agamémnon pictures no less than

> the day . . . Ilion [Troy]
> is <u>given to fire and sword, and Priam perishes,</u>
> <u>. . .with all his people</u>. (4:199ff)

> No fugitive, <u>not even</u>
> <u>the manchild carried in a woman's belly!</u>
> <u>Let them all without distinction perish</u>,
> every last man of Ilion,
> without a tear, without a trace! (6:67ff)

This is not just inflated rhetoric. The Trojans themselves know that their defeat will mean annihilation, as evidenced by Hektor's forecast of genocide (15:557f), or even more vividly by Priam's nightmare vision of his own fate in the conquered city:

> . . . in misery,
> <u>the son of Krónos [Zeus] will destroy my life</u> . . .
> my sons brought down, my daughters dragged away,
> bedchambers ravaged, and small children hurled
> to earth in the atrocity of war,
> as my sons' wives are taken by Akhaians'
> ruinous hands. . . .
> . . . <u>I shall be torn apart</u>
> <u>on my own doorstep by the hounds</u>
> <u>I trained as watchdogs, fed from my own table.</u>
> <u>These will lap my blood with ravenous hearts</u>
> <u>and lie in the entranceway</u>. (22:71ff)

The boundless cruelty of bloodlust unleashed upon the defeated city of Troy is illustrated on a fifth-century B.C.E. red-figure drinking cup now in the Louvre: Achilles' grown son, Neoptolemos, has Hektor's little boy by the ankle and is seen in midswing, apparently in the act of clubbing the aged Priam to death with his own grandson.[12]

Destruction and devastation of the adversary was the normal expectation that both the conqueror and the conquered held in Homeric culture. In the words of Achilles' old uncle Phoinix:

> . . . all the ills that come to men
> whose town is taken: <u>soldiers [i.e., all males] put to the sword;</u>
> <u>the city razed by fire; alien hands</u>
> <u>carrying off the children and the women</u>. (9:719ff)

The terror of Trojan civilians under siege, defenders outnumbered better than ten to one by the invaders (2:144f), must have reached the point of madness, alternating with deathlike numbness.

The poet Adrienne Rich wrote in a 1973 essay, toward the end of the Vietnam War:

> Rape has always been a part of war; and rape in war may be an act of vengeance on the male enemy "whose" women are thus used. . . . Rape [has been] used as a bribe to the peasants being impressed for service, as one of the perquisites of the military: as part of an invading army one has carte blanche to loot property and rape women. . . . Rape is a part of war; but it may be more accurate to say that the capacity for dehumanizing another which so corrodes male sexuality is carried over from sex into war. The chant of the basic training drill: "This is my rifle, this is my gun [cock]; This is for killing, this is for fun" is not a piece of bizarre brainwashing invented by some infantry sergeant's fertile imagination; it is a recognition of the fact that when you strike the chord of sexuality in the . . . [male] psyche, the chord of violence is likely to vibrate in response; and vice versa.[13]

The *Iliad* was composed by a man, for audiences of male soldiers and former soldiers, from inherited epic narratives about the exploits of men. The experience of women is sparsely and selectively represented in the *Iliad*. Where Homer presents it at all, it is that part of a woman's experience that is centered and dependent on men, such as her response to a man's death. He acknowledges the fact of rape, the fact of genocidal slaughter of all males and pregnant women to kill even males in the womb (6:66ff), the fact of enslavement, the fact that every captive woman has lost her home, friends, relatives, community, and local culture after the fall of her city; but he fails to represent the behavioral, emotional, and sensory reality of these atrocities against women.

Homer imagines that Achilles' bride-to-be, Brisêis, mourns only her lost male connections, and he treats her lost relationships with women as nothing, a nullity:

The husband to whom my father and noble mother gave me,
I saw him torn by the sharp bronze before our city,
and my three brothers . . .
. . . all went down to death on the same day . . .
<u>But you, Patroclus, you would not let me weep</u>,
not when the swift Achilles cut my husband down,
not when he plundered the . . . city—
<u>not even weep! No, again and again you vowed</u>
<u>you'd make me godlike Achilles' lawful, wedded wife</u> . . .
So now I mourn your death—I will never stop—
you were always kind. (Fagles trans. 19:341ff, Fitzgerald 316ff)

Even her grief for these lost men is shown in a demeaning fashion. According to Homer's fantasy, a widow's grief can be canceled by substitution of a more powerful, higher-status male, as though men can be traded up without a pang, like automobiles.

There is another, not-so-latent meaning: Because Achilles was stronger and killed Brisêis's husband, she'll like him better anyway. The overall effect is pornographic, a male fantasy that a woman *wants* to be raped by any man strong enough to kill her husband and carry her away. In contrast, Homer's portrait of Achilles' grief for Pátroklos shows that Homer understood that this was the love of a particular person, not replaceable by another second-in-command who might be stronger or braver. When Pátroklos dies, Achilles does not say, "This *therápon* is dead. Bring me another." He grieves, he grants himself "the luxury of tears." It is possible that Homer thought that women's capacity for love was inferior in depth and particularity to that of men. However, I think it is more likely that we are seeing Homer's projection onto women of the culturally imbued habit of dehumanizing them as replaceable objects. Homer attributes to Brisêis the same belief in the replaceability of men as Greek men defined for women.

Civilian casualty data for the defeated side are rarely collected and reported by the victors after a war. Gang or individual rapes by soldiers—whether or not these end in the woman's murder— have *never* been counted as civilian war casualties. Psychological injuries to the surviving rape victims are often lifelong.

Likewise the soldier inflicts lifelong injuries on himself when he makes rape or rape-murder part of his war. Much of the sex practiced upon prostitutes in Vietnam was extremely violent. Many of the women were murdered, but since their lives meant nothing to the South Vietnamese civilian authorities, these cases came to the attention of the American military only under unusual circumstances.

The overwhelming majority of combat veterans whom I have known are painfully aware of the absence of intimacy, tenderness, light playfulness, or easy mutuality in their sex lives. For many, sex is as sure a trigger of intrusive recollection and emotion from Vietnam as the sound of explosions or the smell of a corpse. Sex and anger are so intertwined that they often cannot conceive of tender, uncoerced sex that is free of rage. When successful treatment reduces their rage, they sometimes report that they have to completely relearn (or learn for the first time) the pleasures of sex with intimacy and playfulness.

CHAPTER 8

Soldiers' Luck and God's Will

Chance walks among us
in dark fury
to pause,
choose,
and move on.
With the chosen lying as found.
—*The Chosen,*
    by Vietnam combat veteran
    W. T. Edmonds, Jr.[1]

Luck knows no reason nor "what's right."
—Palladas of Alexandria

The nineteenth-century military theorist Carl von Clausewitz said that the combat soldier is "everywhere in contact with chance."[2]

Battle creates inexplicable events that soldiers experience as luck. These run from astounding good luck to crushing bad luck that taints the very soul.

THE SOCIAL SPECTRUM OF LUCK

Vietnam combat soldiers did not have good demographic luck to begin with. Demographic factors of age, gender, social class, and race brought citizens to or kept them out of Vietnam combat. Each of us lives in an historically definite situation; nobody has a life-in-general. A combat veteran's demographic profile—such as being U.S.-born in 1949, male, of a working-class family— becomes one metaphor of the pervasive role in human existence of luck, of that which simply happens. The numbers,[3] roughly a giant, tapering funnel, are these:

```
- - - - - - - - - The whole Vietnam Generation = 53,100,000 - - - - - - - - -
- - - - - - - - - - - - - - - - - - - Men = 26,800,000 - - - - - - - - - - - - - - - -
- - - - - Served in military during Vietnam era = 8,615,000 - - - - -
- - - - - - - - Served in Vietnam = 3,145,000 - - - - - - - -
- - - - - - - - Served in combat = 776,000 - - - - - -
- - - Casualties = 321,000 - - -
- - Dead = 58,000 - -
```

A civilian looking at this grim funnel may imagine that soldiers who have survived prolonged heavy combat must be intimates of supremely good luck. However, many combat veterans with PTSD regard the men who died as the lucky ones. This does not mean that survivors of war are unaware of their luck but that the complex interplay of conflicting emotions gives rise to the distinctive form of soldiers' black humor, especially when they remember episodes of startling good luck. One airborne sergeant with four combat tours in Vietnam recalls his whole company coming out unscathed after landing from helicopters in an old French minefield:

> We get on the fucking helicopters and we take off and fly for maybe an hour, and we come in, and everybody does *everything right*. Y'know, that was the funny part about it, it went decent. Everybody was in position. We jumped off the helicopter [gestures right, center, left], everybody ran to where they're supposed to— and the first fucking thing over the radio came, "BE ADVISED YOU'RE IN A FRENCH MINEFIELD."
>
> And I remember the first thing I said was, "I don't fucking believe you motherfuckers!" So . . . I said to [my radio man] [whispers], "Pass it on: We're in a minefield." And seventy-two fucking guys get up and ran out of the minefield. I mean everything went so *perfect*, y'know, and I'm standing there, "I don't fucking believe this." We've already been *doing* this shit, we're already *trained*. And I yelled, "Where the fuck yous going?" And they just ran out. And I grabbed the fucking radio man by the fucking harness and awa-a-ay we go. Like, I mean, *I* did it too! We just ran out of a fucking minefield—and nothing went off.
>
> So then, y'know, you're sitting down and the sweat's rolling off

of you. It ain't because of the heat. And everybody talking bullshit, you know. *Now* you're invincible. You just ran out of a fucking minefield. You were taught: You step in a minefield, your ass is grass. So then you get the feeling, "There ain't nothing that can happen to us. We got a shining star with us."

Such stories of astonishing, even comic good luck are told of times when everyone survived extreme danger. This veteran recalls another occasion on which everyone in his team made it untouched out of a banana grove enfiladed by enemy machine guns—"all them banana trees fell down like a fucking mower went through 'em"—and yet another instance of lucky escape, when an accidental attack in the open by an American helicopter gunship left his team unscathed:

> I had a Cobra gunship roll in on me. We worked it out with the fucking pilots that we would all wear boonie caps, and when we'd see a fucking helicopter we would flip the boonie caps. And we had a fluorescent patch inside the thing so them fucking idiots would know who we were on the ground. This fucking gunship must've been bra-a-and new in country. . . . And I'm telling you, that motherfucker can lay some shit down on you. And, didn't hit one of us, but he laid a whole bunch of fucking stuff around us, y'know?
>
> Then you go into that fucking [way of thinking]: "Fucking Americans can't kill me, how [can] the fucking Gooks kill me?" You know, you had a fucking Cobra gunship roll in on us three fucking times and he didn't hit one of us. Y'know? I mean, we were running around, running, "Oh FUCK," y'know, running around an open fucking area. This motherfucker's chasing six fucking different directions. It was fucking stupid. You get to a fucking point where nothing can fucking hurt you.

As with these episodes, most of the good luck in the veteran histories I have heard encompassed the whole social unit to which the soldier felt he belonged. I can think of no episode in the *Iliad* that is directly comparable to the ones from Vietnam that I have just quoted, except for the following passage, which describes some memorable good luck as seen from the point of view of the enemy, for whom it is "no luck at all":

> "Damn this day," he said. "A fool would know
> that Zeus had thrown his weight behind the Trojans. . . .

As for ourselves, no luck at all, <u>our shots
are spent against the ground</u>." (17:713ff)

The reader has certainly noticed that Homer's soldiers attribute
the lucky and unlucky aspects of combat to the gods, and that the
veteran who spoke earlier did not.

Occasionally I have heard stories of purely personal good luck,
such as these parallel episodes from Vietnam and the *Iliad:*

> One veteran was struck in the flesh of his upper arm by a spent
> .50-caliber machine gun bullet. This heavy, high-velocity bullet,
> which can be lethal at a range of three thousand to four thousand
> yards, was projecting from his skin. He simply pulled it out, and
> the corpsman put on a field dressing.

> At the behest of Athêna, Pándaros got off an arrow at Meneláos.
> It penetrated his skin only superficially, with the barbs still outside.
> (4:181) The surgeon, Makháôn, simply pulled it out and dressed the
> wound.

Another veteran recalls a grenade that didn't go off, a trip-wire
booby trap that did not explode, and a Punji stake[4] that tracked
between the layers of his boot rather than into his foot. All survivors of prolonged combat have such stories:

> Y'know, I should've been dead ten times over. And I stepped on
> booby traps. . . . It was just incident after incident after incident. A
> hand grenade that never went off.
> It wasn't that I couldn't be killed. I didn't care if I was killed. . . .
> There was a time, and it might be hard for people out there to
> understand, but I just didn't care if I lived or died.

In these examples, good luck has blessed the whole social unit, or
personal luck has not had repercussions for others. The next point
in the spectrum of luck is also social—but grimmer, as one soldier's good luck means death for a comrade. We hear about the
same sorts of combat incidents both at Troy and in Vietnam.

> To briefly remind the reader of an episode described in chapter 4
> by a former radio man involving another radio man: Usually the
> two alternated nights in the company commander's bunker and
> outside the perimeter wire on ambush. One night the other radio
> man asked our patient to switch. He had a bout of malaria and
> didn't want to go out on ambush, generally the more dangerous

and exhausting duty. During the night the command bunker was mortared and both the company commander and the other radio man were killed.

Another veteran told of his friend who jumped down from a height just moments after he had jumped down at the exact same spot. His friend triggered an antivehicle mine and was obliterated.

Antiphos threw his spear at Aías but hit Leukos instead. (4:592ff) Diomêdês threw at Hektor but hit his charioteer. (8:134f) Teukros got off two arrows at Hektor; both missed and killed other Trojans. (8:344, 352ff) Homer recounts nine more unlucky deaths in this form. (13:209ff, 466ff, 588ff, 14:519ff, 15:600ff, 16:539ff [hits a horse], 844ff, 17:339ff, 689ff)

An episode of luck that was good for the man who was spared but fatal to the next man, as in the thirteen *Iliad* deaths cited above, frequently gave rise in Vietnam to the "ain't nothing that can happen" feeling of invulnerability and to episodes of berserking, as well as to obsessive guilt that "it should have been me."

EQUIPMENT FAILURE

The modern reader who does not know to read the *Iliad* as the soldier's experience is likely to find its elaborate arming scenes to be archaic displays of poetic virtuosity, and nothing more. But the tools of the soldier's craft, his weapons and armor, are more richly invested with emotion and symbolism than any other material objects he is ever likely to use. His life, his honor, and the fulfillment of his purposes depend upon them in combat. These arming scenes play on this emotion, on the loving attention a soldier necessarily devotes to his weapons and armor. They also illustrate Homeric culture's concept of weapons and armor as a store of economic value and as transferable emblems of social honor:

> . . . [Agamémnon] cried out, "Troops in arms!"
> and clothed himself in armor of bright bronze.
> Upon his legs he fitted beautiful greaves
> with silver ankle straps. Around his chest
> he buckled on a cuirass, long ago
> a pledge of friendship from the Lord Kinyrês,
> . . . on the eve

of the Akhaian sailings against Troy . . .
a cuirass with ten bands of dark enamel,
twelve of gold, twenty of tin. Dark blue
enamel serpents, three on either side,
arched toward the neck, like rainbows that Lord Zeus
will pose on cloud as presages to men.
Across his shoulder and chest he hung a sword
whose hilt bore shining golden studs, and bands
of silver glinted on the scabbard, hooked
to a gilt baldric. Next he took his shield,
a broad one and a work of art for battle,
circled ten times with bronze; the twenty studs
were pale tin round the rim, the central boss
dark blue enamel that a fire-eyed Gorgon's
horrifying maw enclosed, with Rout
and Terror flanking her. Silver the shield strap
whereon a dark blue serpent twined—three heads,
put forth by one trunk, flexing every way.
Then Agamémnon fitted on his brow
a helmet double-ridged, with four white crests
of horsehair nodding savagely above it.
Last, two tough spears he took, with brazen spearheads
whetted sharp, and that clear bronze reflected
gleams of sunlight far into heaven. (11:17ff)

Here is an arming scene from a Vietnam veteran:

> We carried enough firepower to act like a company. Six people—that's hard to believe, but we did. We had a small arsenal with us.
>
> I carried six frags, four Willie Peters, two LAWs—that's like a bazooka, a rocket—two belts of [M-]60 machine gun, thirty clips of sub-Thompson ammo, plus two boxes of .45 ammo. I had a thirty-ought-six with two boxes of ammo, my knives, and a .357 pistol. Everybody carried two belts of ammo, and the Sixty [the M-60 machine gunner] would carry, he'd carry two full cases of ammo, plus two belts hooked, and just about everything I was carrying. 'Cept like we all had different weapons. _____ had a 16 [M-16]. I don't know why he walked around with a 16. _____ had the 60. _____ was carrying a grease gun, it's like a Thompson, called a burp gun, German, shot .45 ammo. . . .

I carried a sawed-off shotgun, too. For brush. When I got into thick, thick shit, and the shit was hitting the fan, that's how I blew my hole through. Depending on what area you're working, that's what you took. . . . [The team had] one 60, one Thompson, one burp gun, an M-16, an M-79 thumper, a BAR. Actually we had like two machine guns, because the BAR was just like it. And we all carried Claymores and trip flares and flashlights, three of us carried two LAWs, and a belt of M-79. You carried what you wanted to carry. We had more weapons than the company did.[5]

The reader should not be distracted here by the technical jargon of modern arms. What is important to notice is the "arming scene" tone that carries the echoes of ancient warrior epic.

Equipment failure in combat can mean death. The terror aroused by breakage or malfunction of arms or armor has not changed in three millennia. However, the interpretation of the experience (if the soldier survived to have an interpretation) seems in Homer's world to have been very different from our own. The reactions and interpretations of American veterans of the Vietnam War have already been discussed in some detail in chapter 1. In that chapter we saw that the modern soldier does not supply his own arms and must depend upon his military organization for their design, manufacture, and maintenance. We also saw that American soldiers were demoralized by the failure of their equipment to function properly. For the most part, they did not experience equipment failure as simply another manifestation of luck, or of God's will, but as culpable human betrayal.

Homeric warriors saw equipment failure and other incidents of battlefield luck as the gods' meddling. Clearly, the poet can extend the finger of god wherever he pleases. Sometimes the *Iliad*'s combatants recognize divine intervention when Homer has shown it to us, and sometimes when Homer has all the gods resting in their dressing rooms the soldiers on stage attribute their bad luck to a god anyway:

Drawing his longsword then, Lord Meneláos
reared and struck [Paris] on the helmet ridge,
but saw his blade, broken in jagged splinters,
drop from his hand. Lifting his eyes to heaven
he groaned:
        "O Father Zeus, of all the gods,

none is more cruel to hopeful men than you are!
I thought to make Aléxandros [Paris]
pay for his crime, and what luck have I had? (3:433ff)

Here Meneláos groans that *Zeus Xeínios*, the divine guarantor of
trust between host and guest-friend, has no interest in avenging
Paris's crime of seducing and abducting Meneláos's wife, Helen,
while he was a guest-friend in Meneláos's house. Apart from this
momentary cry of frustration, Meneláos shows no signs of being
demoralized by the idea that Zeus is "cruel to hopeful men" and
neglects to punish the wicked.

ATTRIBUTING BLAME

Homer's soldiers speak as if everything that happens is the pur-
poseful intention of some person or god, so they probably would
have drawn a blank if asked about "pure" luck, chance, or accident. Such an idea is not easy for American veterans either, who
almost always fix the blame somewhere.

Who is to blame? Who allowed all these deaths? Who intended
this? Let's examine some of the common answers to these bedevil-
ing questions as understood by Homeric soldiers and Vietnam
combat veterans.

The enemy: The enemy did this. The enemy is to blame. The
enemy wanted this to happen. Modern Americans and archaic
Greeks alike frequently made this attribution, and frequently they
responded in the same way—by attacking the enemy.

The dead man himself: American soldiers were trained to protect themselves from the enemy and to defeat him. Once trained,
they were responsible for carrying out this training. American soldiers were led and were responsible for obeying their leadership.
If one did not act as he was trained or did not obey his leadership,
runs this line of thinking, it's the soldier's own fault if he dies. He
has caused his own death, even if he did not intend it:

> So certain guys you see die and you say, "Hey, they fucked up.
> Move 'em out."
> And everybody stands there and looks at you, like saying, "Hey,
> . . . where's your fucking compassion? That fucking guy's dead."
> Y'know?

"He's a weak fucking link." Right? "He's a weak link. Don't wind up like him!"

This angry, judging, dismissive tone is never heard in the *Iliad*, even though Homer shows us deaths that were clearly brought on by the victim's own folly, such as that of Hektor's brother Polydôros:

> Akhilleus turned his spear on Polydôros,
> Priam's son. The father had refused
> permission to this boy to fight, as being
> youngest of all his sons and dearest, one
> who could outrun the rest.
> <u>Just now, in fact,</u>
> <u>out of pure thoughtlessness, showing his speed,</u>
> <u>he ran the front line till he met his end.</u>
> <u>The great battlefield runner, Prince Akhilleus,</u>
> <u>hit him square in the back as he flashed by</u> . . .
> Passing through the man, out at the navel
> the spearhead came, and on his knees he fell
> with a loud cry. The blinding cloud of death
> enveloped him as he sprawled out, his entrails
> held in his hands before him. . . . (20:466ff)

Even though the youth was killed by his own grandstanding, the poet's tone is compassionate rather than judgmental.

The surviving comrade: "No, it's not his fault, it's *my* fault," say many veterans, though they often bear even less real responsibility than Achilles had for the death of Pátroklos. This dynamic has been explored in detail in chapter 4. American and Homeric soldiers' emotional responses seem much the same when they take on this self-blame.

Officers and politicians: If the veteran does not blame the enemy, nor his dead comrade for fucking up, nor blame himself for his comrade's death, who or what else is available? A direct military superior may be blamed, rightly or wrongly. The politicians in Washington, the Pentagon generals and paper-pushers, the rear-echelon staff officers living in safety and luxury in Saigon—they too may be blamed.

God: As we have seen, both American soldiers in Vietnam and Greek soldiers at Troy sometimes made God (or a god) the target for attribution of causality, responsibility, and blame. However, even when the attribution was the same, the emotional meaning for the soldier was often very different. American soldiers felt betrayed, abandoned by God; they became spiritual orphans. The Homeric warrior was not orphaned when he saw a god against him; he might be terrified, but he wasn't devalued or dropped into the void.

It is striking how little Homeric warriors were demoralized when they saw a god was against them. In the following example, the Greeks are desperate, the Trojans having broken through to the ships. Aías (Ajax) comforts his brother Teukros, the champion archer, because his new bowstring has just snapped as he was getting a shot off at Hektor. Hektor's death would have saved the day, but in their present tactical position they both may be killed within minutes:

> Aías answered:
>   "Well, old friend,
> just let the bow and sheaf of arrows lie,
> since a god wrecked them, spiting the Danáäns [Greeks].
> Take up a long pike, get a shield, and fight
> the Trojans that way, make the soldiers fight.
> If the enemy is to take the ships,
> they'll know they are in a battle. Let us hold on
> to joy of combat!" (15:547ff)

In this instance the gods are explicitly involved: Zeus himself has snapped Teukros's bowstring.

Gods were multiple, so a Greek or Trojan could hope that the enmity of one god might be offset by the favor of another. Homer's soldiers spent effort and wealth courting divine favor—prayers and sacrifices abound—but they did not expect gods to be other than what they were: powerful, self-centered, arbitrary, unpredictable, heartless, and cruel. Many American veterans still languish in the following demoralizing logic: A positive relationship to God is the foundation of personal value; defeat by the Vietnamese meant that God was against Americans; therefore, I am valueless. "I'm a piece of shit," is specifically how these veterans put it. One said:

> When I came back from Vietnam, I felt like I was underneath a
> toilet, and every five minutes someone had diarrhea on me.

JOB'S PARADOX AND THE POSSIBILITY OF VIRTUE

How does defeat—"the will of God"—affect the soldier's sense of personal value? To what extent is it necessary to believe in God's goodness to experience one's own goodness? Some combat veterans are trapped in the paradox that the biblical Job struggled with: "If God is God He cannot be good; if God is good He cannot be God." One veteran in our program wrote flatly, "Any God that allows what happened in the 'Nam I want nothing to do with." Many Vietnam combat veterans lost both a sense of meaning and a sense of their own value when they felt cut off from God. Their culture had taught them that there was no possibility of meaning or value outside a monotheistic framework.

To explore these questions, I shall contrast the Homeric gods with the biblical Judeo-Christian-Moslem God to help explain why American warriors felt devalued and demoralized when they thought themselves betrayed and abandoned by God, while Homeric warriors kept both their self-respect and their morale. As elsewhere in this book, the object is to learn about ourselves, using Homer like an ultraviolet lamp to see what is ordinarily invisible.

As products of a Judeo-Christian culture, we have been taught that we float in limitless seas of divine loving-kindness:

> One generation to another praises thy works . . .
> They spread the fame of <u>thy great goodness</u>,
> And sing of thy righteousness,
> <u>Gracious and merciful</u> is the Lord,
> Slow to anger and of <u>great kindness</u>.
> The Lord is <u>good to all, and his mercy is over all his
> works</u>.[6]

Such lines from the Psalms, texts like very many others, have prominent and utterly uncontroversial usage in both Jewish and Christian liturgy. Everyone knows that people debate whether God exists, but no one questions the benevolent character of this possible God, if he does exist. Questioning his goodness simply does not enter the mind. Theologians may see the possibility that God is the source of great human suffering, such as his punishment for general or specific sinfulness or jealous punishment for various idolatries, but such suffering is always supposed to strike under the signs of truth and righteousness. I have never met veterans for whom these theologies made any difference.

Homeric soldiers appear to have been better off in two regards. First, things that could be said of a god had not fallen under the censorship that descended after Platonic and Judeo-Christian ideas gained the upper hand. Since it was still possible in Homeric culture to speak of gods as cruel, crooked, or heartless, it's not surprising that the characters in the *Iliad* expect less of them. Second, there was more than one game in town. Apollo might be against you, but Athêna could be on your side, or you might be out of favor with Poseidon but in favor with Arês.

God's love for humankind is one of our present culture's all-pervasive, invisible, unquestioned, and thus unconscious assumptions. When war shattered this assumption, American soldiers in Vietnam lost a sustaining idea. For some, this loss was devastating. The veterans most devastated have had the hardest time rebuilding a personally meaningful world view. One obstacle may be the equally pervasive religious teaching that no other sources of meaning, morality, value, or goodness are possible—or even logically conceivable—in a world without God. The veterans' religious teachers had claimed all these as God's monopoly. For many Vietnam combat veterans, God has vanished and taken it all with him. With God against them or gone, all possibility of virtue seems lost.

CHAPTER 9

Reclaiming the *Iliad*'s Gods as a Metaphor of Social Power

Consider these seemingly "self-evident" statements about the role of gods in human life:

> Gods embody the most sublime human aspirations.
> Gods are the bulwark of morality and public order.
> Gods provide inner peace.
> Gods ennoble and civilize mankind.

Because the *Iliad*'s gods fit none of these generalizations, many modern Western readers find it very hard to take them seriously. Homer's Olympians have powers as impressive as those of the superheroes of television cartoons, but they are just as easy to shrug off. Our own expectations of what may be said about God (now capitalized and singular) are molded by the comprehensive victory of Judeo-Christian teachings. As a result, the Olympians' heartless cruelty, their faithlessness, negligence, and frivolous aims simply don't register with many modern Western readers. After reading the *Iliad*, many modern readers stolidly continue to endorse the above "self-evident" statements about gods as universal, as if the counter-example of the *Iliad* did not exist.

A cultural chasm yawns between us and Homer. When we notice it, we usually bridge this chasm with smug ideas of our civilization's advanced state, or with the sophisticated relativities of cultural anthropology, or with the ethical and religious agnosticism of literary analysis. But as Oxford classicist Jasper Griffin phrases it, "The gods of Homer must be faced as gods, and then we must see what we can make of them."[1]

Homer's overwhelming message concerning the gods is that they are *powerful*. The modern world has achieved so much control over nature that color has been bleached out of the associations we were taught as children between each Greek divinity and a terrifying natural power: Zeus personifies lightning, thunder, and storm; Apollo, sickness; Hêphaistos, fire; Poseidon, earthquakes and water; Artemis, wild animals, and so forth.

Can we reclaim emotional significance for the *Iliad*'s gods? Why would we want to? I shall propose a metaphorical understanding of the Olympians collectively that infuses them with more meaning as we read the *Iliad* and at the same time furthers our quest to understand combat trauma and its post-traumatic consequences. I invite the reader to react emotionally to all the gods together as a metaphor for terrifying *social* power. I propose Homer's gods as symbols of institutions that acquire godlike power, such as armies and the social institution of war itself.

As seen from the combat soldier's perspective, the distant gods are the rear-echelon higher officers and civilian political authorities who control an army and (along with the enemy) are the soldier's *de facto* masters and captors. They have truly godlike power over soldiers in combat.[2] Rear-echelon authorities were known universally among Vietnam combat soldiers as REMFs (pronounced as a word, the "m" formed with the lower lip against the upper teeth, often accompanied by a curl of the upper lip), an acronym for "rear-echelon motherfuckers."

ARMIES AS CREATORS OF SOCIAL POWER

Armies, like families, are institutions that create a world. Both successfully engender the new member's respect, loyalty, love, affirmation, gratitude, and obedience. I speak of armies and families as *creating* social power, because the hold that each of these institutions has over its members comes to greatly exceed its moment-to-moment capacity to reward or punish and usually persists long after significant practical affiliation has ended. The following features are common to both of these world-making institutions, whether the new member experiences them as benign or malevolent:

    Barriers to escape
    Control of body and bodily functions
        What and when to eat
        When, where, and how much to sleep

Body form (clothing, weight, haircut)
When and where to urinate and defecate
Lack of privacy regarding bodily functions
Prolonged daily contact with power-holder in group
Combination of enticement, force, intimidation
Power-holder as source of small rewards, comfort, approval
Inconsistent, unpredictable, capricious enforcement of rules
Monopolization of communication, resources, control
Secrecy regarding some activities and events
Lack of alternative to seeing world through power-holder's eyes
Required repetition of buzz words, songs, slogans, clichés, even if
inwardly disbelieved and rejected

Apply this list to the relationship between recruits and their drill instructors and that between small children and their parents. The fit to both is uncomfortably close. I am aware that my unsoftened choice of words suggests something sinister, which readers may not wish to see applied to normal families or to well-functioning armies. The uncanny, slightly ominous quality comes from the emanation of absolute power that the list embodies, *even if that power is never abused.*

During the Vietnam War, the more elite the unit, the more its training incorporated the psychological techniques of coercive control used on political prisoners. In particular, incessant demands for proof of obedience and loyalty, and intense pressure to ally with the power-holder by forcing recruits to sacrifice and victimize other recruits, seem to have been common features of Marine and airborne training during the Vietnam War. Organized techniques of disempowerment and disconnection were employed to "break them [recruits] down and then build them back up again"—what veterans often quote as the basic goal of military training.

The isolation and virtual captivity of the first stages of military training became explicit for many men when they were about to be sent over to Vietnam or were in transit. One man remembers that the doors of the transit barracks in Oakland, California, were chained shut at night while he was there on his way to Vietnam. Another recalls:

> The next thing I know, we're getting loaded [for unit movement
> to Vietnam]. Nobody knows where we're going—we all knew where
> we are going anyways. Because the battalion commander that we

had—his name was _____ and his code sign was _____—he took barbed wire and he put it around the whole battalion. <u>He isolated us from the whole division. He went and had Conexes made, y'know the Conexes they ship overseas, the big boxes? We had that kind. And he took the doors off and had bars welded on there. He made his own prison, right there in Kentucky.</u>

Once in Vietnam combat, the condition of captivity often worsened to a degree associated with concentration camps. Combat soldiers in the field in Vietnam frequently experienced:

Terror and helplessness
Loss of communication with all others outside combat
    Conviction that others had forgotten or betrayed them
    Renunciation, loss, or destruction of symbolic tokens of connection to others
Inconsistent, unpredictable, capricious, and *violent* enforcement of rules
Threats to close comrades
Debilitation by sleep deprivation, starvation, exposure, drugs, alcohol
Violation of one's own moral principles
Participation in sacrifice or victimization of others
Participation in immoral, disgusting, or illegal practices
Betrayal of one's own basic human attachments[3]

In a political prison these conditions are intentionally created by the perpetrators as a matter of plan. In its fullest form, coercive control is an intentional program used to break the will and to enslave a human being. In a tyranny the perpetrator is usually a unitary state apparatus, but in war the perpetrator's role is divided between the enemy and the soldier's own army. For soldiers, the institution of war itself is the unitary perpetrator. Psychological injuries done to soldiers may happen to be inflicted at one moment by the enemy, at another by the soldiers' own army. The conditions created by ongoing battle create psychologically catastrophic conditions that no single perpetrator has coordinated, but they are no less destructive for the lack of knowing cooperation between organized enemies in breaking the soldier.

Even looking at the American side alone, it is sometimes hard to determine after the fact what was accidental and what was planned. Reread the section on pages 3–4 in which a veteran describes the massacre of civilian fishermen due to an intelligence error, which left him feeling that he had violated his own moral principles by participating in the sacrifice and victimization of others. Another airborne veteran, reading this account, shrugged and said, "They did that to 'blood' the unit. After that everyone thought they were invulnerable." The injury was the same whether an accidental result of the "fog of war" or a calculated step in creating the kind of fighting force the airborne brigade leaders wanted.

Unexpected deliverance from certain death happens by design in political torture (as in the case of mock executions) and by chance or design in war. The psychological impact may be similar. Reread the veteran's narrative of his company landing from helicopters in a minefield and escaping unscathed, on pages 138–139. What is the effect of such an experience? In the veteran's words, "You get the feeling, 'There ain't nothing that can happen to us. We got a shining star with us.'" Also reread the helicopter pilot's account on pages 79–80 of how he "knew he couldn't be killed" after a shell that had been aimed at him "melted" his copilot. In the first instance, the radioed information that the company had landed in a French minefield may have been a fabrication for training purposes, akin to a mock execution. In the second instance, the enemy and battlefield luck created an unexpected deliverance of the pilot from certain death. The goal of mock executions during political torture is to decompose the prisoner's identity and mental reality, substituting the absolute reality of the torturer's world. In battle, these deliverances establish the absolute reality of the institution of war. Just as survivors of political torture often suffer lifelong obsession with their former torturers, unable ever again to think their own thoughts or imagine their own world, survivors of prolonged combat may mentally become lifelong prisoners of war, psychologically missing in action.

Like the Homeric gods, power-holders in armies can create situations that destroy good character and drive mortals mad. Homer presents the gods simply as power, whether behaving well or badly. For humans the most dangerous power—and at the same time the power most able to confer heart-swelling beneficence—has always been other human beings acting together in a social institution.

Homer shows the tragic corrosion of a noble character, the transformation of something good into something vile and evil. The gods can do this; the gods have this power; the gods can drown a human in catastrophic moral luck.

GODS AS REMFS

Vietnam combat veterans' picture of higher-echelon military and political authorities is not pretty. The terms *heartless, crooked, shallow,* and *self-indulgent* constitute a quick portrait of the REMF, but each of these has numerous subheadings and illustrations. The traits in this portrait of the REMF are shown in the *Iliad* as characteristics of gods. A whole territory of meaning for Homer's text springs into view when we read his gods as metaphors for bad military and political leadership. We do not see these traits in the *Iliad*'s human leaders, I presume because they were personally at risk on the battlefield. The *Iliad* shows us war in which the highest military and political authorities fight, risk all, take wounds, and sometimes die in the most dangerous places of the battlefield. Agamémnon, the Greek political and military chief, knows personally and exactly the terror and pain of war for the warrior, as does Hektor, the Trojan leader.[4]

Heartlessness of the Gods

As a dramatic artist, Homer mostly *shows* us the gods' heartlessness rather than *telling* us. The one instance when Homer does tell us that the gods have no compassion for humans is shot through with irony, because he puts the words in the mouth of the god Apollo—no font of loving-kindness himself:

> But now . . . lord Apollo rose and addressed the immortal
>   powers:
> "Hard-hearted you are, you gods, you live for cruelty! . . ."
>   (24:37ff, Fagles trans.)

Let us watch how Homer dramatizes this.

Readiness to "waste" lives

Combat soldiers on both sides of the Trojan War long for it to end. At the opening of Book 3, with the armies facing each other, Hektor tongue-lashes his brother Aléxandros (Paris), the seducer of Helen, and co-thief with her of Meneláos's stored-up treasure, telling him that the Trojans ought to have stoned him for "all the wrong you've done." Paris responds with an offer to sacrifice himself to end the war. He suggests single combat between himself and Meneláos, whom he has wronged by seducing and abducting his wife. He doesn't stand a chance against Meneláos. Hektor jumps at the offer:

> Listening, Hektor felt his heart grow lighter,
> and down the Trojan center, with his lance
> held up mid-haft, he drove, calling "Battalions
> halt!" till he brought them to a stand-at-ease.

> The long-haired Akhaian soldiers bent their bows,
> aiming with arrows and with stones. But high
> and clear they heard a shout from Agamémnon: (3:91ff)

Amazingly, Agamémnon calls for his Greek archers to hold their fire, even though they have the most formidable Trojan fighter "in their sights" with his back to them. This is the morning after Zeus has falsely promised Agamémnon quick victory in a dream (2:1–46), but Agamémnon does not yet know that Zeus was lying. He shouts:

> "Hold on, Argives! Men, don't shoot! This means
> he has in mind some proclamation,
> Hektor, there in the flashing helmet!" (3:98ff)

Meneláos accepts the offer to settle the war by single combat:

> "So death
> to him for whom the hour of death has come!
> The rest of you part peacefully and soon!" (3:119ff)

Homer then shifts his focus to other soldiers on both sides:

> Now all hearts lifted at his words, for both sides
> hoped for an end of miserable war;

and backing chariots into line, the men
stepped out, disarmed themselves, and left their weapons
heaped at close intervals on open ground. (3:132ff)

Everyone sees fairness and good sense in a duel to the death between Meneláos and Aléxandros (Paris). The terms of the duel are as follows: If Meneláos dies, the Greeks sail home, leaving Helen and treasure behind; if Paris dies, the Trojans turn over Helen and treasure and pay annual tribute. Even Agamémnon and Meneláos prefer to end the suffering with a partial settlement and to forgo total victory.

However, the gods act like home-front politicians or rear-echelon generals and thwart the soldiers' dream to end the suffering. Neither champion falls, because the goddess Aphrodítê wraps Paris in a cloud and whisks him off the battlefield, leaving both armies bewildered. Agamémnon claims victory by default, and the Greek soldiers assent to this by acclamation, even though this means they forgo looting the city. After nine years of war and thousands of deaths, the Greeks can go home, having achieved their political objective of reclaiming Meneláos's wife and treasure and winning some punitive damages in the form of annual tribute. The Trojans don't object to their claim.

The Trojans get no chance to accept, however, because the gods once again intervene. Zeus, seeing what has happened down below, says to his wife, Hêra, and daughter Athêna, who work constantly for Troy's destruction:

> "Clearly,
> Meneláos . . . has won
> the single combat. Let us then consider
> how this affair may end; shall we again
> bring on the misery and din of war,
> or make a pact of amity between them?
> If only all of you were pleased to see it,
> life might go on in Priam's town [Troy],
> while Meneláos took Helen of Argos home." (4:15ff)

The two goddesses will have none of it. Asks Hêra:

> "Your majesty, what is the drift of this?
> <u>How could you bring to nothing all my toil,</u>

> the sweat I sweated, and my winded horses,
> when I called out [the Greeks] to bear hard
> on Priam and his sons?" (4:30ff)

Now begins some high-level political horse-trading between utterly heartless gods:

> Coldly annoyed,
> the Lord Zeus, who drives the clouds of heaven,
> answered: . . .
> "Whenever my turn comes
> to lust for demolition of some city
> whose people may be favorites of yours,
> do not hamper my fury! Free my hands
> as here I now free yours. . . ."
>
> And wide-eyed Hêra
> answered:
> "Dearest to me are these three cities:
> Mykênê . . . , Argos, Sparta.
> Let them be pulled down, if you ever find them
> hateful to you. I will not interfere. . . ." (4:37ff)

There is no hint that human suffering in the "demolition of some city" means anything at all to these gods, who are ready to claim recompense in human lives for "the sweat I sweated, and my winded horses."

When Zeus agrees to let Troy be destroyed, he does not mention that he will make the Greeks bleed and bleed and bleed before they finally conquer it. He gives the goddess Athêna permission to sabotage the truce and political settlement. She convinces a Trojan archer to get off an arrow at Meneláos from a concealed position. The narrator comments, "This was Athêna's way, leading him on, the foolish man, to folly." (4:123f)

Enraged that the sacred truce-oaths have been betrayed, the Greeks attack with renewed fury.

Sunk-costs argument

The desire of the combat soldiers at Troy to end the suffering is clear in everything Homer shows us. In Book 2 the Greek army stampedes toward the boats, after Agamémnon puts his troops to a perverted "test" of their loyalty by calling for retreat after his quarrel with Achilles. (2:158ff) As Hêra watches the stampede, she complains to Athêna,

> "Can you believe it? . . .
> will they put out for home this way, the Argives [Greeks]. . . .
> How could they now abandon Helen . . . ?
> <u>Helen, for whom</u>
> <u>Akhaians died by thousands far from home</u>? (2:178ff)

Hêra's rhetoric here, and in her question "How could you bring to nothing all my toil, the sweat I sweated, and my winded horses. . . ?" (4:31f) puts forth what is widely known in business parlance as the "sunk costs" argument. In the context of war it runs as follows: So many men have died that we can't give up now; we've got to go on "so they will not have died in vain." Surprisingly, this argument has no appeal to soldiers actually fighting, even though it is utterly compelling to rear-echelon noncombat soldiers and to civilians.[5] Homer's warriors do not use this argument with each other. When Odysseus turns back the men pouring toward the ships, he never once uses the sunk-costs argument to them (2:216ff), nor does Nestor, who follows him up with a rousing speech to the reassembled army. (2:390ff) The farther removed a person is from real danger, from real consequences, the more appealing this argument becomes. The gods, infinitely distant from real risks of any sort, are irresistibly drawn to it.

Sinister demographic agendas

Some African-Americans have suspected that the Vietnam War contained a secret demographic agenda to kill off young black men. Many of the *white* Vietnam combat veterans whom I have worked with firmly believe that there was a general demographic plan to "thin" the baby-boom generation by holding a war. One white veteran said:

> The stocks [of the M-16] broke [in hand to hand combat]. <u>I start-
> ed feeling like the government really didn't want us to get back,
> that there needed to be fewer of us back home.</u>

I draw attention to this belief because of the striking parallel to a *skhólion*, an ancient explanatory note on some of the *Iliad*'s opening lines: ". . . crowded brave souls into the undergloom, leaving so many dead men . . . <u>and the will of Zeus was done</u>." (1:4ff) The *skhólion* addresses the question, What was the will of Zeus? Its answer:

> There was a time when the countless tribes of men, though wide-dispersed, oppressed the surface of the deep-bosomed earth, and Zeus saw it and had pity and in his wise heart resolved to relieve the all-nurturing earth of men by causing the great struggle of the Ilian [Trojan] war, that the load of death might empty the world. And so the heroes were slain in Troy, <u>and the will of Zeus was done</u>.[6]

The scholiast who wrote this attributes to the highest Greek god the same sinister demographic objective that some veterans believed American power-holders had during the Vietnam War. Zeus, we might say, was the original REMF.

THE GODS AS INCONSISTENT, UNRELIABLE, INATTENTIVE, DISTRACTIBLE

By Book 14, Zeus is well along in fulfilling his promise to Thetis to make the Greeks suffer from Achilles' absence. The main Greek fighters are out with wounds, and the Trojans have penetrated the last perimeter before the ships. Zeus favors the Trojans and lends them strength, but then he is distracted by sexual desire for Hêra. We hear this first from her point of view:

> Then . . . [Hêra] looked at Zeus, who rested
> high on the ridge of Ida bright with springs,
> and found him odious.
>   Her ladyship
> of the wide eyes took thought how to distract
> her lord who bears the stormcloud. Her best plan,
> she thought, was this: to scent and adorn herself
> and visit Ida, hoping hot desire
> might rise in him—desire to lie with her
> and make love to her nakedness—that so
> she might infuse warm slumber on his eyes
> and over his shrewd heart. (14:179ff)

Men die while Zeus dallies and then sleeps. This kind of lapse also happened in Vietnam. A veteran, who was a supply sergeant whose work took him to many isolated landing zones, recalls that no matter how far out in the bush, once the LZ had been in use for a while, women would appear, apparently out of nowhere, and stand quietly outside the wire, waiting for their mute solicitation to be taken up. If the "Old Man," the senior officer at the site, did not specifically forbid this, the women would gradually be brought inside the perimeter, and the men would purchase sex from them. The veteran says he knew of times a corner or a side of the perimeter was left with no one in charge, because the man in question was in a bunker with a prostitute.

For me, Zeus's casual indifference arouses more terror and horror than his lust:

> When Zeus had brought great Hektor and his Trojans
> into the beachhead by the ships, <u>he left them</u>
> <u>to cruel toil of battle, and to grief,</u>
> <u>while he himself with shining eyes turned north</u>. . . . (13:1ff)

What Zeus was looking at or why it mattered is never explained. His mind simply wandered. In Vietnam men died from the distraction of higher officers in control of fire support, of helicopter extraction, of resupply, of backup companies for reconnaissance patrols. One of our veterans, who commanded the unit backing up his best friend's Recon unit, is tortured by the memory of his friend's death. The CO neglected to inform him that the Recon was in trouble. When the unit went to bring in survivors (there were none) and bodies the next day, our patient found his friend at the end of a blood trail hundreds of yards long, with all his ammunition and grenades expended. He had clearly lived for some time after his team was attacked.

HOMERIC IRONY AND GOD'S LOVE

In his own eyes, Zeus cares about men. He says,

> Men on both sides may perish,
> <u>still they are near my heart</u>. And yet, by heaven,
> here I stay, at ease upon a ridge. (20:24ff)

This is not an isolated example of Homer's irony regarding Zeus's loving concern for humankind. In a sense, the whole poem begins and ends with Zeus's messenger proclaiming, "[Zeus] has you in his heart, he pities you now." (Fagles trans.) These words are spoken first to Agamemnon in the dream in which Zeus falsely promises immediate victory (2:31), and then to Priam (24:208). Zeus has terror, defeat, and humiliation in store for Agamémnon, and the second recipient of this message of familylike sympathy and compassion, Priam, will shortly lie dead in his own doorway, eaten by his household dogs, his city in flames around him—an outcome Zeus has just negotiated with Hêra and is well able to prevent.

Homer shows us on several occasions that Zeus sees himself as deeply caring and compassionate, like many higher political and military leaders. Homer was a master of irony.

PART III

CHAPTER 10

The Breaking Points
of Moral Existence—What Breaks?

When a soldier is broken by combat, what breaks? The reader has already had many glimpses of the post-traumatic existence of combat soldiers. It is now time for a more extensive and systematic discussion of combat PTSD. Here is Shakespeare's account of what seems very much like the symptoms of PTSD; the person speaking is a combat veteran's wife:[1]

O, my good lord, why are you thus <u>alone</u>?	Social withdrawal and isolation
<u>For what offense</u> have I this fortnight been <u>A banish'd woman from my Harry's bed</u>?	Random, unwarranted rage at family, sexual dysfunction, no capacity for intimacy
Tell me, sweet lord, what is't that takes from thee <u>Thy stomach</u>, <u>pleasure</u>	Somatic disturbances, loss of ability to experience pleasure
and thy golden <u>sleep</u>?	Insomnia
Why dost thou <u>bend thine eyes upon the earth</u>,	Depression
And <u>start</u> so often when thou sit'st alone?	Hyperactive startle reaction
Why hast thou <u>lost the fresh blood in thy cheeks</u>,	Peripheral vasoconstriction, autonomic hyperactivity
And given my treasures and my rights of thee To thick-eyed musing and cursed melancholy?	Sense of the dead being more real than the living, depression
In thy <u>faint slumbers</u> I by thee have watch'd,	Fragmented, vigilant sleep

And heard thee murmur tales of iron wars,
Speak terms of manage to thy bounding steed,
Cry "Courage! to the field!" And thou hast talk'd
Of sallies and retires, of trenches, tents,
Of palisadoes, frontiers, parapets,
Of prisoner's ransom, and of soldiers slain,
And all the currents of a heady fight.
Thy spirit within thee hath been so at war
And thus hath so bestirr'd thee in thy sleep,

Traumatic dreams, reliving episodes of combat, fragmented sleep

That <u>beads of sweat have stood upon thy brow</u>,
Like bubbles in a late-distrubed stream;

Night sweats, autonomic hyperactivity

THE OFFICIAL DIAGNOSTIC CRITERIA FOR PTSD OF THE AMERICAN PSYCHIATRIC ASSOCIATION

Of the five official criteria that make the diagnosis of PTSD, all but the first (criterion A, which I shall discuss below) are straightforward clinical description, broadly stated to apply to all PTSD, not only to combat PTSD. I believe at this point the reader will be interested in seeing them exactly as they stand in the official diagnostic manual (known as the DSM-III-R). The dry criteria may come to life if the reader tests them against Shakespeare's portrait and decides whether Harry Hotspur, the most formidable fighter among the rebels against King Henry IV, has it:

A. The person has experienced an event that is <u>outside the range of usual human experience</u> and that would be markedly distressing to almost anyone, e.g., serious threat to one's life or physical integrity; serious threat or harm to one's children, spouse, or other close relatives and friends; sudden destruction of one's home or community; or seeing another person who has recently been, or is being, seriously injured or killed as the result of an accident or physical violence.

B. The traumatic event is persistently reexperienced in at least one of the following ways:

(1) recurrent and intrusive distressing recollections of the event (in young children, repetitive play in which themes or aspects of the trauma are expressed)

(2) recurrent distressing dreams of the event

(3) sudden acting or feeling as if the traumatic event were

recurring (includes a sense of reliving the experience, illusions, hallucinations, and dissociative [flashback] episodes, even those that occur upon awakening or when intoxicated)

(4) intense psychological distress at exposure to events that symbolize or resemble an aspect of the traumatic event, including anniversaries of the trauma

C. Persistent avoidance of stimuli associated with the trauma or numbing of general responsiveness (not present before the trauma), as indicated by at least three of the following:

(1) efforts to avoid thoughts or feelings associated with the trauma

(2) efforts to avoid activities or situations that arouse recollections of the trauma

(3) inability to recall an important aspect of the trauma (psychogenic amnesia)

(4) markedly diminished interest in significant activities (in young children, loss of recently acquired developmental skills such as toilet training or language skills)

(5) feeling of detachment or estrangement from others

(6) restricted range of affect, e.g., unable to have loving feelings

(7) sense of a foreshortened future, e.g., does not expect to have a career, marriage, or children, or a long life

D. Persistent symptoms of increased arousal (not present before the trauma), as indicated by at least two of the following:

(1) difficulty falling or staying asleep

(2) irritability or outbursts of anger

(3) difficulty concentrating

(4) hypervigilance

(5) exaggerated startle response

(6) physiologic reactivity upon exposure to events that symbolize or resemble an aspect of the traumatic event (e.g., a woman who was raped in an elevator breaks out in a sweat when entering any elevator)

E. Duration of the disturbance (symptoms in B, C, and D) of at least one month.[2]

Criterion A is not at all as straightforward as the others. The linchpin of this diagnostic standard is its implicit claim to ethically and culturally neutral knowledge of *"usual* experience."

In the twentieth century, combatant deaths in all wars worldwide have averaged 180 per million population per year. This makes war casualties, and their witnessing, sound very rare, less than two in 10,000 (0.02 percent). But life happens in particular, not as a worldwide century average. Four hundred died or were seriously wounded for every 10,000 who served in the U.S. armed forces during the Vietnam era, whether or not they went to Vietnam; 1,200 (12 percent) died or were seriously wounded for every 10,000 who served in Vietnam.[3] The percentage of combat veterans, as defined here, who died or were wounded cannot be determined from the available data, but it is surely higher than the 12 percent for all high- and low-combat-exposure servicemen lumped together. Findings from the *National Vietnam Veterans Readjustment Study* (*NVVRS*), a rigorously designed and executed nationwide epidemiological study of a random sample of Vietnam-era veterans and a random sample of demographically similar civilian controls, showed that 35.8 percent of male Vietnam combat veterans met the full American Psychiatric Association diagnostic criteria for PTSD at the time of the study, in the late 1980s. This many men had grossly unhealed psychological injuries—almost twenty years after their war experience. This is a thirty-two-fold increase in the prevalence of PTSD compared to the random sample of demographically similar civilians. More than 70 percent of combat veterans had experienced at least one of the cardinal symptoms ("partial PTSD") at some time in their lives, even if they did not receive the full syndrome diagnosis.[4]

Given the luck of assignment to a combat unit, it is *not* "outside the range of usual human experience" to undergo "serious threat to one's own life or physical integrity; serious threat or harm to . . . close . . . friends; . . . or seeing another person who has recently been, or is being, seriously injured or killed. . . ." This is the *normal* experience of a combat soldier. "Outside the range of usual human experience" pretends that the "usual" deployments of social power have nothing to do with events that cause psychological injury.[5]

The official definition almost totally fails to convey the ease with which PTSD can be confused with other mental disorders. For example, the numbness, mistrust, hallucinated voices of the dead, and social withdrawal of combat PTSD are easily confused with schizophrenia. Some combat veterans remain in an emotionally deadened, socially withdrawn state for prolonged periods, and many have been misdiagnosed as schizophrenic. Another common misdiagnosis is bipolar affective disorder, the current term for what the general public knows as manic-depressive illness. When intrusive relived experiences predominate and the veteran is flooded with emotions of fear and rage, he may stay awake for many days at a time and engage in driven, frantic activity. He may meet the descriptive criteria for mania and have a history of depression and despair—like Shakespeare's Harry Hotspur—and *voilá*, the diagnosis of bipolar affective disorder is made. A cycle of alternating states of numbness and intrusive reexperiencing is common enough in PTSD for most authorities in the field to regard it as intrinsic to the disorder. Combat veterans in our program who first made contact with the mental health system in the early 1970s were almost universally diagnosed as paranoid schizophrenic, if first seen in the late 1970s as manic-depressive or schizo-affective, and if first seen in the mid-1980s as suffering from PTSD. PTSD can unfortunately mimic virtually any condition in psychiatry.

PTSD AND THE RUINS OF CHARACTER

Regardless of when they were first seen, most of my patients have also been diagnosed with borderline or antisocial personality disorder, as well as other personality disorders. I do not believe the official PTSD criteria capture the devastation of mental life after severe combat trauma, because they neglect the damaging personality changes that frequently follow prolonged, severe trauma. The World Health Organization's *Classification of Mental and Behavioral Disorders* offers the category "Enduring personality change after catastrophic experience," defined as these personality features that did not exist before the trauma:

(a) a hostile or mistrustful attitude toward the world;
(b) social withdrawal;
(c) feelings of emptiness or hopelessness;
(d) a chronic feeling of being "on the edge," as if constantly threatened;
(e) estrangement.[6]

More than simply inflicting the set of symptoms described in DSM-III-R, prolonged combat can wreck the personality.[7]

PERSISTENCE OF THE TRAUMATIC MOMENT— LOSS OF AUTHORITY OVER MENTAL FUNCTION

The everyday experience of authority over mental processes is denied to the survivor of severe combat trauma. Many combat veterans made their first contact with mental health institutions because of fears for their sanity. Much as we expect effortless control over voluntary physical activities of our bodies—and are profoundly disturbed by paralysis, involuntary movements, or loss of bladder or bowel control—so is effortless and confident control over perception, memory, and thought an essential part of feeling sane. Many veterans who sought help could only express their affliction by saying things like, "I ain't right."

UNTRUSTWORTHINESS OF PERCEPTION

A human enemy strikes not only at the body but at the most basic functions of the soldier's mind. The Vietnamese enemy defeated the soldier's perception by concealment and his ability to understand what he saw by camouflage. The basic mental state of intention and will was attacked by ambush, deception, surprise, and anticipation. I recall canoeing with veterans along tranquil meanders of the Saco River in Maine, when one of them, who had served on riverboats in the Mekong Delta, pointed out the tan mudbank on the outside of a curve. He said that such an innocent riverbank would be riddled with tunnels and invisible machine-gun and rocket-propelled-grenade positions. The cumulative effect of prolonged attacks on mental function is to undermine the soldier's *trust* in his own perceptions. Another veteran said:

> Nothing is what it seems. That mountain there—maybe it wasn't there yesterday, and won't be there tomorrow. You get to the point where you're not even sure it *is* a mountain.

In such a situation, "hypervigilance" is a rational response. Everything must be looked at twice, three times, to be sure that it is what it appears to be.

I speculate that a soldier's trust in his own perceptions and cognitions usually recovers spontaneously upon return to civilian life, *unless the soldier has also experienced major betrayals* by his own leaders. Without recapitulating the kinds of betrayal described in chapter 1, I want to focus on the extremely common experience in Vietnam of being told by military superiors, "You didn't experience it, it never happened, you don't know what you know." One multitour airborne veteran recalls a particular denial of perception and experience with great bitterness. I shall start with a portion of this former sergeant's narrative that we have heard earlier, and then allow the reader to hear how it continues:

> Daylight came [long pause], and we found out we killed a lot of fishermen and kids.
>
> What got us thoroughly fucking confused is at that time, y'know, you turn to the team and you say to the team, "Don't worry about it. Everything's fucking fine." Because that's what you're getting from upstairs. The fucking colonel says, "Don't worry about it. We'll take care of it." Y'know, uh, "We got body count! We have body count!" So it starts working on your head. . . .
>
> The lieutenants got medals, and I know the colonel got his fucking medal. And they would have award ceremonies, y'know, I'd be standing like a fucking jerk and they'd be handing out fucking medals for killing civilians. So in your mind you're saying, "Ah, fuck it, they're Gooks."
>
> I was sick over it, after this happened. I actually puked my guts out. You know what had happened, but—see, it's all explained to you by captains and colonels and majors that "that's the hazards of war. They were in the wrong place." Y'know, "It didn't have anything to do with us. Fuck it. They was suspects anyways." And we was young fucking kids. That reasoning didn't come to effect right away, with me anyways. All I could see was anger building up. And what they did is they played on my anger. "You guys did a great job." Y'know, "Get drunk. You guys deserve it." Y'know, "You guys party." Y'know, "If yous wanna go downtown and get laid, go ahead." Y'know, and everything's fine, y'know. "RECON! AIRBORNE!" Y'know, uh, "We made it! We got body count!". . .
>
> As a young fucking kid, which we were, but we were old men. I don't know if you can understand what I'm saying. We were young in the heart and the body but they made us old men. . . . Y'know, "Erase that. It's yesterday's fucking news." "Ain't got nothing to do with us." "Move on."

This man suffered the nullification of perception and experience by his superiors. In high-stakes situations this is a major betrayal in itself. American soldiers in Vietnam experienced repeated erasure and denial of their own experiences. And this was not limited to enlisted men.[8]

Some loss of the trustworthiness of perception may be purely biological and independent of what others say about reality. Some survivors of heavy combat report persistent illusions of movement in their peripheral vision. One veteran tells that after he returned from Vietnam he shot at rats he saw moving out of the corner of his eye. His bedroom wall was peppered with bullet holes—"but there were not rats!" Because of the way our vision works, everyone has a fair amount of jiggling about in the far peripheries of the visual fields. However, our brains effortlessly filter this out before it attracts our attention. The inability to filter out trivial and harmless sensations may relate to chemical or even anatomical changes in the brain. A growing number of medical researchers are currently finding abnormalities of brain chemistry, function, and even gross structure in those suffering from combat PTSD. This is a rapidly advancing field.

MEMORY

Severely traumatized individuals lose authority over memory. Amnesia is common for traumatic events. In amnesia the trauma survivor has no authority over his memories of events because they cannot be recalled at will like ordinary memory. On the contrary, memory has authority over him.

Traumatic memory is not narrative. Rather, it is experience that reoccurs, either as full sensory replay of traumatic events in dreams or flashbacks, with all things seen, heard, smelled, and felt intact, or as disconnected fragments. These fragments may be inexplicable rage, terror, uncontrollable crying, or disconnected body states and sensations, such as the sensation of suffocating in a Viet Cong tunnel or being tumbled over and over by a rushing river—but with no memory of either tunnel or river. In other instances, knowledge of the facts may be separately preserved without any emotion, meaning, or sensory content. Often the only clue to a traumatic event may be an utterly bland statement of fact slipped into another context, such as ". . . just near the ville where Porker got his shit scattered [killed]."

In the overwhelming emotion of a fire fight in which a friend's jaw is shot away and he is seen suffocating on his own blood, words such as *terror*, *rage*, and *grief* do not do justice to the merging of powerful feelings in this hyperaroused state. We must bear in mind that when the traumatic moment reoccurs as flashback or nightmare, the emotions of terror, grief, and rage may be merged with each other. Such emotion is relived, not remembered. The naming of these as separate emotions, creating a *language* of emotion—which may be in plastic and musical arts, not only in words—is an important part of gaining mastery over the traumatic memory. Naming is one of the early stages of the communalization of trauma by rendering it communicable, however imperfectly.

Once reexperiencing is under way, the survivor lacks authority to stop it or put it away. The helplessness associated with the original experience is replayed in the apparent helplessness to end or modify the reexperience once it has begun. Fortunately, some learnable psychological techniques can be taught to survivors to gain substantial mastery over flashbacks and other intrusive phenomena and to mitigate the dangers that they present to the veteran and to others.

So long as the traumatic moment persists as a relivable nightmare, consciousness remains fixed upon it. The experiential quality of reality drains from the here-and-now; the dead are more real than the living. This is a cognitive aspect of the detachment of the trauma survivor from his current life and is intimately connected with the persistence of numbing, one of the basic skills of surviving prolonged, inescapable terror.

PERSISTENT MOBILIZATION FOR DANGER

Vigilance, the mental and physical preparation for attack, is a combat survival skill that needs no explanation. It is difficult, however, for anyone who has never been in combat to grasp the extent to which vigilance invades sleep.

The modern soldier's sleep can hardly be said to be sleep. In Vietnam, one veteran in our program always slept on his back with his rifle across his chest, or sitting up. It is not safe to shut out sounds and shadowy movements, so they are not shut out but instead are acknowledged during the light, unrestorative doze that is the soldier's sleep. By contrast, Homeric warfare was apparently suspended every night from sunset to sunrise. The

Trojans slept in their own beds behind the city walls. The Greeks slept in huts in a permanent encampment. Many veterans continue to sleep the same way they did in combat, on their backs with weapons, facing the door or window, ready to attack. For the veteran with unhealed PTSD, no place is familiar enough to completely shed combat vigilance.

Split-second, unthinking, self-defensive responsiveness when surprised is another combat survival skill. The metallic arming click of an enemy RPG, once heard, meant a searing explosion seconds later. Several of our patients will involuntarily hit the ground to this day when they hear a similar sound. One vet threw himself down on hearing such a sound and fell from a metal walkway where he was working above a post office sorting hall. Family, friends, and co-workers of Vietnam combat veterans have learned that it is most unsafe to approach these men unannounced from behind. The persistence of combat reflexes when surprised is not the same thing as recurrence of the berserk state, although the former may trigger the latter. The link between the two appears to be the adrenaline rush that accompanies surprise, which in turn can trigger the berserk state. Veterans who are prone to going berserk live in dread of such triggering and protect themselves from surprise for this reason. Suppression of the adrenaline rush by adrenaline-suppressing drugs called β-adrenergic blockers has permitted some veterans to venture out of their surprise-proof basement bunkers.

Exposed to the continuous threats of warfare, the body remains mobilized for battle indefinitely. There is no longer any baseline state of physical calm or comfort. Over time the combat veteran's body may seem to have turned against him. He begins to suffer not only from insomnia and agitation but also of numerous types of somatic symptoms. Tension headaches, gastrointestinal disturbances, skin disorders, and abdominal, back, or neck pain are extremely common. He may complain of tremors, choking sensations, or a rapid heartbeat. Some veterans become so accustomed to their condition that they cease to recognize the connection between their bodily distress symptoms and the climate of terror in which these symptoms were formed. It should come as no surprise that Vietnam combat veterans have been hospitalized for physical problems about six times more often than Vietnam-era veterans who never served in Vietnam.

A person "broken" by combat has lost the capacity for a sense of well-being, self-respect, confidence, and satisfaction—all attributes that we lump together in our concept of "happiness." It can come as no surprise that Vietnam combat veterans rate themselves as "very happy/satisfied" less than half as often as civilian counterparts and "very unhappy/unsatisfied" more than six times as often. For roughly a third of Vietnam combat veterans—a proportion 4.5 times as large as that found among civilian counterparts—demoralization is pervasive, encompassing a sense that their bodies are not working right, that they have lost their capacity to think, that they are helpless, hopeless, and full of dread. The word _demoralization_ is very apt for this state of being, because it invites us to think of the social and moral ground of these apparently private miseries.[9]

PERSISTENCE OF SURVIVAL SKILLS

Humans are biologically equipped to learn. The result of learning is persistence through time of the thing learned. Things done to survive in the danger of death and mutilation are learned very well indeed. Survival skills, such as vigilant sleep, brought back into the civilian worlds of family and employment, are actually more destructive of the veteran's well-being than the intrusive persistence of the traumatic moment.

Control over attention is one of the fundamental survival skills of people in captivity everywhere. All modern warfare is a condition of terrorized captivity for the combatants, whether in a static position under bombardment, and constant threat of ground attack, or patrolling from a helicopter landing zone.[10] The latter is no less a condition of inescapable captivity, even though the captive does much moving about in the open. Displacement, restriction, and detachment of attention are fundamental survival skills under all conditions of inescapable terror.[11] One 101st Airborne veteran, who had spent every summer as a child on Plum Island off the Massachusetts coast, literally hallucinated lying on the beach there with his extended family nearby, during any moment it was safe to turn his attention away from the enemy. It is not clear at present what relationship these dissociative skills have to the release of numbing, opiumlike substances in the brain, although under some conditions, both probably happen simultaneously.

The destruction of time is an inner survival skill. These words, written about concentration camp prisoners, apply equally to soldiers in prolonged combat:

> Thinking of the future stirs up such intense yearning and hope that . . . it [is] unbearable; they quickly learn that these emotions . . . will make them desperate. . . . The future is reduced to a matter of hours or days.
>
> Alterations in time sense begin with the obliteration of the future but eventually progress to obliteration of the past. . . . [At first they] cultivate memories of their past lives in order to combat their isolation . . . [and then they] lose the sense of continuity with their past. The past, like the future, becomes too painful to bear, for memory, like hope, brings back the yearning for all that has been lost. Thus prisoners are eventually reduced to living in an endless present.[12]

For combat soldiers, the temporal horizon shrinks as much as the moral and social horizon. Only getting through *now* has any existence. With this loss of a meaningful personal narrative that links past, present, and future comes a shrinkage of volition. Combat restricts and arrests the personal exercise of *will* as absolutely as the harshest imprisonment. A key survival skill in both circumstances is suppression of the will, which goes hand in hand with suppression of thoughts of the future. A depleted state of apathy, an inability to *want* anything, to will anything, often persists into life after combat, when it is no longer needed as a survival skill.

Rules, formal task descriptions, and written orders play a more visible role in the military than in any other setting. The combat soldier's attitude toward them often evolves into one of profound hostility and suspicion, both during and after military service. The soldier in combat experiences his situation in all its life-or-death specificity, where the *general* rule can get him killed. Orders, rules, and procedures often come to the soldier from the vast distance of safety in the rear, rules devised to cover general situations that may be lethally irrelevant:

> So you gotta pull devious shit. Y'know what I'm saying?
>
> Like we changed our [radio] call signs in the middle of fucking things. The Gooks some way or another got the roster of our shit. The fucking yo-yos in the back used to have all these fucking Indigenous Personnel working for them. So we were in the field

and we were called, like, Robin Hood, Robin Hood One, Robin Hood Six, Broken Arrow. And they started to get our fucking call signs. And [the enemy] started talking to us on the fucking radios. . . . So when we went to the field, the six teams going had already talked.

And we said, if the shit hits like it again, we'll all use something that we used back home. So like all of a sudden we became Batman and Robin, Snoopy and Pigpen. Y'know, "Snoopy, have you seen Pigpen?"

"He's with Schroeder." Right? So we knew where everybody was.

And fucking everybody in the rear fucking flipped out, because we weren't using proper radio procedures. And these motherfuckers were on the radio with us, "Use proper radio procedures!" Y'know? "You guys are in deep trouble."

You fucking got the radio, and you're saying, "I'm in deep fucking trouble? You people fucking serious?" Y'know? "What the fuck you going to do? Send me to jail? Do me a fucking favor." I'm out there getting fucking murdered, and they're telling me I'm in fucking trouble.

Other examples are not so benign or funny. Another veteran recalls one instance in which his lieutenant ordered him to take his squad into a senseless death trap in a rice paddy, and he refused. The lieutenant found three other men more compliant and sent them sent across the paddy, rather than around it. All three were killed by mines.

At the deepest level, survival in war trains or selects men for the skills to ignore, deflect, pervert, or circumvent orders, rules, and standard operating procedures. The reason for this lies in the nature of war against a human enemy—who is diligently stealing and studying training manuals, directives, standing orders, procedures, etc. The enemy's power of intelligent observation and thought give rise to what Georgetown University military historian Edward Luttwak calls the "paradoxical logic of war."[13] No matter how sound the rules and procedures in "the book," the enemy will very shortly know "the book" better than you do and will turn "doing it by the book" into a death trap.

The soldier quickly grasps that following rules can get him and the people close to him killed. It is clear that the skill to ignore and subvert rules often persists into civilian life, accounting for antisocial traits apparent in some combat veterans. However, the atmosphere of mortal danger also persists into civilian life and in my view is the main engine behind subversion of institutional rules by combat veterans.

A shared narrative future—as expressed in such statements as "Yes, I'll come to the picnic next Friday"—defines socially shared predictability of behavior. Prolonged contact with the enemy teaches that *predictability is fatal*. Being unpredictable is a basic survival skill in combat, where the enemy is ever observant. Many of the veterans in our program take different routes to the clinic every time they come. Carried into civilian life, this ingrained tie between unpredictability and survival negates the shared narrative consciousness assumed by social life in families and at work.

Readiness to react instantly and violently when surprised, a learned skill in training and combat, often comes to haunt and impair veterans in civilian life. If a veteran instinctively strikes or throws to the ground a family member, friend, or stranger who surprises him, the veteran's mood afterward is usually one of profound shame.

PERSISTENCE OF BETRAYAL

Severe, prolonged traumatization can bring wholesale destruction of desire, of the will to exist and to have a future. Betrayal of "what's right" is particularly destructive to a sense of continuity of value in ideals, ambitions, things, and activities. When some major ideals have been betrayed, the trustworthiness of every ideal or activity may be called into question. Undoubtedly this overlaps a great deal with the other topics in this section, particularly morale, and with the depression that is pandemic among combat veterans, who are seven times more likely to have suffered a major depressive episode than a demographically similar civilian control group, and eleven times more likely to have suffered from dysthymic disorder, a chronic, fluctuating state of depression, hopelessness, loss of self-respect, and loss of energy for living. Sometimes combat veterans appear to have a memory deficit for things, activities, or ideals that once carried intrinsic merit and a sense of satisfaction for them. Even the value of one's own home and possessions and of familiar places can be lost: Vietnam combat veterans are three times more likely to have been both homeless and vagrant than their civilian counterparts. According to a report compiled by the National Coalition for the Homeless, at least one-third of homeless males are veterans, with 150,000–250,000 veterans homeless on a given night and at least twice that number homeless at some time in the course of a given year. Alienation from a valued image of marriage may contribute to the fact that combat veterans are 3.5 times more likely than age-matched civilian controls to be living with partners "as if married" but not legally married.[14]

PERSISTENCE OF ISOLATION

Shrinkage of the social horizon after betrayal of "what's right" may persist long into civilian life. Safe, nonviolent attachments to others can become virtually impossible. The idea of a "freely cooperating partner" ceases to be a conceivable category for others or for oneself. Personal relationships of work, love, or friendship therefore become extraordinarily difficult. In the *National Vietnam Veterans Readjustment Study*, combat veterans were about twice as likely to have a highly unstable occupational history and to have had two or more divorces than demographically similar civilian counterparts.[15]

PERSISTENCE OF SUICIDALITY

Thoughts of suicide are common symptoms of combat PTSD. Paradoxically, they are also signs of life. If a person enters the zombielike state of indifference beyond despair, rage, suicidality, and fear, he or she simply dies. This is the testimony of concentration camp survivors and combat veterans. The ability to kill oneself is the bottom line of human freedom. Many combat veterans think daily of suicide. Knowledge that one has this freedom seems to be sustaining. Vietnam veterans assert that twice as many of their brethren have died by suicide since the war than died at the hands of the enemy. I, for one, have no inclination to dispute this number, though accurately estimating suicides in this population is even more difficult than counting the homeless.

PERSISTENCE OF MEANINGLESSNESS

When a survivor of prolonged trauma loses all sense of meaning-ful personal narrative, this may result in a contaminated identity. "I died in Vietnam" may express a current identity as a corpse. When the "I" who died is understood to be the bearer of a civilized social morality, what remains may reflect a tainted, evil identity, one deserving punishment. I have heard more than one veteran declare that God kept him alive to torture him: If God had loved him, He would have let him die in Vietnam. Many combat veterans speak of the dead as the lucky ones.

Since the earliest studies of concentration camp survivors, it has been known that severe trauma shatters a sense of the mean-ingfulness of the self, of the world, and of the connection between the two. The same obliteration of meaning has subsequently been confirmed for rape victims, Hiroshima survivors, survivors of the Cambodian genocide, and Vietnam combat veterans. In present-day America, religious educators have been extraordinarily suc-cessful in claiming hegemony over experiences of Meaning and Right and Wrong. This is so well entrenched in our culture that many combat veterans have no way of thinking or speaking about these matters apart from God.

DESTRUCTION OF THE CAPACITY
FOR DEMOCRATIC PARTICIPATION

Unhealed combat trauma devastates the civic and political life of the returning veteran. To see how this can happen, let us consider some of the assumed and unnoticed features of mental and social life that make democracy possible.

Democratic process embodies the apparent contradiction of *safe struggle*. Combat veterans with unhealed PTSD have the greatest difficulty conceiving of any struggle apart from killing and dying. Passionate struggle conducted within rules of safety and fairness simply doesn't make sense to them or seems a hollow charade. For them it is psychologically impossible to win a strug-gle without killing or to lose without dying, and they do not want to do either. Many veterans' response is to withdraw and not par-ticipate. Democracy embodies safe struggle over the shape and implementation of a future. An unhealed combat veteran cannot *think* in terms of a future. Democratic political activity presupposes that the future exists and that it is meaningful. Combat taught the survivor of prolonged combat not to imagine a future or to want anything. Prior to seeing the point of one's voluntary participation in a social process, one must feel that it is safe to want something.

Veterans with unhealed PTSD feel that it is not safe to commit to attending political meetings—there may be a crowd, and it may be impossible to cover one's back. Appearing at a known time and place, especially over and over again, invited death in Vietnam. Going to a second meeting, after a first meeting proved tolerable, may provoke a disabling panic attack. The persistent survival skill of unpredictability devastates the simplest forms of democratic participation. "Show up at the polls? Forget it."

Democratic process entails debate, persuasion, and compromise. These all presuppose the trustworthiness of words. The moral dimension of severe trauma, the betrayal of "what's right," obliterates the capacity for trust. The customary meanings of words are exchanged for new ones; fair offers from opponents are scrutinized for traps; every smile conceals a dagger.

Unhealed combat trauma—and I suspect unhealed severe trauma from any source—destroys the unnoticed substructure of democracy, the cognitive and social capacities that enable a group of people to freely construct a cohesive narrative of their own future.

CHAPTER 11

Healing and Tragedy

I will tell you something about stories, . . .
They aren't just entertainment.
Don't be fooled.
They are all we have, you see,
all we have to fight off
illness and death.
                                        —L. M. Silko,
                                          Ceremony, page 2

Anything in the form or substance of an account of combat trauma that offers the reader easy reassurance betrays the truth in the veterans' narratives and in the *Iliad*. Homer ends the *Iliad* with mourning, not reassurance. The aching reconciliation of Achilles and Priam in Book 24 is comfort between men who both know they are doomed. Neither the conclusion of the *Iliad* nor the healing achieved by severely injured combat veterans can be snugly characterized as "the triumph of the human spirit." As Vietnam combat veteran Tim O'Brien wrote in his novel *The Things They Carried*:

A true war story is never moral. It does not instruct, nor encourage virtue, nor suggest models of proper human behavior, nor restrain men from doing the things men have always done. If a story seems moral, do not believe it. If at the end of a war story you feel uplifted, or if you feel that some small bit of rectitude has been salvaged from the larger waste, then you have been made the victim of a very old and terrible lie. There is no rectitude whatsoever. There is no virtue. As a first rule of thumb, therefore, you can tell a true war story by its absolute and uncompromising allegiance to obscenity and evil. . . . You can tell a true war story if it embarrasses you. If you don't care for obscenity, you don't care for the truth;

183

if you don't care for the truth, watch how you vote. Send guys to war, they come home talking dirty.[1]

The *Iliad* tells the tragedy of Achilles. In these pages veterans have narrated their own tragedies. Today, twenty-nine years after the first U.S. combat troops landed in Vietnam and twenty-two years after the last U.S. ground combat battalion was withdrawn, more than 250,000 Vietnam combat veterans currently meet the full DSM-III-R criteria for post-traumatic stress disorder.[2] Time does *not* heal all wounds. Can these veterans ever recover? What treatment will help? What stands in the way?

IS RECOVERY POSSIBLE?

Despair—suffocating despair—occurs in every therapeutic relationship with survivors of severe trauma. This is true in group therapy, in individual therapy, and in every relationship the survivor manages to sustain. Despair is communicable. It communicates itself to mental health professionals, families, employers, co-workers, social service workers, and administrators. Is there any hope? Is recovery possible after severe trauma of the sort described here?

At the risk of seeming evasive, I shall respond to the question "Is recovery possible?" with three answers: (1) Return to "normal" is not possible. (2) We don't know. (3) Yes.

RETURN TO "NORMAL" IS NOT POSSIBLE

Veterans speak of losing their innocence and longing to regain it. They ask: "Why can't I just go back to the way I was?"

> I was eighteen years old. And I was like your typical young American boy. A virgin. I had strong religious beliefs. . . . My religious upbringing was, God was good. Everything good was—it was like obeying your mother and father, y'know. Everything good was what God wanted. Y'know, evil was the Devil's way.
>
> Evil was not going to church, that was a bad thing. Swearing, fighting, hurting people, that was bad. I lived in a very simple world. It was the way you were taught, like, "Whenever you're

alone, make believe God's there with you. Would he approve of what you are doing?" That's basically—sure, I wasn't no angel, either. I mean, I had my little fistfights and stuff. It was, you're only human.

But evil didn't enter it till Vietnam. I mean real evil. I wasn't prepared for it at all. . . .

It was all evil. All evil. Where before, I wasn't. I look back, I look back today, and I'm horrified at what I turned into. What I was. What I did. I just look at it like it was somebody else. I really do. It was somebody else.

Any knowledge is potentially transforming; the knowledge of evil, particularly in trusted authorities, custodians of *thémis*, and within oneself, brings irreversible change. The word *innocent* has the double meaning of having done no harm and of being unacquainted with evil and malevolence. To encounter radical evil is to make one forever different from the trusting, "normal" person who wraps the rightness of the social order around himself snugly, like a cloak of safety. Trust, which was once an unthinking assumption and granted with no awareness of possible betrayal, is now a staggering accomplishment for survivors of severe trauma. Trauma survivors grant trust only as an act of courage, after time and *tests* of trust, one after another, like trials and labors in ancient myth. Blind trust in authority, position, and credentials is a dangerous luxury of the still innocent. If recovery means return to trusting innocence, recovery is *not* possible. Recovered survivors of severe trauma adopt their own lives—including their limitations—with passion and existential authority. These veterans can become profoundly valuable human beings, even if their external accomplishments in the world are often very limited.

WE DON'T KNOW IF RECOVERY IS POSSIBLE

Certain dramatic successes of modern medicine have come to seem like paradigms for real healing: A cancer that is discovered early and cut out by a surgeon never recurs; a bacterial double pneumonia, fatal before the antibiotic era, is cured by penicillin. These and many other examples of notable success in medicine share a certain story line: The problem is identified (diagnosis); a treatment is administered over a brief period of time by a professional (therapy); the patient returns to his prior relationships, occupation, and pleasures without impairment, without ongoing treatment, and without recurrence of the problem (cure). In the sense of regaining lost innocence, combat PTSD is definitely incurable. In the sense of being permanently free of all specific symptoms of combat PTSD, the honest answer is that we *don't know*.

Some of the neurophysiological changes brought about by severe trauma may require maintenance medication, or occasional remediation with a drug that had been discontinued. The same applies to psychological treatments. Entering a new stage of life such as parenthood or retirement, an on-the-job injury, or the death of a spouse may reopen old traumas and require further therapy. Betrayal of *thémis* in life-or-death circumstances has profoundly damaging consequences for the biological makeup of the victim. Restoration of trustworthy community to the survivor will have healthy biological effects, of comparable or greater magnitude than successful medications. Effective psychological therapies change the biological state of the survivor for the better.

We don't know how much recovery a survivor can expect from psychological, social, and pharmacological therapies during his or her lifetime. We are just discovering some modes of healing, and others need to be rediscovered from the vast experience of many ages and cultures.

YES—RECOVERY IS POSSIBLE

Recovery is possible in many areas of life, perhaps in the most important ones for a fulfilling existence. I have seen it. A small number of veterans in our program have achieved lives of great value to others and satisfaction for themselves. By DSM-III-R standards, however, *they remain highly symptomatic*. Several had to be hospitalized during the recent Persian Gulf War because of the overwhelming intrusive symptoms it triggered. Their lives include some very sharp limitations; for example, some recovered veterans are still unable to tolerate public places. Because of such limitations, every one of the most fully recovered veterans I know is financially quite poor. Yet their lives flourish with activity that they find satisfying, usually helping other people. One spends his mornings delivering meals to children with AIDS. Another assists homeless veterans in getting social security and other benefits.

WHAT IS THE BEST TREATMENT?

The essential injuries in combat PTSD are moral and social, and so the central treatment must be moral and social. The best treatment restores control to the survivor and actively encourages communalization of the trauma. Healing is done *by* survivors, not *to* survivors.[3]

The essential first step that a veteran needs to take, which is a precondition of healing, is to establish his own safety, sobriety,[4] and self-care. This is often a protracted struggle, and various means of assistance are available to support the veteran in accomplishing these things for himself. A number of medications safely ameliorate one or another symptom of PTSD and assist in the achievement of safety and sobriety by reducing the pressure toward self-medication with alcohol or street drugs and, even more valuably, by reducing explosive rage.[5]

During the early days of the current era of PTSD treatment, mental health professionals shared the folk belief that simply "getting it all out" would result in safety, sobriety, and self-care. The consequences of these well-intended "combat debriefings" were catastrophic, resulting in many suicides, according to veterans in our program who participated. On this dangerous illusion of instant cathartic cure, Harvard professor of psychiatry Judith Lewis Herman writes:

> The patient may imagine a kind of sadomasochistic orgy, in which [he or] she will scream, cry, vomit, bleed, die, and be reborn cleansed of the trauma.[6]

Combat veterans often hold such an apocalyptic-cathartic idea of healing, but before safety, self-care, and sobriety have been firmly established, active uncovering of trauma history only retraumatizes the survivor. Recovery from severe combat trauma more nearly resembles training to run a marathon than cathartic redemption in faith healing.

Virtually all treatment methods direct the survivor to construct a personal narrative at some time in his or her recovery, although there are powerful disagreements about the timing and venue. Homer, who was considered the first tragic poet, told stories. He created narratives that unfolded in time.

❋ WHY AND HOW DOES NARRATIVE HEAL?

Severe trauma explodes the cohesion of consciousness. When a survivor creates fully realized narrative that brings together the shattered knowledge of what happened, the emotions that were aroused by the meanings of the events, and the bodily sensations that the physical events created, the survivor pieces back together the fragmentation of consciousness that trauma has caused. Such narrative often results in the remission of some symptoms, particularly intrusive symptoms, dissociated bodily sensations, affects, and behaviors that inexplicably intrude into the veteran's life. What I principally want to address, however, is how narrative heals personality changes, how narrative enables the survivor to rebuild the ruins of character. The ancient Greeks revered Homer, the singer of tales, as a doctor of the soul. In the *Odyssey*, Homer paints a (self-)portrait of the epic singer whose healing art is to tell the stories of Troy with the truth that causes the old soldier, Odysseus, to weep and weep again. (*Odyssey* 8:78ff)

Narrative heals personality changes only if the survivor finds or creates a trustworthy community of listeners for it. Several traits are required for the audience to be trustworthy.

Some traits relate to strength. The listeners must be strong enough to hear the story without injury. Combat veterans will never trust a therapist whom they see to be "freaked out" by what he or she hears. In a therapy group doing trauma-centered work, the other members of the group must be strong enough to cope with inevitable triggers to their own memories.

The listeners must also be strong enough to hear the story without having to deny the reality of the experience or to blame the victim. We are so trained to deny the soldier's experience that the normal response to hearing an account of betrayal is to make all the power-holder's excuses: This is a figment of your fantasy; if you knew all the facts, you'd see it was for the best; you've got a hidden agenda in saying this; it never happened; you brought it on yourself; and anyway, it's twenty years ago, so forget it and don't create more problems now.

To be trustworthy, a listener must be ready to experience some of the terror, grief, and rage that the victim did. This is one meaning, after all, of the word *compassion*. Once the veteran sees that the listener authentically experiences these emotions, even though with less intensity than in combat, the veteran often loses the desire to shout in the listener's face, "You weren't there, so shut the fuck up!" A poem by Vietnam combat veteran W. T. Edmonds voices the powerful will to compel others to understand with their heart:

> . . . White-hot anguish stokes the mind,
>   forging words to hammer the emotions
>   and wound the feelings
> of those who did not go and could not see.

> With an adder's stealth,
>   hidden between the covers,
>   deadly letters lie in wait,
>   innocent in their camouflage of black and white,
>   to strike your mind

>   and scar your soul.[7]

Without emotion in the listener there is no communalization of the trauma.

To achieve trust, listeners must respect the narrator. The advice that veterans consistently give to trauma therapists is "Listen! Just listen." Respect, embodied in this kind of listening, is readiness to be changed by the narrator. The change may be small or large. It may be simply learning something not previously known, feeling something, seeing something from a new perspective, or it may be as profound as redirection of the listener's way of being in the world.

Respect also means refraining from judgment. This is standard training for psychotherapists, but it is often difficult to achieve when the victim of severe trauma has also been a perpetrator. People sometimes imagine that soldiers alone are both victims and perpetrators. But veterans are not unique among survivors of severe trauma. Tyrants in all spheres of life, whether domestic, political, or military, have discovered that the most powerful way to break the will of another person is to coerce participation in the victimization of others. Many victims of such situations have done terrible things to survive, with devastating consequences for good character. The child singled out for incest may be forced to participate in the sacrifice of younger siblings, a battered woman in the abuse of her children, a prostitute in the kidnapping of a new coerced prostitute, a political prisoner in the torture of another prisoner. This is the ultimate bad moral luck. Cultural training and wishful thinking lead us to believe that our own good character would have stood firm to the point of death, rather than submit to this final degradation. Or we imagine that our intelligence would have seen a way out that the victim did not. These beliefs lead inevitably to the feeling that the person who was broken by coercion has been defective from the start and deserves neither compassion nor treatment. Our laws even say that under some circumstances a person is culpable for not resisting to the death. If someone who batters a woman is convicted of injuring or killing one of her children, the battered mother usually goes to prison, too, for failure to protect, despite proven duress and well-founded terror.[8]

Narrative time—the idea that an event takes place in a temporal context, with other events happening before, during, and after it—is an ancient cultural construction, originating perhaps in the Indo-European epic tradition that Homer inherited and the Athenian tragic theater transformed. Homer did not invent narrative time, nor did God nor Nature. It is a cultural artifact, very, very old but by no means universal. Chinese novels and opera construct time differently. In some "primitive" societies informants will include notable deeds of their ancestors in their own life stories. Although the *thémis* of narrative temporality is one of the deepest structures of our culture, severe trauma destroys the capacity to think a future or a past. For many Vietnam combat soldiers, a cramped, eternal present, extending no further than the next C-rations, death, cigarette, or fire fight, snuffed out all other temporality.

One of the men in our program, when asked to explain the Larry Burrows photo on the cover of this book, said of the men at the far right, one of whom has his back to the man on the ground:

> These guys don't have a lot to look forward to here, there's not much to look forward to. Maybe the next smoke or someone's got

190

some extra food. That's all that's on their mind. Or dying might be on their mind. Why not die?[9]

The time horizon in the future has shrunk to a few hours and to the timeless shelter of death.

Narrative time is built into the very structure of the family of languages to which English belongs. This may form part of the enormous difficulty that many survivors of severe trauma have in putting their experience into words; their experience is ineffable in a language that insists on "was" and "will be." The trauma world knows only *is*.

We see the paradox that narrative temporality can never be completely true to the timeless experience of prolonged, severe trauma. If narrative is a lie, how can it heal? Is it simply another "noble lie" when we encourage a trauma survivor to tell a story in the form of "This was my life before. . . . This is what happened. . . . This is what I became." The paradox disappears when we look at narration as a step in the survivor's larger move to communalize the trauma by inducing others who were not there to feel what the victim felt when he or she was going through it. The character damage of a trauma survivor can be understood as a reflection both of his or her radical aloneness and of the continued presence of the perpetrator in the victim's inner life.

Trauma narrative imparts knowledge to the community that listens *and* responds to it emotionally. Emotion carries essential cognitive elements; it is not separable from the knowledge. Something quite profound takes place when the trauma survivor sees enlightenment take hold. The narrator now speaks as his or her free self, not as the captive of the perpetrator. The aloneness is broken in a manner that obliterates neither the narrator nor the listener in a reenactment.

Some survivors, having learned the untrustworthiness of words, conclude that the only way to be heard is through action—guerrilla theater. Intimidation, "acting out," and creating impossible situations sometimes aim at coercing the therapist to feel the fear and helplessness that the survivor felt. This is coercive communalization. It recreates terror and helplessness at work, in the family, on the street, or in the clinic. Like Achilles (1:292f), these survivors have flung the herald's staff to the ground. Words mean nothing; only actions count. In this coercive communalization the audience is no longer made up of listeners; the survivor has made them victims. They most assuredly feel the emotions. Aloneness is broken here, too, but the inner presence of the perpetrator has taken over. Healing does not occur.

Peer recognition, which allows survivors of trauma to grasp that they are not freaks and "do not have to go through it alone," usually leads to communication of experience in words, not action. When a healing community of combat veterans forms, the herald's staff can be picked up from the dirt, and veterans once again find they can speak without acting. Initially they speak in unison, as it were. In this earliest form of group communication, individual experience seems to be spoken and heard as part of the discourse of mutual affirmation and recognition: We were all grunts, we all went through the same thing.

Major recovery, however, requires that personal narrative be particular, not general. The friends who died in Vietnam were not friends in general but particular human beings. The survivors who lost them are also particular human beings, and they must be given permission by the community to speak without fear that their particularity will rupture the we-all-went-through-the-same-thing support that they have come to rely upon. In a fully realized personal narrative the survivor grips the herald's staff and speaks as himself.

All who hear should understand that no person's suffering can be measured against any other person's suffering. It can be extremely damaging if anyone makes comparisons. Combat veterans frequently doubt that they are worthy of treatment, knowing other vets who are worse off now or went through worse than they did. Many survivors of appalling trauma obstruct their own healing by placing themselves in "hierarchies of suffering," usually to their own disadvantage.[10]

Narrative can transform involuntary reexperiencing of traumatic events into memory of the events, thereby reestablishing authority over memory. *Forgetting combat trauma is not a legitimate goal of treatment.* Veterans find it morally degrading to forget the dead. To know why this is so, we need only recall what we have seen in the earlier chapters on the existential functions of guilt and rage. The task is to remember—rather than relive and reenact—and to grieve. For combat veterans this means grieving not only the dead but also their own lost innocence in both its meanings, as blamelessness and as unawareness of evil. Also, many prewar relationships with parents, friends, siblings, and spouses are now gone forever. A secure sense of the goodness of the social order is irretrievably lost and must be mourned. One veteran said,

> You're afraid that once you start to cry you'll never stop. And once you do start, it seems like it will never stop. I cried for a whole year.

We must all strive to be a trustworthy audience for victims of abuse of power. I like to think that Aristotle had something like this in mind when he made tragedy the centerpiece of education for citizens in a democracy. However, to do this we must overcome all the good reasons why normal adults do not want to hear trauma narratives. If forced to hear them, normal people deny their truth. If forced to accept them as true, they often forget them. Taken together, I call these good reasons the law of forgetting and denial.

THE LAW OF FORGETTING AND DENIAL

The social morality of "what's right," what Homer called *thémis*, is the normal adult's cloak of safety. The trauma narrative of every person with PTSD and character damage is a challenge to the rightness of the social order, to the trustworthiness of *thémis*. To hear and believe is to feel *unsafe*. It is to know the fragility of goodness.

Trauma narratives show us that our own good character is vulnerable to destruction by bad moral luck.

Normal adults recognize the actual power deployments in their own society. To repeat what one has heard from a "loser," from "damaged goods"—and this is how trauma survivors are often stigmatized—is to risk marginalization, reprisal, or being tainted by the same low status of the trauma survivor. Just as trauma testimony is always a political act, retelling trauma narrative is likewise political. Judith Lewis Herman has persuasively connected the capacity to hear, believe, and retell with a supportive sociopolitical movement.[11]

Trauma narrative confronts the normal adult with the fragility of the body. These stories bring mortality into view. Trauma narratives cause normal adults to imaginatively identify with one or more of the characters in the narrative. The feelings this arouses are almost all unpleasant.

We should not sit in judgment of those who cannot, in the absence of social support, hear the truth of trauma. The reasons to deflect, deny, and forget trauma narrative stem from the social construction of normal human life. They cannot be set aside by wishing them away or by moralizing.[12]

I have been politicized by this work and now see that treatment must be morally engaged—that trauma work can never be apolitical. I cannot contemplate a "professional," affectively neutral posture toward trauma work without misgivings, because, as I have argued here, an affectively neutral position will defeat healing. As much as I love what I do and consider it worthwhile, I cannot escape the suspicion that what we do as mental health professionals is not as good as the healing that in other cultures has been rooted in the native soil of the returning soldier's community. Our culture has been notably deficient in providing for reception of the Furies of war into community. For better or worse, the health care system has been given this role—along with the prisons, where a disproportionate number of men incarcerated since the Vietnam War have been veterans.[13]

We must create our own new models of healing which emphasize communalization of the trauma. Combat veterans and American citizenry should meet together face to face in daylight, and listen, and watch, and weep, just as citizen-soldiers of ancient Athens did in the theater at the foot of the Acropolis.[14] We need a modern equivalent of Athenian tragedy. Tragedy brings us to cherish our mortality, to savor and embrace it. Tragedy inclines us to prefer attachment to fragile mortals whom we love, like Odysseus returning from war to his aging wife, Penelope, and to refuse promised immortality (*Odyssey* 5:209).

Conclusion

I want that this is the last war in my life.
—Twelve-year-old Bosnian
girl in refugee camp

No more fucking wars!
—Four-tour airborne Vietnam veteran

I have written this book because I believe we should *care* about how soldiers are trained, equipped, led, and welcomed home when they return from war. This is our moral duty toward those we ask to serve on our behalf, and it is in our own self-interest as well. Unhealed combat trauma blights not only the life of the veteran but the life of the family and community. In some instances, such as in the Weimar Republic in Germany after World War I, it can substantially weaken the society as a whole.

Economically, unhealed combat trauma costs, and costs, and costs. Recall that more than 40 percent of Vietnam combat veterans sampled in the National Vietnam Veterans Readjustment Study reported engaging in violent acts three or more times in the preceding year. When violence against others results in injury, society incurs the costs of medical care and lost productivity of the victims of this violence. Between a tenth and a quarter of all males in prison are veterans, and it costs an average of about $25,000 per year to incarcerate each of them. When combat trauma results in domestic violence and pathologic family life, there is an intergenerational transmission of trauma. A number of men in our program have children who are currently in prison.

Unhealed combat trauma diminishes democratic participation and can become a threat to democratic political institutions. Severe psychological injury originates in violation of trust and destroys the capacity for trust. When mistrust spreads widely and deeply, democratic civic discourse becomes impossible.

Conclusion

PREVENTION

Can combat PTSD, and particularly the devastating character changes associated with it, be prevented? In the language of public health, primary prevention of combat PTSD requires elimination of the source of the injury, which is to say, elimination of combat. However, moving from international and civil wars to an era that is free of war will take generations or centuries, during which many more soldiers will fight. Is there anything we can do to protect men and women from psychological injury when they must face combat? In public health terminology, this is secondary prevention.

The military's answer to this question usually comes in one word: training. There can be no doubt that rigorous, realistic training does provide significant psychological protection to people who must fight, not to speak of enormously raising their chances of survival. The reader may have noticed that there are no accounts in this book of veterans attributing their psychological injuries to military training. In fact, many Vietnam combat veterans felt deeply betrayed by the *irrelevance* of their training to the actual conditions and enemy they had to face. As with the well-chronicled deficiencies of the M-16 rifle, this perception fostered a bitter conviction among veterans that their country simply didn't care. Negligence in the training of soldiers for Vietnam is one of the deepest sources of anger in Colonel David Hackworth's very angry book, *About Face*.[1]

Thoughtful military people assert that the answer lies in better training *and* leadership. Colonel James Stokes of the U.S. Army Medical Department issued an Information Paper titled "Management of Combat Stress and Battle Fatigue"[2] shortly before the Persian Gulf War. It states tersely, "Control of stress is a command responsibility." The whole of this book's first chapter, "Betrayal of 'What's Right,'" makes the point that bad leadership is a cause of combat trauma. The elements of military leadership that were stated some twenty-four centuries ago by the Chinese warrior-philosopher Sun Tzu still hold true today: "Leadership is a matter of intelligence, trustworthiness, humaneness, courage, and sternness."[3] Tragically, the institutional pressures and cultural milieu of the Vietnam War destroyed or warped each of these military leadership virtues at every level of command.

Support on the home front for the soldier, *regardless of ethical and political disagreements over the war itself,* is essential. This is never easy in the emotionally polarized climate of a war. However, when facing individual soldiers, we must remember that all modern soldiers serve under constraint.[4] The justice of overall war aims and of operational theories—"strategic" bombing of civilians to weaken the industrial capacity to wage war is an example of such a theory—is not within the individual soldier's scope of moral choice, unless he or she is willing to face imprisonment or death by refusing to fight. I cannot hold soldiers to an ethical standard that *requires martyrdom in order simply to be blameless.* I am not arguing against the Nuremberg principles, which say that no person is absolved of responsibility for horrible acts by the fact that he or she was legally ordered to do them. I am speaking from the pain that I feel when I witness in our veterans the ruin of moral life by the overwhelming coercive social power of military institutions and of war itself. If war goals, operational methods, and military culture were so unjust that the Nuremberg principles loomed over every Vietnam combat soldier, we must recognize that the blood is on our hands too. If we had exercised Sun Tzu's virtues of "intelligence, trustworthiness, humaneness, courage, and sternness" toward our representatives in Washington, from the presidents down, our soldiers in Vietnam would not have been in that position. War itself always creates situations in which physical survival contradicts moral survival. Bad moral luck haunts every battle along with the other manifestations of luck. However, wrong-headed civilian/military leadership and destructive cultural patterns bloat isolated bad moral luck into tragedy that can afflict a whole generation.

Primary prevention of combat trauma requires an end to the social institution of war. However, we must not allow despair of bringing this about in our lifetime blind us to the possibilities of secondary prevention of combat trauma. Given that we will continue to send men and women into combat, what can be done to protect them? What existing cultural and organizational patterns need to be changed? The military can do many things to reduce permanent psychological injury.[5]

Conclusion

PROTECT UNIT COHESION
BY UNIT RATHER THAN INDIVIDUAL ROTATION

Preservation of the social and moral cohesion of the soldier's face-to-face combat unit ranks highest among things that must be done. Destruction of unit cohesion by the individual-rotation policy in Vietnam cannot be overemphasized as a reason why so many psychological injuries that might have healed spontaneously instead became chronic.[6]

I am often asked why Vietnam apparently caused such a high rate of long-lasting psychological injuries compared to World War II. We have no data for the Second World War comparable to the *National Vietnam Veterans Readjustment Study* on the prevalence of PTSD among World War II veterans twenty years after that war's end. This is a large and complex subject, but I always begin my answer to the question by focusing on the fact that most World War II soldiers trained together, went overseas together, fought together, had R&R together, and came home together. The typical Vietnam soldier went over alone, integrated himself as the "fucking new guy" in an already formed and highly stressed unit to the extent that luck and his personal traits permitted, went on R&R alone, and came home alone, often leaving behind a unit that was still in combat. He had no chance to "debrief," to talk about what had happened with people he trusted who understood his experiences.

What a returning soldier needs most when leaving war is not a mental health professional but a living community to whom his experience matters. There is usually such a community close at hand: his or her surviving comrades. Men and women returning from combat should "debrief" as units, not as isolated individuals. *Unit rotation is the most important measure for secondary prevention of combat PTSD.*

VALUE GRIEFWORK

I have emphasized the importance of griefwork in chapter 3. The official and folk culture of the American military must change so that grieving enjoys high status—is valued, not stigmatized. The capacity to weep and to feel the pain of sorrow does not weaken a soldier; if the *Iliad* shows us anything, it surely shows us this. Tentative steps are currently being taken to change the cultural valuation of grief in the U.S. military. A military transport plane that crashed at Gander, Newfoundland, in 1985, killing 248 soldiers, seems to have catalyzed a rethinking by the military of its culture of grief. Since then, such terms as "grief leadership" have begun to circulate. I am told that military chaplains are now receiving training in grief leadership.[7] However well intended, a focus on chaplains misses the point. Until meaningful training is required of NCOs and platoon, company, and battalion commanders, little real change can be expected, especially in wartime. If the military service academies fail to offer cadets role models of senior commanders who value sincere and intelligent attention to the griefwork of their troops, better prevention of PTSD is unlikely. The "hierarchy of bereavement," that is, the ranking of intensity of attachment to the dead, rarely coincides with hierarchy of rank or with military occupation specialty. What kind of training will make it "just common sense" for a commander to ask a dead soldier's closest friend to speak or read a prayer at a memorial ceremony, regardless of his or her rank?

I have made a plea to rethink the policies and practices relating to handling and transporting the dead during war. The needs of bereaved families *can* be harmonized with the needs of surviving comrades. These surviving comrades are entitled to a gut certainty that the bodies of their dead friends are handled respectfully by the Medical Corps and by Graves Registration. This was denied to many in Vietnam.

Special communal meals in honor of the dead strike me as more meaningful to combat units than the inevitable Thanksgiving and Christmas meals, which felt like cruel jokes to most of the combat veterans I have known.

Finally, I have argued against defining soldiers' grief as a breakdown, and crudely medicating soldiers because they weep or defining grief as requiring treatment by a mental health professional. If both mental health professionals and chaplains made authentic communalization of soldiers' grief their goal, they would do more good than the best individual counseling. And such advice on communalization will be welcomed by commanders in wartime only if prior training and role modeling have prepared them to be receptive.

Conclusion

DO NOT ENCOURAGE BERSERKING

Nowhere is illumination more needed within military culture than in the matter of fighting spirit and its relation to the berserk state. Fighting spirit, a ringing term that broadly refers to a soldier's readiness to move in on an enemy rather than flee or freeze, is essential for survival in combat. Military training under realistic, fear-inducing conditions has fighting spirit as one of its legitimate goals, and anything less can rob a soldier of his or her life when facing real battle.

However, the folk culture of the American military, especially during the Vietnam War, merged fighting spirit with being berserk. Leadership beliefs encouraged the conversion of grief into berserk rage as a militarily desirable consequence. The *Iliad* speaks with contradictory voices in regard to the military value of the berserker. I have argued that Homer holds up Diomêdês as the ideal warrior who never loses self-restraint. The *Iliad* tells the story of Achilles' tragedy and destruction, not his glorification. On the other hand, when Achilles brings down Hektor, Troy is doomed, which instills the message that a single berserk warrior can bring victory for the whole army. This is the message remembered by American military folk culture.

Thoughtful military commanders have always rejected a positive image of the berserker, noting the degradation of unit effectiveness that comes from the berserker's loss of all social connection, distractibility, suspiciousness of friends, irrationality, and inconsistency in tasks taken on and how they are carried out. Colonel Stokes's Persian Gulf War memorandum, cited above on page 196, reflects the thinking of commanders who doubt that berserking is a good thing. Berserking, it says, "may or may not interfere with specific combat tasks and may even be done by otherwise 'excellent' soldiers, but is harmful to discipline and perhaps to the moral or physical health of the individual." "Excellent" soldiers display "heroism, courage, self-sacrifice, exceptional strength, and endurance"[8]—all traits of the berserk state. "Loyalty to comrades (cohesion)," another signifier of military excellence, is ambiguous if understood as loyalty to living comrades. As we have seen in chapter 5, the berserker's loyalty is often exclusively to the dead.

Most of my patients volunteered to do more than one combat tour and often "re-upped" to get revenge for the death of a special comrade. They had acquired valuable military skills and were willing, even eager, to volunteer to fight for another six months. Such men were usually promoted to sergeant. Their immediate superiors, company grade officers who were highly stressed themselves, could hardly have been expected in the midst of war to turn away an experienced and motivated solider whom he knows (and knows to be somewhat crazed) in favor of an inexperienced replacement whom he does not know. The military culture at the time valued the berserk soldier as "the best."

Allowing a berserk, revenge-driven soldier to return to battle is to send him to probable death and knowingly to send out a man who cannot distinguish atrocities from acceptable military conduct. He has lost the capacity for restraint. If the soldier survives physically, he is certain to be gravely disabled from participation in civilian society—probably for life.

A key preventive policy would be to require an honest psychological assessment at the time a soldier volunteers to extend his combat tour. Berserk soldiers should be regarded as serious psychiatric casualties, denied their request to extend, and given compassionate medical treatment of their psychological injuries. The presence of even one berserker in a unit may indicate that the unit as a whole needs to be rotated, and the other psychiatric casualties, who are virtually certain to be present, identified and cared for. Just as every "friendly fire" incident in a well-run military calls for investigation, I believe that every berserk soldier signals a possible leadership betrayal that, if present, should never pass unnoticed and without consequence for the officer. I am pessimistic, however, that such a policy could survive (or that the mental health officers performing honest assessments could resist) the combined pressures of field commanders who regard these crazed volunteers as "the best," and of the volunteers themselves, who no longer plan to return home alive and want nothing but revenge.

ELIMINATE INTENTIONAL INJUSTICE AS A MOTIVATIONAL TECHNIQUE

There seem to have been many commanders in Vietnam who inflicted intentional injustice and humiliation on their subordinates to inflame their fighting spirit. The belief that rage at superiors is usefully channeled into rage at the enemy is quite ancient and is acknowledged in the *Iliad*. (4:446ff) Because the idea that there is great military advantage in displaced rage is so ingrained and widespread, it has not been critically examined. However, some armies with a reputation for formidable fighting spirit do not share this folk belief and its degrading practices.

From the point of view of subsequent PTSD and character damage, I see nothing but harm flowing from this folk belief. My impression is that its authority in American military culture peaked at the time of the Vietnam War, especially in the Marines and airborne forces. Training practices at that time especially reflected a positive view of humiliation and degradation as motivational techniques. When these attitudes were carried into the field, the moral injury they inflicted worsened the severity and persistence of psychological injury created by war itself. Humiliation and degradation usually *reduce* military effectiveness. A helicopter-pilot veteran in our program continues to suffer great rage and pain at the suicide of a much-admired fellow pilot the night after the following incident: While on a reconnaissance in a free fire zone, the pilot encountered a group of women and children. Upon hearing this over the radio net, the commanding officer ordered him to kill them. When he refused, the CO berated him as a coward and a weakling over the radio, and this was overheard by all the other pilots in the company. That night, the pilot blew his brains out.

Humiliation and degradation as techniques of motivation should be seen as signs of leadership failure and should result in swift, massive, and visible damage to an officer's career. The Israeli army, which is well known for its fighting spirit, does not encourage or value the berserk state, refrains from humiliation as a part of training and motivation, and places a high social value on grief for dead comrades.

RESPECT THE ENEMY AS HUMAN

Another cultural "truth" that I have disputed through my reading of the *Iliad* is the notion that fighting spirit depends upon dehumanization of the enemy. The *Iliad* shows that it is possible to regard the enemy as human and honorable like oneself and still fight with fierce tenacity. I have argued that viewing the enemy as subhuman vermin or nonhuman matter endangers soldiers' physical survival during war and moral recovery after it. I fear that the military folk culture that makes dehumanization of the enemy a self-evident, necessary truth will resist change because it has roots in biblical stories and attitudes. Chaplains would better serve the troops by reminding them that enemy soldiers are extremely dangerous, *because they are human just like us*, rather than perpetuating the image of the enemy as God-hated vermin who hardly know they're alive and "don't value human life like we do."

All levels of authority concerned with making war, from sergeant to president, must acquire the habit of honoring the enemy, if the nation is to avoid future hemorrhage of blood and spirit as in Vietnam—and to avoid defeats. This is one of the vital lessons of Vietnam that I fervently hope the military victory in the Persian Gulf has not obliterated. *The visible respect that the American military leadership had for the Iraqi forces was a necessary precondition for the technical superiority of American arms to be effective.* If the war had been conducted with the "turkey shoot" mentality that characterized the early years of the Vietnam War, the Gulf War could have cost thousands, possibly tens of thousands of American lives, with no less carnage and suffering on the Iraqi side. It is *logical* that the Persian Gulf military victory would strengthen the habit of respecting the enemy, but there is such strong cultural pressure to return to "We're number one!" that a war that was a walkover readily turns people back to the illusion that the next enemy is again "just Gooks," not to be taken seriously.

ACKNOWLEDGE PSYCHIATRIC CASUALTIES

Even with the best training, equipment, and leadership, prolonged fighting will inevitably cause psychiatric casualties. In World War II, one-third of all casualties were psychiatric. The very fact that the military services acknowledged that men *could* be broken by battle and evacuated them may have been a major factor that reduced the rate of life long psychological injuries from that war.

In Vietnam the official psychiatric casualty rate was less than 5 percent. We now know that this low rate did not reflect the true incidence of major psychological injury, but instead reflected a multilayered institutional illusion, denial, and fiat. The reasoning ran this way: Because the required tour of duty had been limited to one year, in response to statistical data from world War II indicating that breakdowns rose sharply after one year of combat, sol diers who break down must therefore be either malingering o suffering from personality disorders (= bad character) acquired during childhood. The ruling psychiatric theories of the day subscribed wholeheartedly to the idea that once a person had formed good character through good nurturing as a child, nothing in adult experience could do permanent harm. Someone who broke down was damaged goods to begin with and should be discharged as unfit or undesirable. The official diagnostic manual of the time did not even have a category for what prior generations had called "shell shock" or "combat neurosis" and the next generation would call "post-traumatic stress disorder." Men broken by combat did not exist—they had been theoretically and administratively ruled out.

WAR IS NOT AN INDUSTRIAL PROCESS

When I point out the harms done to our own soldiers by picturing the enemy as inanimate matter to be ground down by attrition, I am only echoing what Carl von Clausewitz wrote more than 150 years ago:

> War is not an exercise of the will directed at inanimate matter, as is the case with the mechanical arts, or at matter which is animate but passive and yielding. . . . In war, the will is directed at an animate object that *reacts*. It must be obvious that the intellectual codification used in the arts and sciences is inappropriate to such an activity. . . . Laws analogous to those appropriate to the realm of inanimate matter [were] bound to lead to one mistake after another.[9]

The laws that von Clausewitz refers to are the laws of Newtonian mechanics that commanded great prestige in his day. The sophisticated managers of the Vietnam War would have snickered at such a naive notion of military science at the same time as they were falling into precisely the same error. For the mechanical science of von Clausewitz's day, they substituted management science in the 1960s, when the "managerial" approach to warfare permeated the entire armed services. As sociologist James Gibson describes it:

> First, warfare is approached as a problem of organizing *quanti-*. The managerial approach secondly constructs various for the *production of warfare*. Using the model of the individual business firm in a capitalist economy, the defense managers

tried to find "profit maximization" in warfare. . . . A third step was necessary to complete the managerial approach: the foreign Other was conceptualized to act according to the *same* logic of "profit" maximization.[10]

American soldiers in the field knew that the rational economic models of attrition and "crossover" (when the enemy's rate of losses exceeded the rate of replacement, so that the enemy could no longer "afford" to continue the war) were delusory, except that soldiers themselves were a real, not delusory, "cost of production." They knew that their own powers of observation, innovation, and initiative were disregarded by their "better educated" leaders, who would listen to nothing coming from below, mirroring civilian industrial practices. Soldiers in the field knew that the war was managed "by the numbers," that their combat units were socially unreal paper fictions assembled from off-the-shelf "replacements." They grew to believe that all that mattered to military commanders was that things looked good on paper, because it was the numbers on paper that the officers managed. Soldiers saw that their officer-managers were not loyal to the substance of their task. Officers were obsessed with numerical performance that would bring their own advancement, rather than with substantive military accomplishment.

They also saw that their superior officers did not taste the hazards of war.

PISSING CONTESTS

One would think that severe psychological injury would give rise naturally to shared compassion and mutual respect among the many diverse groups of trauma survivors, such as have lived through genocide, political torture, domestic battering, incest, war, abusive religious cults, and coerced prostitution. Unfortunately, it has not. Veterans call it "pissing contests" when one veteran denies the validity of another veteran's war trauma. Different survivor groups eagerly start these competitions as well, each claiming that their experience is the only significant one. An intern in our program approached a battered women's shelter for further training opportunities; when she spoke of her experience with combat veterans, the person at the shelter scoffed and said, "That was twenty years ago. This is now!" Holocaust scholars have disparaged the writings of incest survivors as merely "confessional."[11] These pissing contests only serve the interests of perpetrators, all perpetrators. It gives me great pain whenever I hear such disparagement among veterans or among survivor groups. No person's suffering is commensurable with any other.

SPECIES ETHIC

Homer worked at the beginning of a new era of unification for his people. Recently invented "city-states" that made ceaseless war upon one another began to recognize their commonality, through both joining the Olympic games and seeing the shared culture that traveling singers like Homer made visible or created. I have presented a reading of the *Iliad* that is deeply opposed to war but just as deeply respectful of the soldier. I hope that hating war while honoring the soldier no longer seems like an absurd or impossible contradiction.

Dare we hope that we, like Homer, stand at the beginning of a new era of unification, of worldwide commonality, when wars can be ended by trustworthy structures of collective security? In the face of intractable horrors like the dismemberment of Bosnia, an actual permanent end to wars seems like an impossible dream that only a fool would spend any time or money on. War has always been with us, after all. Perhaps it is intrinsic to human nature. I often despair that the array of cultural, economic, and social forces in support of warfare simply are impossible to overcome, ever. However, as William of Occam pointed out in the fourteenth century: What is, is possible. Just a few centuries ago, the social institutions of chattel slavery and serfdom were supported by powerful interests and seemed just as universal, ancient, and natural as war seems today. Slavery was worldwide, unarguably knit into every corner of every culture, and yet today it is gone, or at least no longer legally condoned.[12] We have achieved a species-wide moral consensus on the subject of slavery, arguably the first component of a species ethic.

The *Iliad*'s prevailing message on what is of value in life is not Achilles' *kléos áphthiton*,[13] "unfailing glory," but rather the social attachments of the domestic world at peace. Here is a collage of Homeric passages that bring out this subtext:

                        On slopes of Ida
descending, by the banks of clear Simóeis,
his mother had conceived him, while she kept
a vigil with her parents over flocks;
he got his name for this. . . . (4:572ff)
                        A rich man
and kindly, he befriended all who passed
his manor by the road. (6:14ff)
                This man had married
Hippodameia, eldest of the daughters,
dearest to her father and gentle mother
in their great hall. In beauty, skill, and wit,
she had excelled all girls of her own age. (13:488ff)
        . . . your sister's husband, who made you his ward
when you were still a small child in his house. (13:530f)
They passed the lookout point, the wild figtree
with wind in all its leaves, then veered away
along the curving wagon road, and came
to where the double fountains well, the source
of eddying Skamánder. One hot spring
flows out, and from the water fumes arise
as though from fire burning; but the other
even in summer gushes chill as hail
or snow or crystal ice frozen on water.
Near these fountains are wide washing pools
of smooth-laid stone, where Trojan wives and daughters
laundered their smooth linen in the days
of peace before the Akhaians came. (22:174ff)

Our animal nature, our biological nature, is to live in relation to other people. The natural environment of humans is primarily culture, not the "natural world," narrowly defined as other species, climate, etc. The sudden and startling growth of the human brain around one million years ago was not in response to saber-toothed tigers, retreating glaciers, nor the intellectual challenge of getting a nutmeat out of its shell, but in response to the emergence of culture itself.[14] The brain mechanisms of self-defense, of predation, of territoriality, of sexual and family group affiliation, and of defending offspring have not been supplanted by culture, but rather speak through it in ways that we poorly understand. Culture is not an illusory, movie-theater projection of bodily "drives" or "instincts," nor is the body a metaphor, wholly constructed by culture. Culture is as biologically real for humans as the body. Unless in a coma, we are always *both* culture bearers and bodies at every moment.

The study of combat trauma and of other severe psychological traumas brings us unavoidably to both the body and to culture. I have emphasized the cultural dimension by focusing on betrayal of "what's right." The specific content of "what's right" varies immensely from culture to culture. Does this mean that everything is relative? The centrality of culture in human life is *not* culturally relative; it is a species universal. But given the diversity in the content of culture, do we have any firm place to stand in discovering a species ethic?

I believe we do. Let me offer a series of propositions:

- We are one species, sharing a common physiology and a common biological disposition to acquire culture.
- When the body is tortured or its boundaries are violated, or it is otherwise assaulted such as by starvation, sleep deprivation, cold, or drugs under conditions in which escape is impossible, the body reacts with fear and rage, and the mind undergoes a distinctive kind of deep learning.
- When "what's right" is violated in a high-stakes situation in any culture, regardless of the specific content of the *thémis* that is violated, the body reacts the same way, with fear and rage, and the mind undergoes deep learning.
- The two together, physical violation and moral violation, destroy the capacity for a flourishing life wherever on the globe they occur.
- After the danger and violation have passed, the deep learning persists as PTSD symptoms and as damage to the best (most highly valued) character as understood within the culture.[15]
- Species-wide ethical rule: Refrain from doing that which causes PTSD symptoms and character damage.

I believe that these propositions are not culturally relative. I believe that they can be derived from biological characteristics of the human species. Unfortunately, nothing in our biology requires assent to these propositions.

Scientific knowledge about how traumatic experience translates into psychological injury can be used to found a science of human rights that is independent of specific cultural bias. *One human being violates the human rights of another by intentionally acting upon the other in a manner that causes PTSD and character damage.* Unfortunately, the same scientific knowledge that can define a science of human rights can be used to perfect a science of tyranny. Anyone who understands the causes of PTSD and character damage can train torturers. Tyrants surround themselves with broken-willed people who flatter, obey instantly, and anticipate the tyrant's wishes. Conditions of coercive control are well suited to produce this kind of human being who, when told to jump, will reply, "How high?"

The social institution of war is a contest of two organized groups, each attempting to exercise tyranny over the other through violence, terror, and threat. In my view, war always represents a violation of soldiers' human rights in which the enemy and the soldiers' own armies collaborate more or less equally. However, until we end wars, we will need men and women to do the military work of collective security that allows the establishment of peace. Peacekeeping and peacemaking will require soldiers. In the face of this necessity, we must protect these soldiers with every strength we have, and honor and care for them when inevitably they are injured by their service.

With what kind of human beings do we want to surround ourselves for our own flourishing? If we want to live among equals with strength and candor, among people with, as Euripides says, "free and generous eyes," the understanding of trauma can form a solid basis for a science of human rights. There is, of course, no scientific basis for preferring to be surrounded by free equals rather than by cowering slaves. When Lincoln wrote, "As I would not be a *slave*, so I would not be a *master*," he did not claim any rational compulsion for what he would not be. This vision of a good life for a human being is an ethical choice and cannot be coerced. It can only be called forth by persuasion, education, and welcoming appeal.

NOTES

INTRODUCTION

1. This is a composite voice of actual veterans in our program, edited to make the composite cohesive and to disguise their identities. All subsequent quotes from veterans are single voices, transcribed and edited from tape, from my notes, or from narratives written by veterans.
2. The statistics of the Vietnam generation are discussed in Chapter 8.
3. Paul Fussell, *The Great War and Modern Memory* (London: Oxford University Press, 1975), 169f.

CHAPTER 1: BETRAYAL OF "WHAT'S RIGHT"

1. Martha C. Nussbaum, *The Fragility of Goodness: Luck and Ethics in Greek Tragedy and Philosophy* (Cambridge: Cambridge University Press, 1986), 397–421. Nussbaum's excellent discussion centers on *nómos*, a word that largely supplanted *thémis* in this semantic range. The word *nómos*, which was much used by the Athenian tragic poets, such as Sophocles, is not found in Homer.
2. Most *Iliad* citations refer to Robert Fitzgerald's translation (New York: Anchor-Doubleday, 1974). They are in the form Book:Line Number(s). Fitzgerald's line numbers are, on average, 16 percent higher than line numbers in the original because of the poetic form of his translation. However, an interested reader will usually have little difficulty in finding quotations in the original. Multiplying Fitzgerald's line number by 0.86 usually yields a line number that is within one or two of the correct one in the original. However, occasional estimates are off by as much as twenty lines. I hope that classicists who read this book will forgive the blunt-edged anachronism of calling Achaeans, Danaäns, and Argives all "Greeks." I have followed Fitzgerald's spelling of proper names with the exception of "Akhilleus"; in this case I used the conventional English, Achilles, instead.
    Where I have used Robert Fagles's excellent new translation (New York: Viking Penguin, 1990), I have so indicated, and the line numberings refer in these passages to his translation.
    When *Iliad* citations indicate that the line numbering is to the Greek original, the edition I used was the two-volume Loeb edition prepared by

1–12 in vol. 1 and books 13–24 in vol. 2. *Odyssey* citations refer to the Fitzgerald translation (New York: Vintage, 1990).

3. Thetis to Zeus, 1:579ff; Brisêis, 9:411ff; also, she was arguably Achilles' betrothed, 19:328ff.

4. This analysis derives from Elaine Scarry, "The Structure of War" in *The Body in Pain: The Unmaking and Making of the World* (New York: Oxford University Press, 1985).

5. My esteemed colleague in the International Society for Traumatic Stress Studies, John Sommer, Jr., who is himself a Vietnam combat veteran and Executive Director of the Washington, D.C. office of the American Legion, has asked me to point out that the treatment experienced by my patients was contrary to the policy of the organization and by no means universal among the 16,000 posts of the American Legion. He describes his own experiences as quite positive and regards the 800,000 Vietnam-era members (out of a total of 3.1 milion) as evidence of widespread support for them in the American legion.

6. Carl von Clausewitz, *On War*, ed. and trans. Michael Howard and Peter Paret (published posthumously in 1832; reprint, Princeton: Princeton University Press, 1984), 113. The title of this section is also von Clausewitz's.

7. Ibid.

8. Paul Fussell, *Wartime: Understanding and Behavior in the Second World War* (New York: Oxford University Press, 1989), 268ff.

9. Ibid., 80.

10. Ibid., 81.

11. Patrols moved single file with space between men. The first man, who was said to be "walking point," was the first to meet mines and booby traps and often the first to be exposed to enemy fire. When enemy ambushers maintained their discipline, they often let "point" and "slack" (the second man) go through and attacked the middle of the file, creating greater shock, confusion, and disruption of unit cohesion than if the first or last ("sweep") man were attacked.

12. Edward Luttwak, *The Pentagon and the Art of War: The Question of Military Reform* (New York: Simon & Schuster, 1985.), 34f.

13. Martin van Creveld, *Command in War* (Cambridge: Harvard University Press, 1985), 255f.

14. This word has now come to mean almost exclusively someone who holds someone else's money in trust. The original meaning of *fiducia*, under Roman law, was the holding of a free *person* in trust.

15. There are numerous writings on the various command pathologies pandemic in the Vietnam War. Among critiques from sources that are impossible to characterize as pacifistic or antimilitary are: Edward Luttwak, *Pentagon and the Art of War*, particularly the first chapter, "The Anatomy of Military Failure"; Martin van Creveld, *Command in War*, particularly chapter 7, "The Helicopter and the Computer"; David H. Hackworth, *About Face* (New York: Simon & Schuster, 1989), 449f on "ticket punching" (Retired General Harold Moore excoriates the practice as well); and Lieutenant General Harold G. Moore and Joseph L. Galloway, *We Were Soldiers Once . . . and Young* (New York: Random House, 1992), 344.

16. Operation Union I, begun by the First Marine Division against NVA in Quang Nam and Quang Tin Provinces on April 21, 1967. Union II followed and ended on June 5.
17. Colonel Harry G. Summers, Jr., *Vietnam War Almanac* (New York: Facts on File, 1985), 234. Moore and Galloway quote one air cavalry trooper as going through three M-16s in the Ia Drang battle before finding a fourth that worked. Another describes the trigger mechanism falling out, another simply that the M-16 he tried to fire was "inoperable." Moore and Galloway, *We Were Soldiers Once*, 89, 97, 100.
18. Gregory Nagy, *The Best of the Achaeans: Concepts of the Hero in Archaic Greek Poetry* (Baltimore: Johns Hopkins University Press, 1979) 75 n. 1.

CHAPTER 2: SHRINKAGE OF THE SOCIAL AND MORAL HORIZON

1. Achilles and Agamemnon seem to have a "history." But what is it? Zanker (*The Heart of Achilles*, 75–79) marshals the evidence that it was a "political" struggle over honor, influence, and power in the army. I have argued that their "history" could also technically have been military disagreements over the conduct of amphibious operations (*Classical Bulletin* 71, no. 1, 1995).
2. Gregory Nagy, *The Best of the Achaeans: Concepts of the Hero in Archaic Greek Poetry* (Baltimore: Johns Hopkins University Press, 1979), 69.
3. The Greek expeditionary force consisted of twenty-nine independent contingents. In Vietnam there were military contingents from the United States, Australia, South Korea, Thailand, New Zealand, the Philippines, and Taiwan.
4. Desertion during the Vietnam War is a complex subject. See Lawrence M. Baskir and William A. Strauss, *Chance and Circumstance: The Draft, the War and the Vietnam Generation* (New York: Vintage Books, 1978), 109–166. Also see Edward Luttwak, *The Pentagon and the Art of War: The Question of Military Reform* (New York: Simon & Schuster, 1985), 34:
   "In Vietnam, the deserter could not blend into the population nor easily leave the country. . . . In 1944, when many Army troops found themselves in France as well as Italy and Belgium, all places then poorly policed, quite hospitable, and undoubtedly attractive, the Army's desertion rate reached 63 per 1,000. . . . During the Vietnam war the rate per 1,000 increased year by year from 29.1 in 1968 to a peak of 73.4 in 1971."
5. Neil Sheehan, *A Bright Shining Lie: John Paul Vann and America in Vietnam* (New York: Random House, 1988), 741.
6. Dolôn, 10:423ff; Adréstos, 6:66ff; sons of Antímakhos, 11:148ff; Kleóboulos, 16:386ff.
7. Martha C. Nussbaum, *The Fragility of Goodness: Luck and Ethics in Greek Tragedy and Philosophy* (Cambridge: Cambridge University Press, 1986), 417. I owe the concept of moral luck to Nussbaum; see in particular the final chapter of *The Fragility of Goodness* and her introduction to C. K. Williams's translation of Euripides' *The Bacchae* (New York: Farrar, Strauss and Giroux, 1990).

8. A Shau Valley, a rugged, remote, and relatively uninhabited area near the Laotian border in the northernmost part of South Vietnam. The best known battle in the area took place on Ap Bia Mountain, remembered as "Hamburger Hill."

9. Homer initiated one broad tradition of tragic narrative. The tragic poets of the Athenian theater continued his tradition and added another: the fatal conflict of two valid claims. King Oedipus must choose between the future of his family (including himself) and an end to the plague in his city; Antigone's valid family piety collides with Creon's valid statecraft; King Agamémnon must choose between the life of his daughter and the lives of his soldiers, who were dying in the wind-locked ships at Aulis, not to speak of the direct command of Zeus to sail against the Trojans. Veterans' experiences described in this book were mainly tragedies of the sort suffered by Achilles. However, the veterans also suffer from the guilt of tragic collisions painfully probed by Sophocles, Aeschylus, and Euripides: guilt from situations where two valid, conflicting claims both lead to fatal actions. One Marine veteran in our program is hounded by the memory of a close friend who was wounded, unable to move, and screaming in agony for someone to please kill him. The North Vietnamese were using him as bait for their ambush and killed one after another would-be rescuer. Our patient, seeing no alternative, shot his friend to prevent more deaths. Another man is tormented by the memory of entering a village from the south while other, inexperienced soldiers were entering it from the east. A Vietnamese baby was sitting in the crossroads at the center of the village. Our patient could see remote trigger wires running to the spot under the baby and began to shout and wave his arms at the other soldiers not to go near the baby. The other soldiers could not hear and simply waved back. Seeing no alternative, our patient fired a burst from his M-60 into the baby, setting off a large explosion. Literary tragedy takes its time and fills in details that show us there was *no* harmless course of action in the conflicts suffered by Oedipus, Agamemnon, or Creon's son Haemon. A soldier's grasp of the possibilities of his situation is always limited in the urgency of battle, and his account to us and our understanding are likewise incomplete. We do our patients terrible injustice if we negate their accounts of tragic conflicts. How easy it is to imagine: *I* would have perceived a nontragic course of action, seen a way out; *I* would have known which moral claim to honor; *I* would have resisted pressures from my emotions, my comrades, my superiors. Nussbaum, *Fragility of Goodness*; particularly instructive are chapter 2, "Aeschylus and Practical Conflict," and chapter 3, "Sophocles' *Antigone*: Conflict, Vision, and Simplification."

10. Elaine Scarry, *The Body in Pain: The Unmaking and Making of the World* (New York: Oxford University Press, 1985), 40f.

11. Carl von Clausewitz, *On War*, ed. and trans. Michael Howard and Peter Paret (Princeton: Princeton University Press, 1984), 605.

CHAPTER 3: GRIEF AT THE DEATH OF A SPECIAL COMRADE

1. It is used between David and Jonathan in the Bible (1 Samuel 1:26) and between Gilgamesh and Enkidu (e.g., *Ancient Near Eastern Texts Relating to the Old Testament*, Third Editions. Edited by J. B. Pritchard. Princeton: Princeton University Press, 1969), 86.

2. Martha C. Nussbaum, *The Fragility of Goodness: Luck and Ethics in Greek Tragedy and Philosophy* (Cambridge: Cambridge University Press, 1986), 354. Citations of the word *philos* and related words in the *Iliad* and *Odyssey* fill a whole page of R. J. Cunliffe's *Lexicon of the Homeric Dialect* (1924; reprint, Norman: University of Oklahoma Press, 1963), 408–409.

3. Pátroklos is not an orphan but rather an alien fugitive, the son of a foreign friend of Achilles' father, Pêleus. Pátroklos's father, Menoitios, apparently spends extended periods in Pêleus's court and is present when Nestor and Odysseus come to recruit Achilles for the expedition against Troy. (11:885ff) Pêleus has virtually, if not legally, adopted Pátroklos.

4. If we were to hand the *Iliad* and no other Greek text to a perceptive reader with no prior exposure to ancient Greece, this reader would declare that according to the text, physical intimacies occurred *only* between heterosexual couples consisting variously of humans, gods, and animals. The sole sexual context involving Achilles and Pátroklos together in the *Iliad* is heterosexual:

> Akhilleus slept in the well-built hut's recess,
> and with him lay a woman he had brought
> from Lesbos, Phorbas' daughter, Diomêdê.
> Pátroklos went to bed at the other end,
> and with him, too, a woman lay—soft-belted
> Iphis, who had been given to him by Akhilleus
> when he took Skyros. . . . (9:805ff)

When Thetis comes to Achilles with Zeus's command to release Hektor's corpse, she observes his intense grief, insomnia, and loss of appetite and advises erototherapy. Note that her assumption is lovemaking with a woman, not with a male youth:

> Thetis . . . found him groaning there,
> inconsolable, while men-at-arms
> went to and fro, making their breakfast ready. . . .
> His gentle mother sat down at his side,
> caressed him, and said tenderly:
> "My child,
> will you forever feed on your own heart
> in grief and pain, and take no thought of sleep
> or sustenance? It would be comforting
> to make love with a woman. . . ." (24:145ff)

But cultures change. Three centuries after Homer, the tragic poet Aeschylus wrote a trilogy called *Achilleis*, now lost, which was famous in antiquity for its erotic explicitness. A surviving fragment has Achilles addressing the dead Pátroklos: "And you felt no compunction for my pure reverence for your thighs—O, what an ill return you have made for so many kisses!" (See Kenneth Dover, *Greek Homosexuality* [Cambridge: Harvard University Press, 1978], 197. This is Dover's translation.) The partygoers in Plato's *Symposium* could not imagine otherwise than their own enthusiasm for homoerotic relationships and projected it backward into the *Iliad*, which was read with as much reverence then as many people today read the Bible. In Plato's time, homosexual love was accorded the same cultural prestige that Christian culture a millennium later would accord to celibacy. (For a precise understanding of how much ancient Greek homosexuality differed from modern ideals of equality and mutuality, see David M. Halperin, *One Hundred Years of Homosexuality and Other Essays on Greek Love* [New York: Routledge, 1990.])

Dover makes the interesting argument that the pederastic love between a mature citizen (*erastes*) and a citizen youth (*eromenos*) was a sort of rite of passage that bound the new generation of boys to the polity/army. Every male citizen was a soldier, and the core duties of the citizen were military. Traits that most perfectly described a beautiful, desirable youth coincide exactly with traits that made him desirable as a potential fighter: strength, speed, endurance, courage, and modesty before his seniors. (Dover, *Greek Homosexuality*, 185ff, particularly 201–203.) Plato has Pausanius argue that an army of lovers could not be defeated, because their bravery in defense of each other would preclude cowardice. (*Symposium* 182a–b) On the subject of sexual couples in ancient Greek military organizations, see Dover, *Greek Homosexuality*, 191ff.

The *Iliad* contributes nothing either way to the debate over whether gay and lesbian soldiers are a good thing for the army in which they serve. The question is irrelevant to the subject at hand. It only provides an excuse to push from one's thoughts the humanity of soldiers and the great love that they feel for one another.

5. Professor Majno's survey of ancient wound management speculates that it was onion, not yarrow. Guido Majno, *The Healing Hand* (Cambridge: Harvard University Press, 1975), 143, 143 n17.

6. E.g., 2 Samuel 13:19 (King James Version): "And Tamar put ashes on her head . . ."

7. See Renato Rosaldo, *Culture and Truth: The Remaking of Social Analysis* (Boston: Beacon Press, 1989), 56–58.

8. This analysis follows that of Seth L. Schein, *The Mortal Hero: An Introduction to Homer's Iliad* (Berkeley: University of California Press, 1984), 129–132. Cloud of death, e.g., 20:479; clawing the earth, e.g., 11:485, 13:593, 17:353; female mourners beating their breasts, 18:33, 18:56; *göoio* = death lament, 24:840, 894, 911; chief mourner holding head, cf. Achilles holding Pátroklos's head, 23:158, and Andrómakhê holding Hektor's head, 24:865. This ritual gesture is seen on Geometric vase paintings contemporary with Homer.

9. Renato Rosaldo, "Grief and a Headhunter's Rage: On the Cultural Force of Emotions," in *Text, Play, and Story: the Construction and Reconstruction of Self and Society*, ed. E. M. Brunner (Washington: American Ethnological Society, 1984), 178–195. Rosaldo stops short of claiming that in the emergence of rage from the headhunter's grief, he has uncovered a biological universal, an emotion unformed by culture.

See also Renato Rosaldo, *Culture and Truth*, 227 n. 12.

10. A short-timer, customarily someone who was within a month of DEROS (Date Eligible to Return from Overseas, also used as a verb, as "When I DEROSed . . ."). A tremendous dread attached to this period as a time of maximum danger of death. In many units it was customary to exempt short-timers from the more dangerous duties, especially during the last two weeks, and often to allow them to return to a base near the main portals, Long Binh, Ton Son Nhut, and Da Nang.

11. This is in addition, of course, to the young age at which the trauma usually occurs and to the massiveness of betrayal of "what's right" in this abuse of power. See Susan Roth and Leslie Lebowitz, "The Experience of Sexual Trauma," *Journal of Traumatic Stress*, 1988, Vol. 1:79–107.

12. Marking bodies for easy spotting from the air is also consistent with a self-protective motive on the part of the NVA, who did not want Americans to track them in order to recover the bodies. Most of the better American units went to great lengths to "leave nobody behind," dead or alive, and would track blood traces and drag marks through the bush to recover dead comrades, sometimes surprising and killing the enemy soldiers who had dragged them away.

13. Graves Registration itself picked up the dead from units in the field by ambulance or helicopter whenever possible. Medevac, Vietnam jargon for medical evacuation, was usually by helicopter; it was also known as Dustoff. The bravery and determination of Dustoff crews in landing almost anywhere, regardless of enemy fire, bad visibility, or dangerous weather, saved very many lives. In the pithy words of a veteran, "Them Dustoff pilots had bra-a-ass balls."

14. See David H. Hackworth, *About Face* (New York: Simon & Schuster, 1989), 633–634, 634 n.

15. The dark side of such unit cohesion is evident in this veteran's willingness, explicitly without their consent, to endanger the lives of the air crew. He acknowledges this:

> I remember when we were leaving the fucking helicopter, the fucking helicopter just almost fucking flipped over, because we all went out at the same fucking time.

CHAPTER 4: GUILT AND WRONGFUL SUBSTITUTION

1. Much has been written about the vast subject of guilt after combat. I limit myself here to the guilt that Homer portrays. Here are some of the other burdens of guilt that Vietnam combat veterans carry: guilt from responsibility for accidental American or Vietnamese civilian casualties, guilt from situations where the only visible courses of action led to fatal outcomes for Americans or civilians ("tragic" guilt), guilt from atrocities committed carrying out orders or while berserk, and guilt from carrying out or failing to carry out a "buddy pact" (an agreement between two comrades that if one is wounded in specific horrible ways, the other will kill him rather than leave him to live as "half a man").

2. Gregory Nagy, *The Best of the Achaeans: Concepts of the Hero in Archaic Greek Poetry* (Baltimore: Johns Hopkins University Press, 1979), 292–295.

3. Danieli speaks of the "four existential functions of guilt": to deny help-lessness, to keep the dead alive by making them ever-present in thought, to sustain loyalty to the dead, and to affirm that the world is still a just place when somebody (even if only the guilt-ridden survivor) feels guilt at what was done. Yaël Danieli, "Countertransference" (paper delivered at the Seventh Annual Meeting of the International Society for Traumatic Stress Studies, Washington, D.C., 1991).

CHAPTER 5: BERSERK

1. From some etymological evidence, it appears the Norse warrior believed that by donning a bearskin he would become a rampaging bear through magical transformation. However, other evidence connects the word to "baresark," meaning "bare shirt," i.e., without armor. J. A. Simpson and E. S. C. Weiner, eds., *Oxford English Dictionary*, 2d ed. (Oxford: Oxford University Press, 1989), II:128, *berserk*; I:953, *baresark*.
2. Katherine C. King has traced the fascinating evolution of the figure of Achilles since Homer in *Achilles: Paradigms of the War Hero from Homer to the Middle Ages* (Berkeley: University of California Press, 1987).
3. Mark W. Edwards, *Homer, the Poet of the Iliad* (Baltimore: Johns Hopkins University Press, 1987), 79.
4. Betrayal, insult, or humiliation by a leader: Achilles 1:1–496, Diomêdês 4:446ff, Agamémnon (by Zeus) 9:16ff, Hektor 17:159 (by Glaukos); death of a friend-in-arms or relative: Hektor (his cousin, Kalêtôr) 15:485, Pátroklos 16:657ff, Achilles 18:20ff; being wounded: Diomêdês 5:113ff, Hektor 14:461ff, Achilles 21:195f; being overrun, surrounded, or trapped: Agamémnon 10:11ff; seeing fellow soldiers' bodies mutilated by the enemy: Achilles 18:20ff (also, anticipated and reported to inflame him, 18:204ff).
5. The appalling aphorism "Don't get mad. Get even!" may also have circu-lated at the time, but this is not what the veterans quote to me.
6. This word occurs ten times in the *Iliad*. Citing line numbers in the Greek original, followed by line numbers in the Fitzgerald translation, the occurrences are these—3:290/342–6: Agamémnon seems to distinguish revenge blood-price [*poinê*] from tribute [*tîmê*] yielded as political settle-ment to end a war. 5:266/308: Zeus gives horses to Trôs as "fee" for Ganymede. 9:633, 636/77, 774: Aías tells Odysseus that a normal man takes blood-price for a killed brother or son: "<u>Fury and pride in the bereaved are curbed when he accepts the penalty [blood-price]</u>." 13:659/755: A father grieves—no blood-price has been received for a son killed in battle. 14:483/544: Akámas kills Prómakhos, "and no delay in the penalty for my brother's death. See why a soldier prays that a kinsman left at home will fight for him?" 16:398/462: Pátroklos is shown "taking toll for many dead Akhaians." 17:207/231: Zeus gives Hektor superior fighting power for the time being as recompense for his wife, Andrómakhê, never receiving Achilles' arms from him, i.e., returning alive. 18:498/572: On shield of Achilles, satisfaction owed for a (kins-man's) murder. 21:28/32: Achilles takes twelve young men alive to pay the price for dead Pátroklos, his foster brother.

7. Diomêdês, Agamémnon, and Hektor compared to a lion: 5:158ff, 11:199ff, and 12:48ff, respectively; Pátroklos compared to a hawk: 16:671f; Achilles eating Hektor: 22:410.

8. See Martha C. Nussbaum, Introduction to Euripides' *The Bacchae*, trans. C. K. Williams (New York: Noonday Press, 1990), xvii–ix. She writes:

> God seems to have something in common with beast, and neither really has the moral virtues. . . . This complex idea makes its first appearance in the Greek tradition in Homer, leading to a depiction of the gods as rather light and frivolous beings, lacking the ethical seriousness that comes to mortals through their constant engagement with death and other limits. [Gods are] incapable therefore of true courage, grief, or risk-taking loyalty. . . . Throughout this complex tradition, then, the gods, insofar as they lack ethical seriousness and compassion for suffering, touch hands with the bestial.

9. Cf. Martha C. Nussbaum, *The Fragility of Goodness: Luck and Ethics in Greek Tragedy and Philosophy* (Cambridge: Cambridge University Press, 1986), 340ff; Aristotle, *Nicomachian Ethics*, Book X, 1178b. For further clarification of the Aristotelian dependence of virtue on mortality, see Martha C. Nussbaum, "Non-Relative Virtues: An Aristotelian Approach" in *The Quality of Life*, ed. Martha C. Nussbaum and Amartya Sen (Oxford: Clarendon Press, 1993), 242–269.

10. The phenomenon I explore here is an isolating, individual phenomenon. However, it clearly overlaps in some respects with the psychological and physiological state of frenzy that takes hold during mob violence. The exact relationship between the two, and particularly the question of whether the postfrenzy consequences are similar, deserve serious study.

11. Just as *aristeía* is too broad to be an exact equivalent of berserk, *aidôs*—shame, respect, social restraint—is too narrow a description of what the berserker loses when he "loses it."

12. Diomêdês' father was the same Tydeus who, as he was dying, cannibalized Melanippos after their mutually fatal battle.

13. Clinicians working with combat veterans need to be aware that berserking may arouse a lust to eat the enemy. Even the remembered wish is extremely disturbing to veterans, and when it has been carried out, the ensuing post-traumatic stress disorder is particularly devastating and intractable.

14. The *Odyssey*, 11:91, 147–149. See Gregory Nagy, *Greek Mythology and Poetics* (Ithaca: Cornell University Press, 1990), 92.

15. The ghost of Pátroklos, 23:80ff; the gods, 24:39ff and 135ff; the narrator, 22:466ff and 23:19ff.

16. This has the ring of naked racism, devoid of substantive military content. However, it reflects a factual report of the role of smell in detecting the enemy *by both sides*. The diet of the Vietnamese enemy included the nutritious but highly fragrant fermented fish and garlic sauce called *nuoc mam*. A sign of American negligence was the use of aftershave lotion and perfumed soaps ("Aren't you glad you use Dial!"), which could be scented by the enemy hundreds of yards downwind and for lesser distances upwind. One newly arrived airborne veteran was rejected by the sergeant

of the platoon he was first assigned to; the sergeant said, "I don't want him. I can *smell* him"— meaning that he smelled "clean" and so would endanger everyone he was with. American reconnaissance teams operating for prolonged periods in enemy territory not only banished Dial soap but smeared *nuoc mam* on their gear.

17. Tells mother, 18:92f; has spear, 16:162f. The schoolchild story of Achilles' "invulnerability" is a mockery of Homer and should be dropped. I speculate that Homer is unable to send Achilles into battle until his lost armor is magically replaced because of the enormous economic value and social significance that Homeric warriors (and Homer's noble audience) invested in armor. Fitzgerald's translation uses the words *armor* seventy times and *gear* forty-two times. Achilles' berserk state makes fighting without armor not only possible but even attractive for him. I believe that Homer understood the berserker's readiness to go into battle naked of any armor. It would not have been beyond this poet's power to create scenes of convincing mayhem by an unarmored Achilles with nothing but his spear and other weapons picked up from men he killed along the way. However, Homer's audience would have felt that a naked Achilles devalued the wealth, honor, and political legitimacy embodied in their own captured and inherited armor. When a Homeric warrior stopped in the middle of a raging battle to strip armor from a fallen enemy, he was not showing lack of discipline, as it appears in modern eyes. He paused to acquire the very substance of honor, which is largely why he fought at all.

18. R. A. Kulka et al., *National Vietnam Veterans Readjustment Study*, VII-20-1f: Distinguishing combat veterans from other veterans by "high warzone stressor exposure."

19. Rudyard Kipling, *Diversity of Creatures* (Garden City, NY: Doubleday, Page and Co., 1917), 264.

CHAPTER 6: DISHONORING THE ENEMY

1. William P. Mahedy, *Out of the Night: The Spiritual Journey of Vietnam Vets* (New York: Ballantine Books, 1986), 15.
2. This corrects misstatements in the hardcover edition about which a number of reviewers have raised critical questions. I had given the location as Hue and the time as after Tet, 1968, from my notes made from memory early in my work with Vietnam veterans. I misremembered the facts. I had asked the veteran who gave me this narrative three times to check over what I was using of his story for his permission and for accuracy. He apparently dissociated while reading the manuscript and did not notice my error. He now informs me that it was the Pat Smith Hospital (or clinic) for Montagnards in Kontum and that it was after Tet, 1969. I have so far been unable to verify this story.
3. Princeton professor Richard P. Martin argues on the contrary that Diomêdês's speech throughout is insulting and mocking, not respectful. See his *The Language of Heroes: Speech and Performance in the Iliad*

(Ithaca: Cornell University Press, 1989), 126–30.
4. Direct speech between enemies:

1.) Trojans to Greeks (respectful): Pándaros to Diomêdês, 5:321; Glaukos to Diomêdês, 6:168; Hektor to Aías, 7:275, 339; Sôkos to Odysseus, 11:490; Hektor to Achilles, 20:499; Asteropaíos to Achilles, 21:180; Aineías to Achilles, 20:231.
2.) Trojans to Greeks (contemptuous, critical, or insulting): Hektor to Diomêdês, 8:186; Hektor to Aías, 13:946; Akámas to unnamed Trojans over Prómakhos's corpse, 14:538; Aineías to Meríonês, 16:707.
3.) Greeks to Trojans (respectful): Diomêdês to Glaukos, 6:140, 254; Meríonês to Aineías, 16:710.
4.) Greeks to Trojans (contemptuous, critical, or insulting): Tlêpólemos to Sarpêdôn, 5:723; Diomêdês to Hektor, 11:413; Diomêdês to Aléxandros, 11:439; Idómeneus to Dêíphobos, 13:511; Meneláos to corpse of Peísandros, 13:709; Pátroklos to corpse of Kebríonês, 16:856; Achilles to many, books 20–22.

5. Soldiers talk to each other about the enemy:

1.) Trojans about Greeks (respectful): Glaukos to Hektor about Achilles, Aías, 17:184; Hektor to Trojan army about Achilles, 20:420.
2.) Trojans about Greeks (contemptuous, critical, or insulting): none.
3.) Greeks about Trojans (respectful): Agamémnon to Meneláos about Troy, 4:200; Diomêdês to his company about Hektor, 5:685; Agamémnon to Greek army about Hektor, 9:154; ghost of Pátroklos to Achilles about Trojans, 23:96.
4.) Greeks about Trojans (contemptuous, critical, or insulting): Agamémnon to Meneláos about Trojans, 4:190, 216; Aías to companions about Trojans, 15:592.

To put negative comments about the enemy in context, compare their relatively objective tone with the abuse that the Greeks heaped on each other: 1:145, 175, 183, 265; 2:229; 4:290, 327, 446; 8:104, 260; 16:9; 19:300.
6. Later Greeks did debase foreign, "barbarian" enemies every bit as much as modern Americans. See Edith Hall, *Inventing the Barbarian* (New York: Oxford University Press, 1991).
7. The most likely date for the composition of the *Iliad* is in the years from 725 to 675 B.C.E., which is also the time of the earliest Greek writing. This borrowed the Semitic alphabet of the Phoenicians, who the Greeks imagined were descended from Phoinix, Achilles' father-surrogate on the expedition to Troy. Archaeological evidence for Phoenician imports into Greece dates from the ninth century B.C.E., and an example is mentioned in the *Iliad* at 23:852ff: "Never a mixing bowl in all the world could match its beauty: artisans of Sidon had lavished art upon it. Phoinikians had brought it out by sea." Rf. Bernard Knox, Introduction to the *Iliad*, trans. Robert Fagles (New York: Viking, 1990), 8, 19, 21.

If we date Saul around 1010 B.C.E., it is plausible that Goliath's Philistines shared a common culture with the Greek and Trojan warriors of the *Iliad*. Around the time of the Trojan War (ca. 1200 B.C.E.), the Philistines, an Aegean people from Crete, colonized the southern coast of Palestine. Crete also sent to Troy the large contingent under Idómeneus in support of Meneláos and Agamémnon. (2:765ff, 3:274ff) The Cretans/Philistines figure on the Trojan side as well: The cities of Philistia included Achish, an Aegean name that some scholars have related to Anchises, father of Aineías. It is plausible that the Philistines, whom Saul and David went up against, bore a polytheistic culture and warrior ideals similar to what Homer depicted. This common culture may have encompassed epic stock scenes and concepts of warrior honor, among much else. The narrative in 1 Samuel 17 quoted here attacks that culture at many levels. Such antipagan polemic may well date from the very earliest times of the Hebrew religion. (Yeheskel Kaufmann, *The Religion of Israel from Its Beginnings to the Babylonian Exile*, trans. Moshe Greenberg [Chicago: University of Chicago Press, 1960].) But by the time the Hebrew Bible was edited and translated into Greek for the huge Jewish population of Alexandria, which numbered from 200,000 to 400,000, Homer was at the center of the prestigious Hellenistic culture that the rabbinic Bible editors were fighting against. It would not have taken much editorial body English to make a more ancient picture of Goliath remind the hearer of Aías and Hektor, for example. I do not argue that the antipagan polemic in this biblical passage was created against Homer, but that the older anti-Philistine polemic was given an anti-Homeric spin.

The Philistines rapidly adopted the Phoenician language after their arrival. This language was known in the Bible as the language of Canaan, which was also quickly adopted by the Hebrews after their entry into Canaan from Egypt—hence David and Goliath could yell at one another across the battlefield in a mutually intelligible tongue. It is ironic that these enemies, the Philistines and the Hebrews, substituted the same indigenous Canaanite language for their own original tongues.

The source for facts in this note is the *Encyclopedia Judaica* (Jerusalem: Keter Publishing, 1972). Biblical chronology, 8:766; Achish and Anchises, 2:210f; archaeological conclusions concerning the origins of the Philistines, 13:399ff; Phoenicia the Greek equivalent of Canaan, 13:471; esteem for Homer among Hellenized Jews, 8:944; the provenance of 1 Samuel, 5:1577 and 14:788ff; the ideological enmity between the editors of the Bible and the surrounding Hellenistic culture, 3:189f and 7:885f; parallel process of translating Hebrew Bible into Greek and final editing of the Hebrew text, 4:826; Jewish population of Alexandria, 2:590 and 13:871.

The Egyptians practiced circumcision, so calling someone "uncircumcised" was not a general-purpose term for idolater. The conventions of Greek vase painting required that the male genitals be displayed if at all possible. Circumcision was a practice known to Greeks from Egypt and aesthetically disapproved. A circumcised penis was regarded as ugly, brutish, and outlandish. See Kenneth J. Dover, *Greek Homosexuality*

(Cambridge: Harvard University Press, 1978), 125–135.

8. John Cooney, *The American Pope: The Life and Times of Francis Cardinal Spellman* (New York: New York Times Books, 1984), 238f, 240, 242.

9. J. Glenn Gray, *The Warriors: Reflections on Men in Battle* (New York: Harper & Row Torchbook, 1970) 152–153.

10. John W. Dower, *War without Mercy: Race & Power in the Pacific War* (New York: Pantheon Books, 1986), 94–111.

11. Clay Blair, Jr., *Silent Victory: The U.S. Submarine War against Japan* (New York: Lippincott, 1975).

12. Dower, *War without Mercy*, 260f.

13. Virgil does take sides: the Greeks are the *bad* guys.

CHAPTER 7: WHAT HOMER LEFT OUT

1. A general discussion of privation in combat can be found in Richard Holmes, *Acts of War: The Behavior of Men in Battle* (Glencoe: Free Press, 1985), 108–135.

2. RIF, or reconnaissance in force, was an attempt to induce the enemy to reveal their presence by attacking the patrolling force, usually platoon size or larger. Recon, or reconnaissance patrol, was intended to locate the enemy by observation, not by engagement.

3. R. A. Kulka, et al., *National Vietnam Veterans Readjustment Study*, C-2 through C-8. **Combat**—"48 items in the study covering, for example, how often the respondent received small arms fire, encountered mines and booby traps, engaged in firefights, saw enemy or Americans being killed or wounded, personally killed enemy, was respondent wounded, did respondent receive personal combat awards or medals. . . . [**Abusive violence and related conflicts**]—24 items, including degree of involvement in torturing, wounding, or killing hostages or POWs; involvement in mutilation of bodies of enemy or civilians; witnessed or involved in situations where women, children, or old people were injured or killed by Americans or South Vietnamese soldiers; personally saw or heard about an American soldier being tortured by the enemy; helping someone who asked to be allowed to die; and knew Americans who were casualties of "friendly fire.". . . [**Deprivation**]—12 items, including how often experienced not having shelter from the weather, enough water, adequate food, adequate equipment or supplies; how often physically fatigued or emotionally worn out/exhausted; how unpleasant found bad climate, loss of sleep, insects, disease, and filth. . . . [**Loss of meaning**]—9 items, including how unpleasant found sense of purposelessness, not counting as an individual, feeling out of touch with rest of world, loss of freedom of movement."

4. David H. Hackworth, *About Face* (New York: Simon & Schuster, 1989), 594. For a perspective on casualties from friendly fire in World War II, see Paul Fussell, *Wartime: Understanding and Behavior in the Second World War* (New York: Oxford University Press, 1989), 17–35.

5. Holmes, *Acts of War*, 329f. Holmes subsumes fragging under the more

general heading of mutiny.

6. *Ibid.*, 329.

7. Richard A. Gabriel, *No More Heroes* (New York: Hill and Wang, 1987), 55f.

8.

	VIETNAM (Americans only)	TROY (Greeks + Trojans)
Killed in Action (KIA)	38,436	214
Died while POW or missing (KIA)	3,639	—
Died of Wounds (KIA)	5,169	—
Wounded in Action (WIA) Total	303,704	24
Hospitalized	153,329	—
Not Hospitalized	150,375	—
Ratio All KIA to All WIA	**0.16**	**8.15**
Died of disease, accident	10,446	"pyres burned day & night" (1:60)

Vietnam data are from Harry G. Summers, Jr., *Vietnam Almanac* (New York: Facts on File Publications, 1985), 113. Trojan War figures are for named officers only; there were also twenty-six unnamed casualties, and casualties in other ranks were not recorded. From Mark W. Edwards, *Homer, the Poet of the Iliad* (Baltimore: Johns Hopkins University Press, 1987), 78.

The reader may be curious about the size of the Greek army. The Greek order of battle given in Book 2 names twenty-nine contingents bringing a total of 1,186 ships. If we accept this without discount and assume they were all the pre-trireme pentakontor, each with fifty rower-soldiers, we arrive at a minimum of 59,000 men. The Greeks outnumbered the Trojans more than ten to one, but this doesn't include the Trojan allies (2:144ff). Comparing Vietnam and Trojan War casualty rates is impossible, since the *Iliad* only reports officers' casualties. Assuming two officers per ship, the officer combat death rate at Troy was about one in eleven. Overall in Vietnam the rate of KIA was about one in sixteen combat troops. Adding in the wounded that required hospital care brings the certain-death-without-modern-medicine rate to about one in four.

9. See Guido Majno, *The Healing Hand: Man and Wound in the Ancient World* (Cambridge: Harvard University Press, 1975).

10. Nineteenth and early twentieth century Homer scholars were struck by this also. See Glen W. Most, *"Disiecti Membra Poetae*: The Rhetoric of Dismemberment," in *Innovations in Antiquity*, edited by Ralph Hexter and Daniel Selden (New York: Routledge, 1992), 413 ff.

11. Jasper Griffin, *Homer on Life and Death* (Oxford: Oxford University Press, 1980), 140–145. This is an excellent survey of this subject.

12. Reproduced in Eva C. Keuls, *The Reign of the Phallus: Sexual Politics in Ancient Athens* (New York: Harper & Row, 1985), 401. This was a fairly common motif of vase paintings of this period, possibly reflecting an antiwar movement at the time. *Ibid.*, 395ff.
13. Adrienne Rich, "Caryatid: Two Columns," in *On Lies, Secrets, and Silence: Selected Prose 1966–1978* (New York: Norton, 1979), 114f.

CHAPTER 8: SOLDIERS' LUCK AND GOD'S WILL

1. By permission of the author, who retains all rights.
2. Carl von Clausewitz, *On War*, ed. and trans. Michael Howard and Peter Paret (Princeton: Princeton University Press, 1984), 120.
3. This topic is comprehensively reviewed, also for race and class, in Lawrence M. Baskir and William A. Strauss, *Chance and Circumstance: The Draft, the War and the Vietnam Generation* (New York: Vintage Books, 1978). I have not attempted to resolve the discrepancies between this accounting and that given in note 8 to page 127. The number of combat veterans comes from the *National Vietnam Veterans Readjustment Study*, "High War Zone Stress" Males, p B-41. The *NVVRS* estimate is almost certainly low, having drastically undercounted incarcerated veterans and veterans with "bad paper," i.e., dishonorable, undesirable, or bad-conduct discharges. Also, the *NVVRS* data apply only to veterans *alive* at the time of the study. The uncounted dead by suicide and homicide are missing from this number. However, I have not used Baskir and Strauss's much higher but less meaningful estimate of 1,600,000. The exact number of dead is controversial. I have used the round number of names on the Vietnam War Memorial. This figure includes those classified as Missing in Action.
4. A sharpened bamboo or metal stake fixed vertically in the ground at the bottom of a camouflaged pit big enough to step or fall into. Usually the tip was smeared with feces to insure that the resulting wound would become infected.
5. Willie Peter—white phosphorous grenade; LAW—light antitank weapon, conceptually equivalent but functionally inferior to the enemy's RPG; Thumper—break-open shotgunlike weapon that fired a 40mm grenade cartridge that exploded on impact, or a load of buckshot; BAR—Browning automatic rifle.
6. Psalm 145, *Daily Prayer Book*, trans. Philip Birnbaum (New York: Hebrew Publishing Co., 1949), 127ff. Its use in Jewish liturgy is much more prominent than in Catholic liturgy. Cf. *Christian Prayer: The Liturgy of the Hours*, trans. International Commission on English in the Liturgy (Boston: Daughters of St. Paul, 1976), 527, 993, 1,505. Protestants make similar liturgical use.

CHAPTER 9: RECLAIMING THE *ILIAD*'S GODS AS A METAPHOR OF SOCIAL POWER

1. This chapter is multiply indebted to Griffin's excellent *Homer on Life and Death* (Oxford: Oxford University Press, 1980), here in particular, 145. Griffin reminds us very effectively of the impressiveness of Olympian power from the earliest lines of the poem, when the plague god, Apollo, is angered:

   > Apollo
   > walked with storm in his heart from Olympos' crest,
   > quiver and bow at his back, and the bundled arrows
   > clanged on the sky behind as he rocked in his anger,
   > descending like night itself. Apart from the ships
   > he halted and let fly, and the bowstring slammed
   > as the silver bow sprang, rolling in thunder away.
   > Pack animals were his target first, and dogs,
   > but soldiers, too, soon felt transfixing pain
   > from his hard shots, and [funeral] pyres burned night and day. (1:51ff)

   As Griffin says, "This description surely presents a god who must be taken seriously." Further refutations of the idea that the Homeric gods are only lightweights are given on pages 150ff of his book.

2. The gods can also be seen as an extended abusive family with several generations of severely traumatized, abusive adults and their spouses and children. Prior generations of this pattern of family violence are in Hesiod, *Theogony*, trans. H. G. Evelyn-White (Cambridge: Harvard University Press [Loeb Classical Library], 1914), 91f (Zeus's father castrates his grandfather as he rapes his mother), 113f (Zeus's father kills all his sons born before Zeus, who survives through his mother's trickery). The main description in the *Iliad* of the Olympian gods as an abuse-bound family is at 1:611. A *partial* list of additional citations:

   > Family violence: 21:493ff, 20:37ff, 21:559ff
   > Frequent threats or anticipation of violence: 8:453ff, 15:151ff
   > Manipulation by sex: 14:179ff
   > Crude bribery and "you owe me" models of reciprocity among family members: 14:261ff (by Hesiod's theogony, Hêra is Sleep's second cousin once removed)
   > Role locks (e.g., Hêphaistos as the family doormat, whom everybody can boss around)—14:268, 18:159; Arês as the out-of-control violent teenager—5:870, 5:1014ff; Aphrodítê as the out-of-control promiscuous teenager, etc.

   I am grateful to Dr. Aphrodite Matsakis for a glimpse at her manuscript in preparation, "The Three Faces of PTSD: Arês, Hêphaistos, and Dionysos—Aggression, Depression, and Ecstasy," in which the Olympian genealogy of family violence is laid out in detail.

3. This and the previous list, on pages 150–151, are culled from Judith Lewis Herman, *Trauma and Recovery: The Aftermath of Violence from*

Domestic Abuse to Political Terror (New York: Basic Books, 1992), 74–95.

4. Not all American higher officers succumbed to the leadership patholo-gies so evident in Vietnam. Colonel Harold Moore landed at LZ X-Ray in the Ia Drang Valley with the first flight of helicopters and did not leave this ferocious battle until he came out in the last chopper when his bat-talion was relieved by another. Lieutenant General Harold G. Moore and Joseph L. Galloway, *We Were Soldiers Once . . . and Young* (New York: Random House, 1992).

5. Paul Fussell, *The Great War and Modern Memory* (London: Oxford University Press, 1975), 216ff; and Robert Graves, *Good-bye to All That*, 2d ed. (Garden City: Doubleday, 1957), 228ff. The sunk-costs argument is pivotal to the rhetoric of Lincoln's Gettysburg Address.

6. The Greek words are identical in the two underlined portions. The *skhólion* is translated by Hugh G. Evelyn-White in *Hesiod, the Homeric Hymns and Homerica* (Cambridge: Harvard University Press [Loeb Classical Library], 1932), 497.

CHAPTER 10: THE BREAKING POINTS
OF MORAL EXISTENCE—WHAT BREAKS?

1. *Henry IV, Part I*, act 2, sc. 3, lines 40–62. This has been effectively used as a teaching text by others, e.g., David Grady's Epilogue in R. A. Kulka et al., *Trauma and the Vietnam War Generation* (executive summary of the *National Vietnam Veterans Readjustment Study*) (New York: Brunner/Mazel, 1990), 284f.

2. American Psychiatric Association, *DSM-III-R: Diagnostic and Statistical Manual of Mental Disorders*, 3d ed. revised (Washington, D.C.: American Psychiatric Association Press, 1987), 250. By permission.

3. These rates are based on the figures given in chapter 8, page 138.

4. Kulka, R. A. et al., *National Vietnam Veterans Readjustment Study* (New York: Brunner/Mazel, 1992). In the statistical comparisons cited here, the civilian control sample was matched during the sampling and analy-sis for age, gender, and race/ethnicity to the group with high combat exposure. Blacks and Hispanics were respectively 63 percent and 43 per-cent more likely to have experienced high combat exposure than whites (C-20). Current full PTSD: *NVVRS* IV-1-1. Here I am using the *NVVRS* "High Warzone Stressor Exposure" as the working distinction between combat and noncombat veterans (*NVVRS* IV-1-2). Lifetime partial PTSD: *NVVRS* III-2-1, III-3-1, III-4-1. This total has to be assembled from the tables cited and should not be confused with the lower figure of 53.4 per-cent for all veterans who had been in Vietnam, whether they had high combat exposure or not, given in the *NVVRS* executive summary, R. A. Kulka et al., *Trauma and the Vietnam War Generation*, 63.

5. Coercive sexual exploitation, such as incest and rape, is likewise difficult to honestly picture as "outside the range of usual human experience." According to sociologist Diana Russell, in the U.S. 12 percent of girls have been the victims of sexual exploitation by relatives before the age of

fourteen. Twenty percent are similarly victimized before the age of fourteen by people outside the family. The total rate of sexual victimization of girls before age fourteen is 28 percent. The lifetime risk of completed rape, defined narrowly as forced vaginal intercourse, for American women is 24 percent. When attempted rape is added, the proportion nearly doubles to 44 percent, of whom half have been assaulted more than once. If one is female now in the United States, sexual assault, starting in childhood, cannot be said to be "outside the range of usual human experience." From Diana Russell, "The Socio-Cultural Causes of Incest and Other Forms of Sexual Assault" (Paper delivered at the World Conference of the International Society for Traumatic Stress Studies, Amsterdam, June 1992).

6. World Health Organization, *The ICD-10 Classification of Mental and Behavioral Disorders: Clinical Descriptions and Diagnostic Guidelines* (Geneva: World Health Organization, 1992), 209. Inexplicably, these WHO criteria exclude PTSD, as though personality changes occur only after symptoms somehow burn themselves out. This is factually incorrect, as has been demonstrated by the DSM-IV field trials.

7. My presentation in this chapter of how severe trauma wrecks the personality is multiply indebted to Judith Lewis Herman, *Trauma and Recovery: The Aftermath of Violence from Domestic Abuse to Political Terror* (New York: Basic Books, 1992).

8. See, for example, Colonel David H. Hackworth, *About Face* (New York: Simon & Schuster, 1989), 533f.

9. Physical problems, NVVRS IX-1-1f; report of happiness/unhappiness, NVVRS VII-16-1f (this was a seven-point scale, not a dichotomy, so the percentages do not add to 100 percent); demoralization, NVVRS VI-1-1f.

10. The classic evocation of the miasma of terror is Michael Herr's *Dispatches* (New York: Alfred A. Knopf, 1977), especially the chapter on Khe Sanh.

11. Also note that control over attention is one of the most fundamental manifestations of human freedom.

12. Herman, *Trauma and Recovery*, 89.

13. Edward N. Luttwak, *Strategy: The Logic of War and Peace* (Cambridge: Harvard University Press, 1987).

14. Dysthymic disorder: *National Vietnam Veterans Readjustment Study* VI-2-1f, VI-6-1f; homelessness: NVVRS VII-18-1f. 10.6 percent reported that they had been homeless or vagrant or both at some time. *Homeless* was defined as one month or more of having no regular place to live; *vagrant* as traveling around with no arrangements ahead of time and without knowing how long the veteran would stay or where he or she would work. Kulka et. al., *Trauma and the Vietnam War Generation*, 178. "Heroes Today, Homeless Tomorrow?: Homelessness among Veterans in the United States," publication of the National Coalition for the Homeless (Washington, D.C.: November 1991), 6ff. The definition of homelessness (for example, is a veteran who sleeps in the spare room of his sister's house homeless that night?) and measurements of homelessness are notoriously fraught with controversy and methodological night-

mare. The National Coalition for the Homeless study cites two government reports as the source of these figures: U.S. Department of Veterans Affairs, "Reaching Out across America: The Third Progress Report on the Homeless Chronically Mentally Ill Veterans Program" (West Haven: December 31, 1989), and the Interagency Council on the Homeless, *1990 Annual Report* (Washington, D.C.: 1991), 248. Cohabiting, not married: *NVVRS* VII-10-1f.

15. Job instability: *National Vietnam Veterans Readjustment Study* VII-9-1f; divorces: *NVVRS* VII-11-1f.

CHAPTER 11: HEALING AND TRAGEDY

1. Tim O'Brien, *The Things They Carried* (New York: Viking Penguin, 1990), 76–77. Lawrence L. Langer's *Holocaust Testimonies: The Ruins of Memory* (New Haven: Yale University Press, 1991) contains a devastating critique of the genre of trauma narrative as reader reassurance.

2. *National Vietnam Veterans Readjustment Study*, data cited above, page 168 and note 4 above .

3. I became aware of James Redfield's fascinating and virtuosic *Nature and Culture in the* Iliad: *The Tragedy of Hector* too late to benefit from it in this book. His Chapter 5, "Purification," is especially relevant to the communal context of healing from trauma.

4. According to the *NVVRS* (VI-13-1f, VI-15-1f), Vietnam combat veterans are almost twice as likely as their civilian counterparts to have experienced alcohol abuse or dependence (45.6 percent) and more than twice as likely to have experienced drug abuse or dependence (8.4 percent).

5. The psychopharmacology of PTSD is a rapidly advancing field. Anything I write here is likely to be out of date by the time this book is published. The field is also fraught with controversies, on which I have strong opinions, but which are out of place here. Without going into any specifics, I will state that the most desirable goal of pharmacotherapy in combat PTSD is to reduce the propensity toward explosive violence without sedating or otherwise disabling the veteran. The goal is to increase the veteran's capacity to decide what he wants to do in any given situation, rather than to mechanically explode. Far from being a chemical straitjacket, such medication *increases* the veteran's freedom, thus restoring some of his dignity. A number of medications currently offer partial accomplishment of this goal in some veterans. My own modest contribution to progress in the pharmacotherapy of combat PTSD is described in my article "Fluoxetine Reduces Explosiveness and Elevates Mood of Vietnam Combat Vets with PTSD," *Journal of Traumatic Stress*, 1992, 5:97–101.

6. Judith Lewis Herman, *Trauma and Recovery: The Aftermath of Violence from Domestic Abuse to Political Terror* (New York: Basic Books, 1992), 172.

7. W. T. Edmonds, Jr., *Histories*. Unpublished poem, used by permission of the author, who retains all rights.

8. "Domestic Violence: Moving beyond the Headlines," transcript of Harvard School of Public Health "working luncheon," published in the *Harvard University Gazette*, July 10, 1992, 13–17. Two thousand children a year are killed in the United States from abuse in the home. This is about one every four hours.

9. Katherine and Mick Hurbis-Cherrier, *History Lessons* (Ann Arbor: University of Michigan Department of Communication, 1992), video documentary.

10. Vera Work and Frieda Grayzel, "Hierarchies of Suffering" (Paper delivered at the World Conference of the International Society for Traumatic Stress Studies, Amsterdam, 1992).

11. Herman, *Trauma and Recovery*, 7–32.

12. In the everyday context of trauma therapists doing their work, this means support and living community *in the workplace*. Communalization is as needful for therapists as it is for their patients. Trauma therapists cannot go through it alone. They should not have to.

13. The proportion who are specifically combat veterans in our prisons is not currently known, but in the mid-1970s it was more than half of all incarcerated veterans.

14. The ancient Greeks had a distinctive therapy of purification, healing, and reintegration that was undertaken as a whole community. We know it as Athenian theater. While a complete presentation is beyond the scope of this book, I want to summarize my view that the distinctive character of Athenian theater came from the requirements of a democratic polity *made up entirely of present or former soldiers* to provide communalization for combat veterans. Despite Athens's slaveholding and denial of franchise to women and descendants of resident aliens, it *was* a democracy for adult male citizens, among whom there was universal military service in a time of constant warfare. The Athenians communally reintegrated their returning warriors in recurring participation in rituals of the theater. The key elements of my argument are: the notable military backgrounds of Aeschylus and Sophocles; the prominence of military matters in the processions and ceremonies held before and between theatrical events; the use of the theater (according to Aristotle) for military training graduations; Stanford University classicist John Winkler's hypothesis that the chorus in Athenian tragedy was made up of young soldiers, ephebes, just at the completion of their military training; the distinctively transgressive character of the actions of the powerful main characters, played against the *themis* voiced by the disempowered chorus; and that the centuries-old controversy over what Aristotle meant when he said that tragedy brings about *katharsis* of compassion and terror can be resolved by reference to the experience of combat veterans.

   In the broadest sense, learning the paradoxical logic of war overturns every *thémis*. The soldier returning to a democracy must find some way to restore *thémis*. The combat soldier who has been through betrayal, grief, guilt, and rage comes home a Fury. I have speculated that the Athenian theater was the community's principal means of his reception and reintegration into the social sphere as Citizen.

See the following sources:

Robert Fagles and W. B. Stanford, "The Serpent and the Eagle," introduction to Aeschylus's *The Oresteia*, trans. Robert Fagles (New York: Penguin, 1977), 13.

Aristotle, *Constitution of Athens*, §42, trans. F. G. Kenyon, in *The Complete Works of Aristotle: The Revised Oxford Translation*, ed. Jonathan Barnes, vol. 2 (Princeton: Princeton/Bollingen, 1984), 2367f.

John J. Winkler, "The Ephebes' Song: *Tragôidia* and *Polis*," in *Nothing to Do with Dionysos? Athenian Drama in Its Social Context*, ed. John J. Winkler and Froma I. Zeitlin (Princeton: Princeton University Press, 1990).

A. M. H. Jones, *Athenian Democracy* (Baltimore: Johns Hopkins University Press, 1986).

Stephen G. Salkever, "Tragedy and the Education of the *Demos*," in *Greek Tragedy and Political Theory*, ed. J. Peter Euben (Berkeley: University of California Press, 1986), 274–303.

Martha C. Nussbaum, *The Fragility of Goodness: Luck and Ethics in Greek Tragedy and Philosophy* (Cambridge: Cambridge University Press, 1986), particularly 378ff, 388–391, 416 (honorable reception of the Furies into Athens).

Aristotle, *Poetics*, 1448b, trans. I. Bywater, in *Complete Works of Aristotle: The Revised Oxford Translation*, ed. Jonathan Barnes, vol. 2 (Princeton: Princeton/Bollingen, 1984), 2320; 1453b, 2326.

Herodotus 6.21.2, quoted in Anthony J. Podlecki, "*Polis* and Monarch in Early Attic Tragedy," in *Greek Tragedy and Political Theory*, ed. J. Peter Euben (Berkeley: University of California Press, 1986), 76f.

CONCLUSION

1. David H. Hackworth, *About Face* (New York: Simon and Schuster, 1989).
2. Colonel James Stokes, MC. "Management of Combat Stress and Battle Fatigue" and "Definitions and Clarification of U.S. Army Combat Stress Terminology" (U.S. Army Medical Department, November 5, 1990).
3. Sun Tzu, *The Art of War*, trans. Thomas Cleary (Boston: Shambala, 1988), 45.
4. Michael Walzer, *Just and Unjust Wars* (New York: Basic Books, 1977), 313ff.
5. The use of medication to *prevent* PTSD is conceptually possible but remains speculative for the present.
6. See chapter 3 of this book, pages 55 ff.
7. Gander crash: Mary P. Tyler and Robert K. Gifford, "Fatal Training Accidents: The Military Unit as a Recovery Context," *Journal of Traumatic Stress*, 1991, no. 4:233–249. Chaplains: A. David Mangelsdorff, United States Army Health Services Command, personal communication.
8. Stokes, "Army Combat Stress Terminology." Stokes is in the Medical Corps, and thus not an infantry commander, but he voices the view of

commanders who do not regard berserkers as "assets."

9. Carl von Clausewitz, *On War*, ed. and trans. Michael Howard and Peter Paret (Princeton: Princeton University Press, 1984), 149 (emphasis in original).

10. James William Gibson, *The Perfect War: The War We Couldn't Lose and How We Did* (New York: Vintage, 1988), 79f (emphases in original). This book provides an excellent discussion of the cultural domination of economic, technological, and managerial metaphors operating at every level of civilian and military leadership.

11. Kali Jo Tal, "Bearing Witness: The Literature of Trauma" (doctoral dissertation, Yale University, 1991), 286f. Forthcoming from Cambridge University Press as *Worlds of Hurt: Reading the Literature of Trauma*. New York: Cambridge University Press, 1994.

12. Some readers will justifiably observe that what is gone is the legally recognized purchase and sale of adult male slaves, but that around the world scores of millions of women and children live under conditions of *de facto* slavery, often concealed in family businesses, in households, as contract labor, and in businesses such as prostitution, which is legal in some countries. Purchase and sale of women and children are regular features of the latter. In many parts of the world, readers may also rightly point out, adult male slavery also persists in fact if not in law, as prison labor and some contract labor, and in businesses employing illegal immigrants.

13. 9:413 in original, 504 in Fitzgerald, "unfading glory."

14. The appearance of human culture was a momentous biological event crowding out other environmental selective pressures on the human gene pool. Biological evolution is driven by the probability of one's genes passing to the next generation. Ever since human culture emerged, nothing has influenced the likelihood of a given human's genes being perpetuated as strongly as his or her social position and culturally constructed interactions with other humans. These factors have largely determined, for example, access to fertile sexual partners, food, shelter, and protection from the most dangerous predators on the human species—other humans. See R. I. M. Dunbar, "Neocortex Size as a Constraint on Group Size in Primates," *Journal of Human Evolution* 20 (1992): 469–493.

15. Perceptive readers will question my claim that this proposition is culturally universal, citing for example that a culture that sanctions slavery will define the broken personality of a normatively abused slave as good character—for a slave. I see this problem, but I have smuggled in a solution by making the most highly valued character the reference point. Treating a master in a manner in which that culture would treat a slave would damage the master's good character as defined by that culture as good character—for a master. Note that I claim that these propositions are correct empirical statements, not that I have arrived at a formula that is culture-free in the sense that all cultures would subscribe to it. Cultures which weave the inferior value and domination of particular categories of people into their cosmologies cannot be logically compelled to assent and would probably reject the Kantian universalism I have smuggled in.

BIBLIOGRAPHY

American Psychiatric Association. *DSM-III-R: Diagnostic and Statistical Manual of Mental Disorders*. 3d ed., rev. (DSM-III-R) Washington, D.C.: American Psychiatric Association Press, 1987.

Aristotle. *Constitution of Athens*. Translated by F. G. Kenyon. In *The Complete Works of Aristotle: The Revised Oxford Translation*, edited by Jonathan Barnes. Vol. 2. Princeton: Princeton/Bollingen, 1984.

———. *Poetics*, 1448b. Translated by I. Bywater. In *The Complete Works of Aristotle: The Revised Oxford Translation*, edited by Jonathan Barnes. Vol. 2. Princeton: Princeton/Bollingen, 1984.

Baskir, Lawrence M., and William A. Strauss. *Chance and Circumstance: The Draft, the War and the Vietnam Generation*. New York: Vintage Books, 1978.

Blair, Clay, Jr. *Silent Victory: The U.S. Submarine War against Japan*. New York: Lippincott, 1975.

Cooney, John. *The American Pope: The Life and Times of Francis Cardinal Spellman*. New York: New York Times Books, 1984.

Cunliffe, R. J. *A Lexicon of the Homeric Dialect*. London: Blackie and Son Limited, 1924. Reprint. Norman: University of Oklahoma Press, 1963.

Dover, Kenneth. *Greek Homosexuality*. Cambridge: Harvard University Press, 1978.

Dower, John W. *War without Mercy: Race and Power in the Pacific War*. New York: Pantheon Books, 1986.

Dunbar, R. I. M. "Neocortex Size as a Constraint on Group Size in Primates." *Journal of Human Evolution* 20 (1992): 469–493.

Edwards, Mark W. *Homer, the Poet of the Iliad*. Baltimore: Johns Hopkins University Press, 1987.

Encyclopedia Judaica. Jerusalem: Keter Publishing, 1972.

Fagles, Robert, and W. B. Stanford. "The Serpent and the Eagle." Introduction to Aeschylus's *Oresteia*, translated by Robert Fagles. New York: Penguin, 1977.

Fussell, Paul. *The Great War and Modern Memory*. London: Oxford University Press, 1975.

———. *Wartime: Understanding and Behavior in the Second World War*. New York: Oxford University Press, 1989.

Gabriel, Richard A. *No More Heroes*. New York: Hill and Wang, 1987.

Gibson, James William. *The Perfect War: The War We Couldn't Lose and How We Did*. New York: Vintage, 1988.

Graves, Robert. *Good-bye to All That*. 2d ed. Garden City, New York: Doubleday, 1957.

Gray, J. Glenn. *The Warriors: Reflections on Men in Battle*. New York: Harper & Row Torchbook, 1970.

BIBLIOGRAPHY

Griffin, Jasper. *Homer on Life and Death*. Oxford: Oxford University Press, 1980.

Hackworth, David H. *About Face*. New York: Simon & Schuster, 1989.

Hall, Edith. *Inventing the Barbarian*. New York: Oxford University Press, 1991.

Halperin, David M. *One Hundred Years of Homosexuality and Other Essays on Greek Love*. New York: Routledge, 1990.

Herman, Judith Lewis. *Father-Daughter Incest*. Cambridge: Harvard University Press, 1981.

———. *Trauma and Recovery: The Aftermath of Violence from Domestic Abuse to Political Terror*. New York: Basic Books, 1992.

Herr, Michael. *Dispatches*. New York: Alfred A. Knopf, 1977.

Hesiod. *Theogony*. Translated by H. G. Evelyn-White. Cambridge: Harvard University Press (Loeb Classical Library), 1914.

Hesiod, the Homeric Hymns, and Homerica. Translated by Hugh G. Evelyn-White. Cambridge: Harvard University Press (Loeb Classical Library), 1982.

Holmes, Richard. *Acts of War: The Behavior of Men in Battle*. Glencoe, IL: Free Press, 1985.

Homer. *Iliad* (in Greek). Prepared by A. T. Murray. Vol. 1, books 1–12; vol. 2, books 13–24. Cambridge: Harvard University Press (Loeb Classical Library), 1924–1925.

———. *Iliad*. Translated by Robert Fitzgerald. New York: Anchor-Doubleday, 1974.

———. *Iliad*. Translated by Robert Fagles. New York: Viking Penguin, 1990.

Hurbis-Cherrier, Katherine and Mick. *History Lessons*. Ann Arbor: University of Michigan Department of Communication, 1992. Video documentary.

Jones, A. M. H. *Athenian Democracy*. Baltimore: Johns Hopkins University Press, 1986.

Kaufmann, Yeheskel. *The Religion of Israel from Its Beginnings to the Babylonian Exile*. Translated and abridged by Moshe Greenberg. Chicago: University of Chicago Press, 1960.

Keuls, Eva C. *The Reign of the Phallus: Sexual Politics in Ancient Athens*. New York: Harper & Row, 1985.

King, Katherine C. *Achilles: Paradigms of the War Hero from Homer to the Middle Ages*. Berkeley: University of California Press, 1987.

Knox, Bernard. Introduction to Homer's *Iliad*, translated by Robert Fagles. New York: Viking Penguin, 1990.

Kulka, R. A., William E. Schlenger, John A. Fairbank, Richard L. Hough, B. Kathleen Jordan, Charles R. Marmar, and Daniel S. Weiss. *National Vietnam Veterans Readjustment Study: Tables of Findings and Technical Appendices*. (*NVVRS*). New York: Brunner/Mazel, 1990.

———. *Trauma and the Vietnam War Generation*. New York: Brunner/Mazel, 1990.

Langer, Lawrence L. *Holocaust Testimonies: The Ruins of Memory*. New Haven: Yale University Press, 1991.

Luttwak, Edward N. *The Pentagon and the Art of War: The Question of Military Reform*, 34f. New York: Simon & Schuster, 1985.

BIBLIOGRAPHY

————. *Strategy: The Logic of War and Peace*. Cambridge: Harvard University Press, 1987.

Mahedy, William P. *Out of the Night: The Spiritual Journey of Vietnam Vets*. New York: Ballantine Books, 1986.

Matsakis, Aphrodite. "Three Faces of PTSD: Ares, Hephaistos, and Dionysos—Aggression, Depression, and Ecstasy." Unpublished paper.

Majno, Guido. *The Healing Hand: Man and Wound in the Ancient World*. Cambridge: Harvard University Press, 1975.

Moore, Lieutenant General Harold G., and Joseph L. Galloway. *We Were Soldiers Once . . . and Young*. New York: Random House, 1992.

Nagy, Gregory. *The Best of the Achaeans: Concepts of the Hero in Archaic Greek Poetry*. Baltimore: Johns Hopkins University Press, 1979.

————. *Greek Mythology and Poetics*. Ithaca: Cornell University Press, 1990.

National Coalition for the Homeless. "Heroes Today, Homeless Tomorrow?: Homelessness among Veterans in the United States." Washington, D.C., 1991.

Nussbaum, Martha C. *The Fragility of Goodness: Luck and Ethics in Greek Tragedy and Philosophy*. Cambridge: Cambridge University Press, 1986.

————. Introduction to Euripides' *The Bacchae*, translated by C. K. Williams. New York: Farrar, Strauss and Giroux, 1990.

————. "Non-Relative Virtues: An Aristotelian Approach." In *The Quality of Life*, edited by Martha C. Nussbaum and Amartya Sen. Oxford: Clarendon Press, 1993.

O'Brien, Tim. *The Things They Carried*. New York: Viking Penguin, 1990.

Oxford English Dictionary. 2d ed. Edited by J. A. Simpson and E. S. C. Weiner. Oxford: Oxford University Press, 1989.

Redfield, James M. *Nature and Culture in the* Iliad: *The Tragedy of Hector*, expanded ed. Durham: Duke University Press, 1994.

Rich, Adrienne. "Caryatid: Two Columns." In *On Lies, Secrets, and Silence: Selected Prose 1966–1978*. New York: Norton, 1979.

Rosaldo, Renato. "Grief and a Headhunter's Rage: On the Cultural Force of Emotions." In *Text, Play, and Story: The Construction and Reconstruction of Self and Society*, edited by E. M. Brunner. Washington, D.C.: American Ethnological Society, 1984.

————. *Culture & Truth: The Remaking of Social Analysis*. Boston: Beacon Press, 1989.

Roth, Susan, and Leslie Lebowitz. "The Experience of Sexual Trauma." *Journal of Traumatic Stress* 1 (1988): 79–107.

Russell, Diana. "The Socio-Cultural Causes of Incest and Other Forms of Sexual Assault." Paper presented at the World Conference of the International Society for Traumatic Stress Studies, Amsterdam, June 1992.

Salkever, Stephen G. "Tragedy and the Education of the *Dêmos*." In *Greek Tragedy and Political Theory*, edited by J. Peter Euben. Berkeley: University of California Press, 1986.

Scarry, Elaine. *The Body in Pain: The Unmaking and Making of the World*. New York: Oxford University Press, 1985.

Schein, Seth L. *The Mortal Hero: An Introduction to Homer's Iliad*. Berkeley: University of California Press, 1984.

BIBLIOGRAPHY

Shay, Jonathan. "Learning about Combat Stress from Homer's *Iliad*." *Journal of Traumatic Stress* 4 (1991): 561–579.

———. "Fluoxetine Reduces Explosiveness and Elevates Mood of Vietnam Combat Vets with PTSD." *Journal of Traumatic Stress* 5 (1992): 97–101.

———. "Achilles: Paragon, Flawed Character, or Tragic Figure." *Classical Bulletin* 71, no. 1 (1995), special issue: *Understanding Achilles*.

Sheehan, Neil. *A Bright Shining Lie: John Paul Vann and America in Vietnam*. New York: Random House, 1988.

Summers, Colonel Harry G., Jr. *Vietnam War Almanac*. New York: Facts on File Publications, 1985.

Sun Tzu. *The Art of War*. Translated by Thomas Cleary. Boston: Shambala, 1988.

Tal, Kali Jo. *Bearing Witness: The Literature of Trauma*. Ph.D. diss., Yale University, 1991. Forthcoming as *Worlds of Hurt: Reading the Literature of Trauma*. New York: Cambridge University Press, 1994.

Tyler, Mary P., and Robert K. Gifford. "Fatal Training Accidents: The Military Unit as a Recovery Context." *Journal of Traumatic Stress* 4 (1991): 233-249.

van Creveld, Martin. *Command in War*. Cambridge: Harvard University Press, 1985.

von Clausewitz, Carl. *On War* (1832). Edited and translated by Michael Howard and Peter Paret. Princeton: Princeton University Press, 1984.

Walzer, Michael. *Just and Unjust Wars*. New York: Basic Books, 1977.

Winkler, John J. "The Ephebes' Song: *Tragôidia* and *Polis*." In *Nothing to Do with Dionysos? Athenian Drama in Its Social Context*, edited by John J. Winkler and Froma I. Zeitlin. Princeton: Princeton University Press, 1990.

Work, Vera, and Frieda Grayzel. "Hierarchies of Suffering." Paper presented at the World Conference of the International Society for Traumatic Stress Studies, Amsterdam, June 1992.

World Health Organization. *The ICD-10 Classification of Mental and Behavioral Disorders: Clinical Descriptions and Diagnostic Guidelines*. Geneva: WHO, 1992.

Zanker, Graham. *The Heart of Achilles: Characterization and Personal Ethics in the* Iliad. Ann Arbor: University of Michigan Press, 1994.

INDEX

INDEX

David (biblical) (*cont.*)
 image of enemy as subhuman, 112
 religious merit in contempt for the
  enemy, 113–14
dead comrades, *See comrades, dead*
defeat
 and soldier's sense of personal
  value, 147
 as abandonment by God, 8, 146
 as stolen victory, 8
 consequences of, in *Iliad*, 132
 honorable, possibility of, 106, 113
  link to images of the enemy, 115
 suffering of civilians, 131
 suffering of women, 129, 132–33
 Vietnam veterans' images, 7
degradation, as motivational technique, 201–2
demographic agenda
 Troy, 158–9
 Vietnam, 158–9
democratic participation, 180–81,
  195
 mental and social capacities
  required for, 180–81
demoralization
 apparent absence among defeated
  Greeks, 143–44, 145–46
 consequence of perceived betrayal,
  143
 by God, 147
dependency, 14–15, 18–19, 36
 of modern soldier, 17–18, 124
  compared to that of a child, 5, 18
depression, 165, 169, 178, *See also
  despair*
deprivation, 19, 49, 51, 86, 121,
  122–23, 152
 sleep, 121, 150, 152, 173, 208
DEROS, 55, 217n10
despair, 122, 169, 179, 184
*Diagnostic and Statistical Manual of
  Mental Disorders, See DSM-III-R*
dignity, *See self-respect*
Diomêdês, 30, 80, 83, 87, 104, 107,
  108, 126, 141
 aristeía of, 80, 87
 contrast to Achilles, 89, 97, 118,
  200
 no simplification of values, 87
 restraint of, 87, 89
disease, 20, 24, 124, 125, 126, 131,
  224n8

domestic abuse, 227–28n5, *See also
  battering; incest*
Dover, Kenneth J., 215–16n4,
  221–23n7
Dower, John W., 118, 223n10, 12
DSM-III-R, 166–67, 169, 184, 186
Dunbar, R. I. M., 232n14

Edmonds, W. T., Jr., 137, 189
Edwards, Mark W., 224n8
emotional numbing, *See PTSD, emotional numbing*
Encyclopedia Judaica, 221–23n7
enemy, images of, 103–4
 American, in Vietnam, 104, 105,
  110
 David (biblical), 112–13
 expected conduct of victorious
  enemy, 104
 Homeric, 109–10
enemy, Vietnamese, xvii, xix, 17–18,
  31, 34, 56, 57, 60, 78, 79–80,
  104, 105–6, 117–18, 123, 172
enslavement, 7, 35, 36–37, 56, 131,
  133, 152, 109
equipment failure, 37, 78, 141, 143,
  158, 196
 in *Iliad*, 18
Euripides (Athenian tragic poet),
  209, 214n9
evil, 31, 32, 33, 93, 103, 118, 154,
  180, 183, 184–85, 192
existential functions, 192
 of guilt, 72–73, 192
 of rage, 89–90, 192

Fagles, Robert, 211n2, 221n7,
  230–31n14
families
 abusive, 168, 226n2, 227–28n5
 as metaphor for closeness of soldiers, 39, 40–42, 71
 bereaved, 67, 129, 130, 199
 of veterans, 117, 174, 175, 178, 195
fear, 10, 11, 20, 21, 36, 49, 60, 74,
  91, 92, 106, 131, 133, 143, 152,
  154, 161, 169, 172–73, 174, 175,
  179, 189, 190, 191, 200, 208,
  209
 loss of, 53, 73, 82
fiduciary
 assumption, 15
 definition and word origin, 15

INDEX